WHERE TO WATCH
BIRDS IN
EASTERN
EUROPE

HAMLYN BIRDWATCHING GUIDES

WHERE TO WATCH BIRDS IN EASTERN EUROPE

GERARD GORMAN

HAMLYN

CONTENTS

First published in 1994 by Hamlyn Limited,
an imprint of Reed Consumer Books Ltd
Michelin House, 81 Fulham Road,
London SW3 6RB and Auckland, Melbourne,
Singapore and Toronto

Copyright © Reed International Books Limited
1994

Text copyright © Gerard Gorman 1994
Colour artwork copyright © Clive Byers 1994
Black-and-white artwork copyright © Mark
Andrews 1994
Maps copyright © Reed International Books
Limited 1994

ISBN 0 600 57976 X

A CIP catalogue record for this book is available
from the British Library

Page design by Jessica Caws
Maps by John Gilkes
Produced by Mandarin Offset
Printed in Hong Kong

INTRODUCTION

The first birdwatching trip I ever made out from Budapest is indelibly printed on my memory. I was almost overwhelmed by the birds I saw that spring day, but the one that always comes to mind first is the White Stork that peered down at me from its telegraph-pole nest at Dinnyés. That day-trip sparked off a series of further excursions across Hungary and it was not long before I branched out into neighbouring Romania and Czechoslovakia (as it was then known), and a little later on into Poland and then Bulgaria. Although I certainly was not to know that things would change as rapidly as they did, I always believed that 'Eastern Europe' would sooner or later be on the agenda of most birdwatchers from the west of Europe once the word was out on the wonderful birds here. As everyone now knows, it was sooner. And then came the collapse of the Soviet Union and the forming of new, easily visited states which has added endless opportunities for birdwatchers to the equation. There is now unparalleled interest in everything in this half of Europe, birds and birdwatching included. Eastern Europe's appeal is understandable. The countries included in this guide have certain birds which are extinct, absent or only rare vagrants farther west. Whether it be lekking Great Snipe in Poland, flocks of Red-breasted Geese in Romania, Pied Wheatears in Bulgaria, Sakers in Hungary, Pygmy Owls in Bohemia, White-backed Woodpeckers in Slovakia or Paddyfield Warblers in the Crimea, this is *the* place to see some of the continent's best birds, and there are also other draws: the numerous large tracts of habitat to explore, the sense of space and the chance of making a discovery. To a greater or lesser degree all the countries in this guide have areas where little is known of the birdlife to be found there and there are many species which local ornithologists have not had the time or finance to study. Areas can be huge, or remote, and there are just too few ornithologists and birdwatchers. In Romania and Bulgaria in particular, much remains to be discovered. Do Lesser Short-toed Larks breed? Do Moustached Warblers winter? Are there any Dotterels left? There are dozens more questions like these, and thus ample opportunities for visiting birdwatchers to add to the overall knowledge of Europe's avifauna.

It is in many ways now easier to visit and explore the countries included in this book than it was before the incredible events of 1989, although it has actually always been possible to find Dalmatian Pelicans, Pygmy Cormorants, Spotted Eagles, Sakers, Great Snipe, Ural Owls, White-backed Woodpeckers, Paddyfield and Aquatic Warblers, Pied Wheatears, Thrush Nightingales and all the other special birds that visitors from the west of Europe come to see. From another perspective, however, the beauty of watching birds in this part of Europe lies not in these specialities but in the *abundance* of other species: White Stork, Lesser Spotted Eagle, Red-backed Shrike, Hawfinch and Tree Sparrow immediately come to mind. But we cannot afford to be blasé. Old problems remain and new threats have arrived alongside the benefits of political change. Thankfully, each country dealt with in this book has a core of very special people who are already taking steps, in sometimes incredibly difficult circumstances, to preserve the wonderful wildlife habitats of their respective countries. Whenever possible these people and the organizations they belong to should be supported.

Now, an explanation: this book's title is, as with all guidebooks, one of convenience. The countries covered are gathered under the familiar 'Eastern Europe' heading. Geographically the term is incorrect, as Czechs and Hungarians in particular will tell you over a glass of *pivo* or *pálinka*. Even the most cursory glance at the map of Europe will reveal that most of the Czech Republic and a large chunk of Poland, for example, lie well to the west of Vienna. The fact is that the perfect title, one which would have embraced all the preferred terms for the region, would have been far too long and confusing. For all its inadequacies the chosen name for this part of Europe is the one most easily understood. Nevertheless, apologies to all my friends who prefer to be known as 'Central Europeans'.

In selecting the sites for inclusion I concocted a recipe of several ingredients. First, as far as was practical, a **nationwide spread** for each country, as I know that birdwatchers like to bird *en route* to their final destination (or one may be in a corner of a country far from the famous sites for reasons other than birds but wish to pick up a few local species). Second, a range of **typical habitats** for each country, as I believe that a knowledge of habitats is an essential element of successful birdwatching. Third, sites where the **birds visitors will want to see** occur. To a certain extent this is subjective and I have presumed, for example, that if two wheatears fly past a British birdwatcher on the Bulgarian Black Sea coast, he or she will follow the Pied Wheatear rather than the one seen regularly back home. Fourth, the final selection obviously includes **famous sites** such as the Hortobágy, Białowieża and the Danube delta, but there are also equally excellent, if perhaps **less well-known areas** such as Šumava, Biharugra and Sandanski, and I have to admit to including one or two which are **personal favourites** and where I have yet to come across another 'foreign' birdwatcher. Last, I have also tried to balance the needs of the well-travelled lister whose aim is to *get* the specialities of each country and then move on, with those of the more casual birdwatcher, perhaps a businessperson on a brief visit to a capital city who has a day free, or the birdwatching couple on a package holiday with the children. Thus common birds are mentioned alongside rarities. In general, however, it is those birds that are rare or totally absent from western Europe that receive most attention. Whatever style of birdwatching one goes in for, it is an undeniable fact that everyone wants to see new species. I have never met a visitor birdwatching who was not in the first place keen to see a new bird. I hope *Where to Watch Birds in Eastern Europe* helps to contribute a few to everyone who uses it.

Gerard Gorman
Budapest

ACKNOWLEDGEMENTS

Sincere thanks are due to Josef Chytil, Jan Lontkowski, Dan Munteanu and Tadeusz Stawarczyk for their invaluable comments, time and enthusiasm. It is a pleasure to have such dedicated and talented people as friends and I cannot thank them enough for their contributions.

Thanks are also due to the authors of *Important Bird Areas In Europe*, Richard Grimmett and T.A. Jones, and through them to the many contributors to that book, which was an invaluable source of facts and figures. Nikolai Diltchev of Pandion (Bulgaria) and Maciej Zimowski of Bird Service (Poland) supplied me with maps and other information on their respective countries. Many other individuals have contributed to the guide in both direct and indirect ways, occasionally through casual conversations which later filled a gap in knowledge, sometimes by introducing me to their local patches and accompanying me on excursions, and often through just taking the time to root out and send notes and answers to my question-filled letters. In particular I would like to thank Gabriel Bánicá, Jósef Büki, Petr Bürger, Chris Fenton, Gábor Firmánszky, Jiri Flousek, Jan Hora, Jirí Janda, László Kalabér, Zsolt Kalotás, Bohuslav Kloubec, Gábor Kovács, Gábor Magyar, John O'Sullivan, András and Egon Schmidt, Arthur Shaw, Jósef Szabó, Guy Thompson, Zoltán Waliczky and Peter Weber. I am also indebted to Mark Andrews and Clive Byers for their excellent work in illustrating the book and bringing it to life.

Last, but certainly not least, are Ivett and Martin. Perhaps now we can go tobogganing or something like that.

HOW TO USE THIS GUIDE

Each country is introduced by a **map** indicating the locations of the sites covered. It should be remembered, however, that the maps in this guide are meant to complement, not replace, more detailed maps produced in the countries concerned.

A **general information** section follows, sprinkled with anecdotes and suggestions which I consider may be of use to the visiting birdwatcher. There are background details on the country's **importance for birds**, advice on **getting there** and details of **bird conservation organizations**.

A section on the main bird **habitats** outlines the places where certain birds live and the key terrain types in each country.

The section on **seasons** contains a few lines on the climate, weather and birdwatching highlights throughout the year.

Each site begins with a **general description**, sometimes accompanied by a site-map, and the most interesting and typical birds found there. **Calendar** outlines weather and best times to visit for certain species. Under the heading **species** brief comments, statistics and tips focus on selected birds. **Access** explains exactly where the site is, how to get there and what permission, if any, is needed. At the very end of each site entry there is a note on whether or not it is listed as an IBA (Important Bird Area). This refers to the Important Bird Areas In Europe inventory of BirdLife International.

CODE OF CONDUCT FOR BIRDWATCHERS

When birdwatching in Eastern Europe behave as one would anywhere else. Remember the **Code of Conduct for Birdwatchers**. Well-behaved birdwatchers are an important lobby for nature conservation, and in Eastern Europe there are ample opportunities to set a good example by respecting habitats, laws and the rights of local people.

KEY TO MAPS

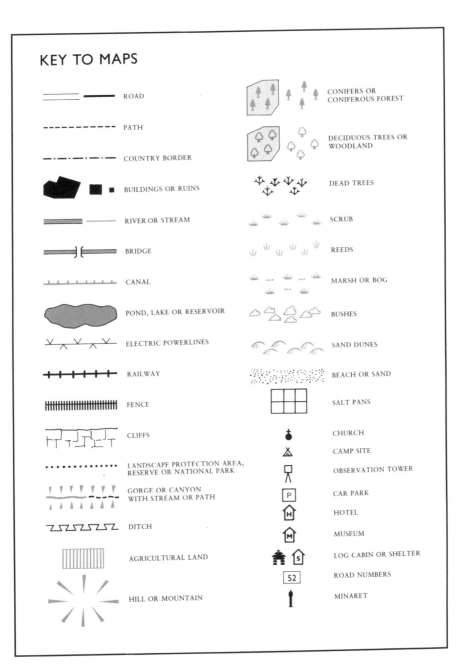

ROAD

PATH

COUNTRY BORDER

BUILDINGS OR RUINS

RIVER OR STREAM

BRIDGE

CANAL

POND, LAKE OR RESERVOIR

ELECTRIC POWERLINES

RAILWAY

FENCE

CLIFFS

LANDSCAPE PROTECTION AREA, RESERVE OR NATIONAL PARK

GORGE OR CANYON WITH STREAM OR PATH

DITCH

AGRICULTURAL LAND

HILL OR MOUNTAIN

CONIFERS OR CONIFEROUS FOREST

DECIDUOUS TREES OR WOODLAND

DEAD TREES

SCRUB

REEDS

MARSH OR BOG

BUSHES

SAND DUNES

BEACH OR SAND

SALT PANS

CHURCH

CAMP SITE

OBSERVATION TOWER

CAR PARK

HOTEL

MUSEUM

LOG CABIN OR SHELTER

ROAD NUMBERS

MINARET

POLAND

GENERAL INFORMATION

By any standards Poland is wonderful. It is also a huge and diverse country needing several visits to do it and its birds justice. It is almost a rule in eastern Europe that the farther east one travels in a country, the poorer it becomes. This is true of Poland where roads and accommodation in the east and north-east (arguably the best areas for birds) are of a lower standard than in the west of the country. Still, there is nothing to worry the experienced travelling birdwatcher and today Poland is probably worked by more visiting birdwatchers than any of the other countries in this book. Accommodation, from *zimmer frei* and small *pensions* to large state-owned hotels, is plentiful and generally inexpensive outside cities, although, as is the trend in the region, prices are increasing rapidly. Only large hotels and tourist offices will handle credit cards and in the countryside small denominations of foreign currency are preferable to traveller's cheques. The unit of currency is the zloty.

In such a large country, temperatures, of course, vary around the regions according to season and depending on whether one is in the mountains, lowlands or on the Baltic coast. January is the coldest month with an average of around 0 °C (32 °F) in Warsaw and often well below that in the east. In July and August temperatures nationwide are around 24 °C (75 °F). But these are only average figures; in high summer a sun-hat and insect repellent will be needed by most and in winter it is as well to prepare for what at times may seem like Arctic conditions.

A reciprocal agreement between Poland and Britain means that free emergency health care is available for British citizens. Basic medicines, toiletries and, if one is visiting wetlands, mosquito repellent should be taken along as pharmacies outside large towns cannot be relied upon. Stock up with essentials in Warsaw, which is nowadays a bustling hive of business.

Few people speak English, although in Warsaw and in other tourist centres it is usually known by waiters and hotel staff. Generally, German is more useful, especially in the west and Silesia. A little Russian or any other Slavic tongue is also useful. Almost anyone connected to nature conservation and/or birdwatching will speak good English. Life is generally more organized in Poland than in some of the other countries of the region, so permission should be sought before wandering around meadows and fish-ponds. Guidebooks almost always refer to locals as being friendly but in this case it really is true; Poles are traditionally very helpful and hospitable, and in the main birdwatching areas they are familiar with the sight of visiting binocular-toting foreigners. Birdwatching is an increasingly popular hobby amongst young Poles, which is not surprising given the delights that they have on their doorstep.

IMPORTANCE FOR BIRDS

Poland is an extremely important country for many bird species which are extinct or under pressure elsewhere in Europe. Four globally threatened species: Red Kite, White-tailed Eagle, Corncrake and Aquatic Warbler have crucial and healthy populations in Poland. Indeed, Red Kites seem to be flourishing in several areas of the country and the White-tailed Eagle population now stands at almost 300 pairs with more wintering. With thousands of pairs of Corncrake, Poland is *the* European stronghold. Aquatic Warbler is another species which has most of its European, if not world, breeding population in this country's marshes and wet-meadows. Besides these high-priority birds, Poland also boasts major populations of both Black and White Storks (30,000 pairs of the latter), Honey Buzzards, Montagu's Harriers, Lesser Spotted Eagles, Cranes and Black-tailed Godwits amongst many others. The country's importance for breeding Great Snipe is well known. There are also a few pairs of Spotted Eagles, another very rare bird in Europe. Poland's forests and upland areas support significant populations of owls, woodpeckers and grouse. In addition, Poland has numerous sites which are important for passage, moulting and wintering species. Grebes, swans, grey geese and ducks congregate in large flocks, and waders, raptors and passerines move along the Baltic coast on migration, and this stretch of coast is also one of Europe's major wintering areas for wildfowl.

GETTING THERE

Daily flights come into Warsaw Okecie Airport from London Heathrow. From the domestic terminal a few miles away, about a dozen Polish cities and the other countries covered in this book can be reached. Fares on LOT, the state airline, between Warsaw and other capitals in the region are usually very reasonable. There are also numerous trains from Germany and from Vienna via Prague, although these can be a little slow. Although extensive, the domestic rail and bus system is not really recommended for a birdwatching trip, as it is slow and often crowded. For most areas, particularly the forests and marshes of the east, the Baltic coastline and the mountains of the south, a car is essential, as large distances are involved. Conditions are changing and improving rapidly in Poland; for instance, over the last couple of years petrol stations have appeared throughout the country, and Warsaw airport has all the usual car-hire firms. If one is intent on a mad clean-up of Poland's famous birds, then so be it, but take into consideration the condition of country roads, the horse-drawn vehicles in the east and inevitable encounters with 'tired and emotional' locals. But why rush? All of these add, in my opinion, to the beauties of a visit. Give Poland, its rural pace of life and its bird sites plenty of time and respect.

CONSERVATION

Poland has a great tradition of ornithology and nature conservation in general, and its birdlife has been studied by generations of dedicated ornithologists. The country has many reserves and parks of various kinds as well as tracts of unprotected but excellent habitat. Political change has moved the responsibility for protected areas away from central government and into the hands of a hopefully more sympathetic environmental ministry. The North Podlasie Society For Bird Protection is a nongovernmental organization which has started to establish a network of reserves in north-east Poland for Aquatic Warblers, Great Snipe and other threatened species. For more information write to them at: 17–230 Białowieża, PO Box 32, Poland. The Polish Society for the Protection of Birds (OTOP), which was founded in 1991, has a rapidly growing membership and can be contacted at PO Box 335, PL-80-358 Gdańsk 50, Poland. Records and unusual sightings are welcomed by the long-established and respected Polish Avifaunistic Commission (Rarities Committee) at the Museum of Natural History, Sienkiewicza 21, 50–335 Wrocław, Poland.

HABITATS

Poland has many important wetlands, from fish-pond systems in the south and west to innumerable lakes in the north and east, reservoirs scattered around the country and large lagoons along the Baltic. All of these habitats are internationally important in terms of both species and numbers of birds. Poland is perhaps most famed for its large tracts of marsh and peatbog which support some of Europe's rarest birds; the river basins of the north-east are particularly important for Black Grouse, Aquatic Warblers, Great Snipe and both Lesser Spotted and Spotted Eagles. There is much forest habitat, of varying age, including the famous pristine deciduous woodland at Białowieża in the east with its flycatchers and wood-peckers. Most forests are, however, conifer plantations which are nevertheless important for species such as Nutcracker, Hazelhen, Crested Tit and Pygmy Owl. Even agricultural land is an important bird habitat in Poland because of the structure and methods of farming employed throughout this century. Montagu's Harriers, Red-backed Shrikes and Corncrakes have all benefited from a lack of 'progress'. Indeed, despite having snow-capped mountains with ski resorts in the south, Poland is predominantly a low-lying agricultural country.

SEASONS

SPRING
Overall this is probably the best time to visit Poland for birds. In April and early May there are good bird movements along the coast, as well as lekking grouse, and songbirds and raptors are back from their winter quarters. As with most of continental Europe, May is an exciting month but few countries in western Europe can rival Poland at this time.

SUMMER
The weather is at its most reliable, and there are plenty of birds in song as well as good opportunities for raptor watching during this season. Woodpeckers and owls are almost silent as they nest early and, once their young have fledged, become rather elusive. Insects can be a problem in the marshes but not enough to put one off for long. The end of August sees the start of major migration along the Baltic coastline.

AUTUMN

This is *the* season to visit the Baltic, September and October being particularly good for migrating waders, warblers and raptors. Rarities often occur right across the country, especially on reservoirs and fish-ponds. White Storks and, later, Cranes congregate before heading south in groups.

WINTER

Generally, winters are very harsh in Poland, especially in the north and east; therefore most birds move on. From December to March many lakes and marshes are frozen over and there are few birds that are more visible now than in other more hospitable seasons. Yet a visit to Białowieża, for example, offers several resident forest birds some of which, like Hazelhens and owls, are easier than in summer, and also gives the chance of encountering large mammals.

BIRDWATCHING SITES

SZCZECIN BAY

53°46N 14°28E

This huge estuary is probably the best place in Poland for seabirds, but that is not the whole story. Several rivers drain into the bay and there are islands, reedbeds, marshes, peatbogs, forests, thickets and agricultural land all around the area. With such a diversity of habitats, all kinds of birds are present. The bay itself has thousands of Goldeneyes, Goosanders, Red-breasted Mergansers and Smews in winter and dozens of White-tailed Eagles. This is also one of Europe's most important stop-overs in autumn. Breeding species include Dunlin, Oystercatcher, Common and Little Terns, Red Kite and White-tailed Eagle. Sea-walls in the port of Świnoujście, between the bay and the sea, are good spots for seawatching. Just about anything is possible here in autumn. South of the port Karsibór Island has an estimated 300 pairs of Aquatic Warblers, as well as Corncrakes, Ruffs, Dunlins, Black-tailed Godwits and occasionally Mediterranean Gulls. Karsibór was the first reserve to be established by OTOP. The Wolinski National Park lies on the coast at the north-east corner of the bay. Here high cliffs, small lakes and pine forests host most of the typical birds of the Baltic Coast. Other sites for Aquatic Warbler are the marshes in river valleys around the spa town of Kamien Pomorski to the east of the park. South of the E65 at Wolin, to the east of the bay, are numerous marshes, meadows and coniferous forest with White Storks, Black and Red Kites, Marsh and Hen Harriers, Short-toed Eagles, Spotted Crakes, Corncrakes, Cranes and Black Terns. On the other side of the bay, between the curiously named town of Police and the German border, is the vegetation-covered Lake Swidwie. There is an ornithological station here where the staff may be able to help with local news. Many of the above-mentioned birds are here, as well as both bitterns, Montagu's Harriers, Ospreys and Lesser Spotted Eagles. The Szczecin Bay area and its birds deserve a visit of several days at least.

CALENDAR

A visit at any time of year will be rewarding. May to July are good for the breeding species of the surrounding marshes and forests. September and October see grey geese, Cranes and waders passing through. There are also large numbers of passerines moving along the coast at this time. Winter is best for thousands of ducks, particularly sawbills, in the bay itself.

SPECIES

- *Red Kite* There should be no difficulty seeing this species as it is widespread in the whole bay area and some overwinter.
- *White-tailed Eagle* Around twenty pairs breed in the region and up to sixty winter.
- *Smew* Thousands winter along with other ducks but across such a large body of water that counts are done by plane.
- *Dunlin* This is one of the few breeding areas in Poland.
- *Oystercatcher* A few pairs breed in the delta of the River Swina and from here seem to have started to expand inland down the River Odra.
- *Aquatic Warbler* In some places on Karsibór and in valleys around Kamien Pomorski this species is quite numerous.

ACCESS

The area is in the very north-west corner of Poland along the German border. The city of Szczecin is at the south of the bay. Berlin is around 150 km (93 miles) to the south-west and Warsaw 500 km (310 miles) to the south-east along the T81. Ferries from Scandinavia dock at Świnoujście. The Wolinski National Park can be explored from a coast road littered with resorts. Karsibór Island can be reached via a bridge to the south of Świnoujście. Lake Swidwie is near Stolec on the border north-west of Szczecin. Ask at the ornithological station here for permission to visit the reserves. Most of the areas which were closed to visitors, being against the former East German border, are now accessible although paths are few and many places wild and boggy. There are several IBAs in and around the bay.

GDAŃSK AREA
54°22N 18°40E

Although Gdańsk itself is an industrial port, it lies at the heart of a famous and wonderful coast for birds. As well as Gdańsk Bay and the Baltic Sea itself, there are coastal meadows, sandy beaches, coniferous forests and the estuary of the River Vistula. The last site is a changing complex of sandbanks, dunes, lakes and marsh with various gulls, ducks, passage waders and breeding Sandwich, Common and Little Terns. In summer there is a ringing camp at Swibno just to the west of the river mouth. The Vistula Spit, Mierzeja Wiślana, is a long sandy coastal strip in the east of Gdańsk Bay. Millions of birds pass this way in autumn, with all kinds of waders and warblers on offer. At the very beginning of the spit, near Kąty Rybackie, there are large colonies of Cormorants and Grey Herons, and breeding ducks including Gadwall, Garganey, Shoveler and Ferruginous Duck. There are also hundreds of Common and a few Arctic Tern pairs. Large reedbeds on the southern shore of the Vistula Lagoon hold Little Bitterns, Marsh Harriers and Spotted and Little Crakes, but are difficult to work. In the west, at the other side of the bay north of Gdynia, is the Bay of Puck. This is a haven for wildfowl and gulls in spring and autumn. At Rewa the River Reda enters the bay amidst ponds and salt-marshes, with Dunlin, Ruff and Oystercatcher. There is another summer ringing camp on the small peninsula here. Farther north at Władysławowo, the Hel Peninsula begins. This is one of the best sites in the Baltic for rarities; pine woods offer the chance of Parrot Crossbill and the port of Hel itself is a good duck and gull spot.

CALENDAR

Interesting all year round, although the lakes and lagoons do freeze over in hard winters. Worth a visit in spring (best for raptor passage) and summer for a good selection of breeding birds, but exceptional in autumn when millions of birds pass along the coast, especially on the Hel Peninsula. September and October for vagrants. Four species of diver, five grebes and just about any duck or gull are possible from mid-September through to April.

SPECIES

- *Wood Sandpiper* So far as is known, their only regular breeding site in Poland is Bielawskie Bloto, to the west of Władysławowo.
- *Dunlin* The Rewa area has Poland's largest number of breeding birds.
- *Mediterranean Gull* Breeds on the Vistula Lagoon.
- *Arctic Tern* Poland's only breeding pairs are in the mouth of the Vistula.
- *Parrot Crossbill* Has bred and may still breed in the forests of the Hel Peninsula.
- *Greenish Warbler* Regular along the Gdańsk coast in June.

ACCESS
Gdańsk is 360 km (223 miles) north-west of Warsaw along the E77 or less than one hour by internal flight. Ferries from Scandinavia also dock here. Gdańsk Bay has numerous resorts and birdwatching from public roads is more or less straightforward. The ringing centre at Swibno operates from August to October and staff may be able to put one onto something. A road runs along the Vistula Spit and the south of the lagoon can be approached via Elbląg. A road and a railway run to Hel and back (sic!) at the tip of the peninsula. There are plans to build hides by meadows near Jastarnia on the Hel Peninsula, which is a noted raptor and rarity spot. Several sites are IBAs.

Słońsk Reserve

52°34N 14°43E

This vast, impressive wetland reserve in the west of Poland at the confluence of the Odra, Postomia and Warta Rivers, is a mosaic of flood-plain woodland, shallow temporary waters with islands and trees, meadows, pastures and a reservoir when levels are high. The fluctuating water levels dictate the birdlife, but there is always something special whether it be species or numbers or both. Breeding

Poland is the country for Aquatic Warbler and one doesn't have to head too far east as the Słońsk and Karsibór reserves are two good sites in the very west of the country.

birds usually include Red-necked and Black-necked Grebes, both bitterns, Black Stork, Shelduck, Black Kite, White-tailed Eagle, Marsh and Montagu's Harriers, Spotted Crake, Corncrake, Crane, Oystercatcher, Ruff, Whiskered, Black and White-winged Black Terns, River, Aquatic, Icterine and Barred Warblers and Penduline Tit. In spring and autumn hundreds of thousands of waterfowl use the area. Whooper, Mute and some Bewick's Swans occur, ducks include Gadwall, Garganey and Shoveler, although almost anything is possible and waders of almost every type pass through. Autumn is generally best for geese with tens of thousands of Bean and some White-front. Słońsk is a spectacular and internationally important site for wetland birds and also proves that one does not have to travel too far into Poland to be impressed.

CALENDAR
Good for a visit all year round but particularly excellent in winter and spring when thousands of swans, geese and ducks congregate with attendant White-tailed Eagles.
SPECIES
- *Whooper Swan* An important wintering site for several hundred birds.
- *Shelduck* Around twenty pairs constitute the only inland colony in Poland.
- *Crane* Does breed but Słońsk is more a feeding and roosting site.
- *Oystercatcher* This inland colony marks an extension in breeding range up the River Odra from the Baltic Sea.
- *Aquatic Warbler* An irregular breeder, but this is nevertheless another western Polish site contradicting the general idea that one has to visit the north-east to stand a chance of seeing this much sought-after bird.
ACCESS
The area lies mostly along the flood-plain of the River Warta north of road 17 between Kostrzyn and the village of Słońsk. There is a new border crossing with Germany at Kostrzyn which is 100 km (62 miles) south of Szczecin and only 110 km (68 miles) east of Berlin. A dam runs from Słońsk northwards to the river. Ask the pump-station staff here for permission to walk along it. The wetland is rather inaccessible and mostly a reserve but birds can always be seen from the dam and public roads. An IBA.

MIDDLE WARTA VALLEY
52°09–52°15N 17°39–18°43E
The flood-plain of the meandering River Warta between Poznan and Konin is a mosaic of marshes, wet woodlands, peat-bogs, sand dunes and agricultural land, much of it prone to seasonal floods. Widespread breeding birds include Black-necked Grebes, Bitterns, Little Bitterns, Garganeys, Spotted Crakes, Corncrakes, Ruffs,

Black-tailed Godwits, Redshanks, Black Terns, Bluethroats and Ortolan Buntings. Although not as common, Ferruginous Ducks, Pintails, Little Crakes, Cranes, Great Snipe, Tawny Pipits and Rollers are also possible in summer. Raptors include both kites and Montagu's Harrier. This is an important area for passage waders, ducks and geese, with large flocks of Greylag Geese and huge numbers of Teal in spring. As one would expect, White Storks nest in many of the region's villages.

CALENDAR
April and May are spectacular for passage, and from May on for summer visitors. August sees the beginning of return passage. The area is probably worth a visit in any season.
SPECIES
- *Ferruginous Duck* Not a common breeder but more occur on passage.
- *Great Snipe* This is certainly not a stronghold for the species, but a few pairs are said to breed.

ACCESS
Poznan is one of Poland's main cities, and lies to the north-west of the flood-plain. Road 38 crosses the Warta and from here there are numerous minor roads from which the area can be worked. Two IBAs are listed.

MILICZ FISH-PONDS
51°27–52°33N 17°00–17°32E
As is often the case in Eastern Europe, fish-ponds created by monks in the Middle Ages are today important wetlands for birds. Some of the ponds in this famous area along the River Barycz are 700 years old. Some are reserves and managed for birds, although most are not, but all have good birds. There are two basic complexes: the west and east, with Milicz at the centre. Stawno in the eastern complex is the largest and probably the best system. A great diversity of habitats here includes various ponds with emergent vegetation, reedbeds, ash woods and beech woods and wet-meadows. Red-necked and Black-necked Grebes, Little Bitterns, Purple Herons, Black Storks, Greylag Geese, Gadwalls, Garganeys, Ferruginous Ducks, White-tailed Eagles, Marsh Harriers, Spotted and Little Crakes, Green Sandpipers, Woodcocks, Black Tern, River, Grasshopper, Savi's, Great Reed and Icterine Warblers and both nightingales are all here. Grabownica in the north-east is the largest pond and a good site for Crane but needs to be viewed from the road as access is difficult. The garden of the nearby ornithological station at Ruda Milicka has Red-backed Shrikes, Barred Warblers and Thrush Nightingales. There are Tawny Pipits in fields behind the station. In the western complex the Radziadz system has typical forest-ponds as well as having good reedbeds and the chance of Red and Black Kites. Ponds

The ponds enclosed by forest at Milicz provide ideal breeding habitat for Green Sandpipers.

around Ruda Zmigrodzka are good for Ferruginous Duck, Common and Black Terns and the ubiquitous White-tailed Eagle. The beech forest by the road southwards from Milicz is good for Black and Grey-headed Woodpeckers and Red-breasted Flycatchers. Species that can be found throughout the whole region include Cormorant, Bittern, White Stork (the village of Ruda Sulowska has up to a dozen pairs), Honey Buzzard, Goshawk, Middle Spotted Woodpecker, Whinchat, Penduline and Bearded Tit, Great Grey Shrike, Serin and Scarlet Rosefinch. If the winter is mild, thousands of geese, Goldeneyes, Goosanders, Smews and as many as twenty White-tailed Eagles occur.

CALENDAR
This wonderful area is worth a visit at any time of year. Large numbers of wildfowl pass through in spring and autumn; summer is simply spectacular and winter, if the weather permits, is a warming experience with White-tailed Eagle seemingly everywhere.

SPECIES
◆ *Whooper Swan* Often around and will occasionally nest in the valley.
◆ *Purple Heron* The only regular pair in Poland breeds here.
◆ *White-tailed Eagle* Always present unless the winter is too harsh for the ducks upon which it preys.

◆ *Thrush Nightingale* The south-western border of its range is here along the River Barycz and many birds in the area have elements of the songs of both nightingale species.

ACCESS
Milicz is 56 km (35 miles) north of Wrocław. Most ponds can be easily watched from public roads, which is all that is really needed. For permits for strictly protected areas, such as the heart of the Stawno system, ask at the ornithological station in Ruda Milicka about 5 km (3 miles) east of Milicz. Several of the fish-pond systems are IBAs.

ODRA VALLEY

51°01–51°03N 17°05–17°10E

The Odra winds its way through southern and western Poland before entering the Baltic Sea at Szczecin Bay, and many good birdwatching sites, such as the Słońsk Reserve, lie along its route. The river is often lined with stretches of woodland and two such areas occur before and after it passes through Wrocław. Just outside the city, between the villages of Kotowice and Siechnice, oak, beech, alder and willow woodland with clearings, backwaters and agricultural land are good for Black Storks, Honey Buzzards, Red and Black Kites, Grey-headed and Middle Spotted Woodpeckers, Icterine and Barred Warblers, Red-breasted and Collared Flycatchers and Golden Orioles. This is a small area, and a network of farm tracks and paths make exploration easy. Farther downstream beyond Wrocław, the River Kaczawa enters the Odra. The Odra south of this point is lined with woodland and is a good area for raptors; White-tailed Eagles are possible. Both kites can often be seen from a bridge over the Odra between Kawice and Lubiaz. Crane, Nightingale and River Warbler are also around and this is another excellent place for Middle Spotted Woodpeckers and Collared Flycatchers.

CALENDAR
May and June are the best months to visit as the flycatchers and warblers are singing and the kites are back from winter quarters.

SPECIES
◆ *Middle Spotted Woodpecker* Probably the most common woodpecker species in the riverine woodland.
◆ *Collared Flycatcher* Very common in the oak and beech woodlands along this stretch of the Odra.

ACCESS
Wrocław, the largest city in south-west Poland, is the best base. The Kotowice-Siechnice area almost touches the suburbs of the city, being only 8 km (5 miles) to the south-east, and lies just to the north of a railway line which runs between the two villages. There is a network of paths through it. The Kaczawa area is 45 km (28 miles) north-west of Wrocław to the east of Legnica, south to Malczyce. Both sites are IBAs.

TURAWA RESERVOIR

50°42–50°43N 18°05–18°11E

Turawa is set amongst forests and agricultural land and in summer is a water-sports centre. There are also reedbeds and exposed sandy banks. Much depends on water levels; in spring the water is usually high, and suitable for local sports enthusiasts, and in autumn rather low, making it a key migration stop-over. Thousands of ducks, 'shanks', stints and Green, Marsh, Broad-billed, Wood and Curlew Sandpipers occur here from August on in some of Poland's highest concentrations. Turawa is also a site noted for vagrants and rarities; several North American waders have been recorded. Breeding birds include Red-necked and Black-necked Grebes, Little Bittern, Bittern, various ducks, Common and Black Terns, Great Grey Shrike, Penduline Tit, Scarlet Rosefinch and woodland birds in the surrounding forests. In general the south-eastern shores of the reservoir are best, although some walking may be necessary as roads here are few and far between. This is one of several excellent reservoirs in Lower Silesia, all of which have their particular bird attractions. A large reservoir near the town of Nysa, to the south-west of Turawa, is another good site in autumn. Great Black-headed Gull and Slender-billed Curlew have occurred here.

CALENDAR

Although there are interesting birds around in the breeding season there is arguably nothing here to compete with the fish-pond systems of Lower Silesia. The reservoir is usually at its best from August to October for passage birds and vagrants.

Scarlet Rosefinch is one of the most familiar birds of the countryside around Turawa.

SPECIES
- *White Stork* Nests in surrounding villages with more stopping over at the end of summer.
- *Wood Sandpiper* Hundreds pass through in autumn.
- *Scarlet Rosefinch* Quite common in suitable habitat around the reservoir.

ACCESS
The Turawa Reservoir lies near the village of the same name 16 km (10 miles) east of Opole in Lower Silesia. Wrocław is 100 km (62 miles) to the north-west along road 34. The eastern part of the reservoir from Szczedrzyk on the southern shore to Dylaki is best though difficult to work as there are no roads near the water. The area is unprotected and can be more or less freely explored. An IBA.

BABIA GÓRA
49°32N 19°32E
This mountain range on the border with Slovakia is home to Lynx, Brown Bears and an impressive selection of montane and Alpine birds. Forests cover most of the range and are determined by altitude. The lower slopes are mostly fir and beech with, for example, Grey-headed Woodpeckers and Red-breasted Flycatchers, then comes spruce forest with Hazelhens, Three-toed Woodpeckers and Nutcrackers, followed by more open areas with dwarf pine and Redpolls. Finally, a treeless Alpine zone is the haunt of Water Pipits and Alpine Accentors. Birds such as Capercaillie, Ural, Tengmalm's, Eagle and Pygmy Owls, Black Woodpecker, Redwing, Ring Ouzel, Willow and Crested Tits and Crossbill are possible at various levels.

CALENDAR
Visit from May one when the weather and the birds are arguably at their best.

SPECIES
- *White-backed Woodpecker* If it is here, old stands of spruce and beech, of which there are plenty, are usually the preferred habitats.

ACCESS
Babia Góra is about 75 km (50 miles) south of Cracow via the E77 and then minor roads. The tourist centre of Zawoja is the gateway to the range. The National Park's Head Office is at 34–223 Zawoja, Poland, and may be able to arrange guides. An IBA.

TATRA NATIONAL PARK
49°15N 19°56E
The Tatras are the highest mountain range in Poland reaching 2499 m (8199 ft) at Mount Rysy on the border with Slovakia. Most of the mountains are covered in forest with deciduous trees and fir, spruce, larch and pine up to about 1250 m (4100 ft), spruce beyond that and dwarf pine reaching 1800 m (5900 ft). Higher still are meadows and rocky terrain with permanent snow cover. There are also picturesque

tarns and numerous streams, where the red-spotted race of Bluethroat is possible. The only alpine habitat in Poland, this is the place for a special flora and Marmots, Chamois and Brown Bears. Not surprisingly it is also good country for Three-toed Woodpeckers, Water Pipits, Alpine Accentors and Wallcreepers. A road runs along the border of the National Park outside Zakopane and is the starting point for walks up various forested and craggy valleys which have Hazelhen, Pygmy and Tengmalm's Owls, Black, Grey-headed and White-backed Woodpeckers, Red-breasted Flycatcher, Nutcracker, Crested Tit and Crossbill. A path links the top of each valley, *dolina* in Polish, to the south and east of Zakopane, with the exception of the dead-end Dolina za Bramka which is itself an excellent spot, good for the above birds as well as Capercaillie, Eagle Owl, Firecrest, Ring Ouzel and Raven. Golden Eagle and Peregrine are also possible. Kuznice, to the south-east of Zakopane, can be reached by road and a cable-car from there will take you to the high tops for Water Pipit, Alpine Accentor, Wallcreeper and Redpoll. If one wants a break from the snow, to the east of Zakopane between Jaszczurówka and Chlabowka is an area of ponds, wet meadows and woodland with River and Icterine Warblers, Thrush Nightingales and Scarlet Rosefinches.

CALENDAR

Winter usually lasts from November to April and the snow can be deep. The mountains are also usually crowded with skiers at this time. Visit from April on, the earlier the better for owls, although there is no guarantee of good weather, especially above the tree line. For summer birds June is perhaps best.

SPECIES

- *Pygmy Owl* In April males call before dusk from exposed perches at the tops of trees.
- *White-backed Woodpecker* The mainly beech woods at the foot of Dolina za Bramka are a good site.
- *Three-toed Woodpecker* Widespread in spruce forest at all altitudes.
- *Wallcreeper* The Tatras are the only place in Poland for this species.
- *Redpoll* The *cabaret* race occurs, mainly at higher altitudes in scrubby open areas.
- *Nutcracker* The mountain tarn of Morskie Oko is a popular tourist spot where Nutcrackers can be quite tame.

ACCESS

Zakopane, 110 km (68 miles) south of Cracow, is the gateway to the National Park. This is a major winter sports and tourist centre and a good base from which to explore the mountains. Almost all of the area can be explored on miles of marked paths, although you should equip yourself with a good map beforehand. Trails should be kept to for safety as well as to prevent further erosion, which is a serious problem here. Higher altitudes can be reached by cable-car and ski-lift. The National Park is an IBA.

BIESZCZADY NATIONAL PARK

49°05N 22°44E

It is hard to imagine a place in Europe which is as out of the way as the Bieszczady. Tucked into a notch of Poland which juts into the Ukraine with Slovakia just to the south, these mountains have seen few 'western' visitors. The trip is worth it, however, as this is a beautiful region of rolling hills, meadows, mountain pastures, areas of pine, spruce and larch and vast beech forests. The forests are the home of Black Storks, Black, Grey-headed and White-backed Woodpeckers and Collared and Red-breasted Flycatchers. An impressive selection of raptors includes Honey Buzzard, Short-toed, Lesser Spotted, Golden and possibly Booted Eagles. This is also one of Poland's, and Europe's, very few sites for Spotted Eagle. There may also be Sakers here; this is an under-watched area and much needs to be confirmed. Another speciality is Ural Owl, with Eagle Owl also possible. Spruce forests are good for Hazelhen, Three-toed Woodpecker, Crested Tit and Nutcracker. Bieszczady is unique in Poland in having large alpine-type pastures. Corncrakes and, at higher altitudes, Ring Ouzels are birds of such places, which are also hunting grounds for the various raptors. The National Park mostly covers these upland areas; Połonina Carynska between Ustrzyki Górne and Brzegi Górne and Połonina Wetlinska north-east of Wetlina are both typical and scenic. But good birds occur all over the range, with the beech forests of Puszcza Bukowa on the border with Slovakia being one example of an almost unexpected area.

CALENDAR

May to August is probably the best time to visit. Winter can be harsh in the Bieszczady, sees an influx of skiers and lacks the key raptors.

SPECIES

- *Spotted Eagle* Breeding has not been confirmed but is highly likely.
- *Ural Owl* Relatively common, but often difficult to track down given its habits and the vastness of the area.
- *Rock Thrush* Another species that may breed. The Polish Avifaunistic Commission would welcome any records.

ACCESS

In the very south-east corner of Poland. The National Park section is around 90 km (56 miles) south-east of Sanok. A minor road, from which marked walking trails begin, runs through Wetlina, Brzegi Górne, Ustrzyki Górne and ends at Wolosate near the highest peak in the Bieszczady Tarnica at 1346 m (4416 ft). Given its location and local conditions, the Bieszczady is certainly not the place for a thrash, rather a trekking holiday of discovery through a scenic region. The National Park is an IBA.

PRZEMYŚL

49°48N 22°47E

This little-known and seldom visited corner of Poland is unique for the country in terms of its rather mild climate and thus specialized birdlife. There are several habitats around the town of Przemyśl itself: wooded hills, forests, orchards, meadows and reedbeds. The attractive flood-plain of the River San to the north is the home of Little Bitterns, Ferruginous Ducks, Spotted Crakes, Corncrakes, River Warblers, Thrush Nightingales, Kingfishers and Bee-eaters, the last a very rare bird in Poland. White-winged Black Terns pass through in spring. A fish-pond complex on the border with the Ukraine near Starzawa offers Black Storks, Black Kites, Marsh Harriers and Bluethroats. There is also the chance of White-tailed Eagle here. The town itself has its attractions, with Syrian Woodpeckers in gardens and orchards, and the town park has the distinction of being an occasional site for Ural Owls. The birds of the Przemyśl area are perhaps more typical of neighbouring Ukraine and Slovakia to the south.

CALENDAR

As usual, the ideal time to visit depends on the weather and what one wants to see. Przemyśl is arguably at its best from May to July when

Found in Poland for the first time in 1978, Syrian Woodpecker is gradually expanding its range north and west.

the summer visitors such as Bee-eaters are around, although May is best for calling Corncrakes and earlier still for Ural Owl.

SPECIES
- ◆ *Corncrake* This is one of the few places in Europe where this species might be regarded as common.
- ◆ *Syrian Woodpecker* One of the best regions in the country for this most elusive of Polish woodpeckers.
- ◆ *Ural Owl* Has even bred in the town park.
- ◆ *Bee-eater* Small colonies are scattered along the river valley here and constitute the only regular breeding populations in Poland.

ACCESS
Przemyśl is in south-eastern Poland 14 km (9 miles) from the Ukrainian border at Medyka. Cracow is 250 km (155 miles) to the west via the E40. Most of the area can be freely explored as long as due respect is given to private orchards and gardens. The Bee-eater colonies are under some pressure and should not be disturbed. There are three IBAs here.

Janów forest
50°40N 22°30E
This vast forest of mostly pine is home to an impressive but at times secretive range of birds. Black Stork, Red and Black Kites, Lesser Spotted Eagle, Hobby, Goshawk, Hazelhen, Capercaillie, Nightjar,

Black, Grey-headed and Middle Spotted Woodpeckers, Red-breasted Flycatcher, Crested Tit, Firecrest, Ortolan Bunting and Crossbill are all here. There are also fish-ponds and peat-bogs dotted around where Cranes, Black Grouse and Scarlet Rosefinches can be found. One such bog with scattered clumps of trees and plenty of elk is *Imielty Lug*, which lies to the south of Łazek Ordynacki. Some miles to the west of here a minor road crosses the River San north of Stalowa Wola and cuts through the forest passing fish-ponds after Lipa. This is a good area for Honey Buzzard, White-tailed and Short-toed Eagles and Osprey. With both storks, crakes and warblers, the fish-ponds are worth a look, too.

CALENDAR

Although the grouse and woodpeckers are resident, it is probably best to visit in summer when all the migrants are in place.

SPECIES

◆ *Capercaillie* A healthy population is said to be here, but a fair amount of luck and/or local knowledge is needed to track them down.

ACCESS

Janów Forest proper lies along road 26 south of Janów Lubelski, but similar forest continues in almost all directions. Stalowa Wola, about 20 km (12.5 miles) to the south-west, is the nearest large town. There are two IBAs in the area.

CHEŁM MARSHES
51°10N 23°30E

The whole of the sparsely populated region between Chełm and the Ukrainian border is dotted with marshes, peat-bogs, hay fields and grazing meadows. This is what eastern Poland is all about, with Aquatic Warblers seemingly common, White Stork nests adorning most villages and Lesser Spotted Eagle, Marsh and Montagu's Harriers, Crane, Woodcock, Ruff, Black-tailed Godwit, White-winged Black Tern, Corncrake, Grasshopper and River Warblers, Whinchat and Scarlet Rosefinch never far away. With sufficient effort, rarer birds like Spotted and Little Crakes, Black Grouse and Great Snipe may be found, too. A typical remote farming landscape with most of the above birds is around the village of Strzelce, north of Hrubieszów. Suitable woodlands have Wrynecks, Golden Orioles, Barred Warblers, Red-breasted Flycatchers and Ortolan Buntings.

CALENDAR

The region is at its best for birds from April to August.

SPECIES

◆ *Montagu's Harrier* Seems to be doing very well in a variety of habitats.

ACCESS
Chełm is in the south-east of Poland 67 km (42 miles) east of Lublin. A general drive between settlements, birding from minor roads is the best option. There are currently two IBAs listed for the region.

URSZULIN AREA

51°20N 23°05E
The settlement of Urszulin lies at the heart of a bird-rich rural landscape typified by meadows, fens, bogs, marshes, copses and traditionally managed small farms. To the east, near the hamlet of Wincecin, are marshes dotted with woods, patches of reed and pine stands where Aquatic Warblers are far from rare and birds such as Black Grouse, Montagu's Harriers, Cranes, Spotted Crakes, Short-eared Owl, Thrush Nightingale, Grasshopper and Icterine Warblers and Scarlet Rosefinch can all be found. To the south-west of the region towards Lake Uściwierz, there are more Aquatic Warblers and Black Kites, Montagu's Harrier and Corncrake. The lake itself has large reedbeds and all the birds one would expect. To the north of Urszulin, a patchwork of wetlands and forests is good for Black Storks and hunting White-tailed and Lesser Spotted Eagles, Buzzards and Honey Buzzards, Hobbies and Black Kites.

One of Poland's great attractions, Great Snipe are, however, restricted to very local, often inaccessible, leks.

CALENDAR
Summer is the season to visit.
SPECIES
- *Black Grouse* Small scattered leks are best sought on early
mornings in April and May.
- *Great Snipe* This certainly looks like the kind of place where leks
could exist.
ACCESS
The area lies about 25 km (16 miles) to the north of road T12,
roughly half-way between Lublin and Chełm. Access is determined by
the going underfoot. Lake Uściwierz is an IBA.

TYŚMIENICA
c. 51°25N 23°00E
This is one of what at times seems like a multitude of small rivers
which criss-cross south-east Poland. The stretch of the Tyśmienica to
the north-east of Lublin is particularly rich in birds as it is lined with
marshes, meadows, fish-ponds, lakes, willow and alder copses,
woodlands and smallholdings. Lake Siemień is a fish-pond system
through which the river passes and has, amongst others, Little
Bitterns, Ferruginous Ducks, White-tailed Eagles, Spotted Crakes,
White-winged Black Terns and Thrush Nightingales in summer.
Farther south, fish-ponds near the villages of Tyśmienica and Tulniki
have Red-necked and Black-necked Grebes, White Storks, Penduline
Tits, River Warblers and good passage of waders and terns. Eagle
Owls inhabit nearby copses, as do Wrynecks and Icterine Warblers.
Farther south still bogs, meadows and marshes near Krasne have
Crane, Great Grey Shrike and Scarlet Rosefinch, although the going
can be boggy and areas often impenetrable.

CALENDAR
Visit from April through to September
SPECIES
- *Aquatic Warbler* Almost certainly here. The Krasne area seems the
best bet.
ACCESS
The area lies about 30–40 km (20–25 miles) to the north-east of
Lublin, and can be worked from adjacent villages and tracks. The
fish-pond system at Siemień is an IBA.

KAMPINOS NATIONAL PARK
c. 50°22N 20°22E
Besides pine forest, which covers most of the park, there are high
dunes, wet-meadows, some stands of oak, marshes with willow and
alder, peat-bogs and numerous settlements. Taking in all these
habitats in summer can produce White and Black Storks, Honey
Buzzard, Lesser Spotted Eagle, Corncrake, Crane, Woodcock,

Wryneck, Black Woodpecker, Woodlark, Tawny Pipit, Collared and Red-breasted Flycatchers, Barred and Icterine Warblers, Hawfinch and Ortolan Bunting.

CALENDAR
Worth a visit at any time of year if one is passing through Warsaw, but summer is best.

SPECIES
◆ *Corncrake* This is not the best place for this species in Poland, but it is certainly the nearest to the capital if one is pushed for time.

ACCESS
Kampinos begins in the north-western suburbs of Warsaw. The National Park's Head Office at ul. Krasinskiego 49, 05-080 Izabelin, Warsaw, is in the south-eastern corner of the park and issues permits and offers guides for restricted zones. An IBA.

BIAŁOWIEŻA FOREST

52°40N 23°50E

Białowieża is a vast forest with Poland's most famous national park at its eastern edge nestling along the Belorussian border. The national park is primeval forest of oak, lime, hornbeam, ash and spruce, much dying and fallen wood and swampy areas with alder and pine. This is only a fraction of the whole area and many birds are easier to locate in the 'managed' forest although the primeval forest is particularly good for Collared and Red-breasted Flycatchers and Black, Middle Spotted and White-backed Woodpeckers. There are also open meadows, clearings and marshes along several streams and the River Narewka. Birds of prey here include Honey Buzzard, Montagu's Harrier and Short-toed, Booted and Lesser Spotted Eagles.

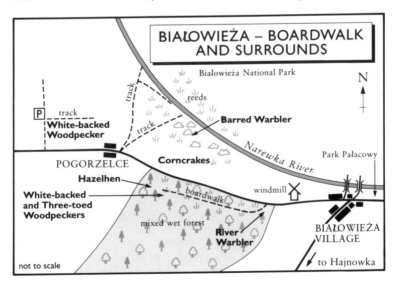

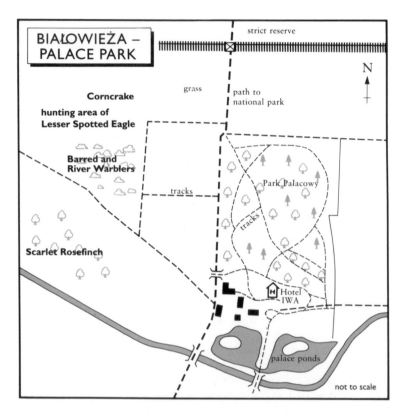

Hazelhens, Pygmy Owls, Three-toed Woodpeckers, Crested Tits and Nutcrackers favour the extensive spruce forests. The Palace Park at Białowieża is home to the National Park Head Office, a hotel and restaurant, Grey-headed Woodpeckers, Wrynecks, Thrush Nightingales, Icterine Warblers, both Collared and Pied Flycatchers and Red-backed Shrikes. A profitable walk from the village towards Pogorzelce usually produces raptors, calling Corncrakes, Barred and River Warblers, Thrush Nightingales and Scarlet Rosefinches. A rather dilapidated boardwalk heading from this road through boggy forest, with Hazelhen, White-backed and Three-toed Woodpeckers and Collared Flycatcher, is worth a try but can be frustrating as one has to also watch one's feet and fend off mosquitoes. When one mentions other birds such as Black Stork, Crane, Eagle and Tengmalm's Owls, Nightjar and Ortolan Bunting, all of which also breed at Białowieża, it should be clear that this is a vast and rich area deserving a stay of several days at least.

CALENDAR

From the end of April to July for most species although woodpeckers and owls are more active and thus easier early on in the year and some migrants only return in the middle of May. This can be a tranquil, but harsh place in winter, although some forest birds, as well as large mammals, may be more confiding. Do not expect to be alone in summer as Białowieża is now the destination of birdwatchers from all over Europe.

SPECIES
- *Lesser Spotted Eagle* Quite common and often seen hunting over the meadows between the Palace Park and the main gate of the National Park.
- *Hazelhen* Try the spruce forest with thick undergrowth south of the railway line at Czerlonka, about half-way between Hajnówka and Białowieża.
- *Black Woodpecker* In all areas of the forest.
- *White-backed Woodpecker* Probably easiest to find with the help of a guide in the National Park proper.
- *Scarlet Rosefinch* Common along the River Narewka.
- *Greenish Warbler* Besides occurring in the primeval forest this species often turns up in and around settlements, even the Palace Park.

ACCESS
Białowieża lies on the border with Belorussia in the east of Poland 222 km (138 miles) from Warsaw. The town of Hajnówka sits at the western edge of the forested area. The National Park can be entered only with a guide which the park administration at Park Palacowy, 17–230 Białowieża, can arrange more or less on the spot. Most of the managed forest can be explored at will though there are some closed reserve sections. The road from Hajnówka to Białowieża village cuts right through the forest and a surprising amount can be seen along this route and the tracks branching off it. The National Park and several adjacent reserves are IBAs.

SIEMIANÓWKA RESERVOIR

52°55N 23°50E

This artificially created huge wetland along the flood-plain of the River Narew offers a birding contrast to the surrounding famous forest areas. Being so close to Białowieża, it is certainly worth fitting into the agenda of any visit there. In the past its proximity to the border and a railway line carrying Soviet troops and equipment meant that this was definitely out of bounds, but now no one seems to mind. Parts of the reservoir have steeply sloping concrete banks, especially at the north-west; other parts have grassy, muddy slopes. The eastern end of the reservoir, where there are vegetation-clad areas, is best. In general the south-eastern shore is easiest to work as roads run nearby. Summer birds include Red-necked and Black-necked Grebes, White and Black Storks, Gadwall, Teal, Garganey, Goldeneye, Osprey, White-tailed Eagle, Crane, Common, Black, White-winged Black and Whiskered Terns, Hoopoe, Crested Lark, Ortolan Bunting and Scarlet Rosefinch. In spring good numbers of waders pass through, particularly Ruffs, but also Green and Wood Sandpipers, Spotted Redshank and Black-tailed Godwit.

CALENDAR

From April to August the place is alive with breeding birds. May and June are probably the best months, but if one happens to be in the region in autumn it may be worth visiting for wildfowl and waders. In winter it can be very harsh.

SPECIES

- ◆ *White-tailed Eagle* A pair hunts at the eastern end of the reservoir in summer.
- ◆ *Osprey* Regular on spring and autumn passage and a pair fish here in summer.
- ◆ *Marsh Sandpiper* A few pairs have recently been found breeding here and it seems that this species may be gradually colonizing eastern Poland.
- ◆ *Whiskered Tern* Poland's largest colony, with up to sixty pairs.
- ◆ *Ortolan Bunting* Scattered around the reservoir. The farm at the southern foot of the railway bridge near Siemianówka station is one regular spot.

ACCESS

The reservoir lies north of the villages of Tarnopol and Siemianówka around 30 km (18 miles) north-east of Hajnówka, the gateway to the Białowieża National Park, and 60 km (37 miles) south-east of Białystok along minor roads. As old maps do not show the reservoir and it is close to the Belorussian border it is probably wise to carry one's passport. The railway bridge across the water from Siemianówka station is a good vantage point and can be followed on a cat-walk. The area east of the bridge is best. A road runs around the northern shore but this area is wild and difficult to work. Not an IBA.

BIAŁYSTOK FISH-PONDS

53°10N 23°10E

North-eastern Poland has numerous wetlands, many in remote locations and several of international importance for their birdlife. Nevertheless, these apparently uninviting fish-ponds lying at the edge of the region's largest city and part of which throng with Poles at play in summer, prove that one need not tramp for miles through bogs and marshes to see good birds in Poland. The main attraction is that all five European grebe species breed. Great Crested and Little are on all four main ponds, Red-necked and Black-necked are scattered around and there is a pair of Slavonian Grebes in stunning breeding plumage every year. There can be few European wetlands that offer a chance of seeing these five colourful birds displaying close to each other. There are other birds, too, with Bittern, various ducks, Water Rail, Little Crake, Whiskered and Black Terns, River, Marsh and Great Reed

Warblers, Penduline Tit and Marsh Harrier all around. Convenient dykes with footpaths cross the system, allowing views of the open water, patches of willow, scrub and reedbeds. Despite the complex being at the edge of a busy city, being also strategically placed for passage birds means that the complete list of species which have occurred here reads like a checklist of eastern Poland's specialities.

CALENDAR
The best time to visit is from May to July when all the grebe species are present in breeding plumage. Occasional divers, grebes and some ducks winter, and there is some wader passage in autumn.

SPECIES
◆ *Slavonian Grebe* This is almost certainly the most southerly breeding site in Europe. If there is another one, it is more than likely to be in Poland, too.
◆ *Marsh Warbler* Common in bushes on dykes between the ponds.

ACCESS
Białystok is 193 km (120 miles) north-east of Warsaw. The fish-ponds are just to the south-east of the city between Zascianki and Dojlidy. A road runs along the northern edge of the system to the village of Sobolewo. The area can be easily and freely explored via a series of paths on dykes between the ponds. Not an IBA.

Careful scrutiny of the grebes at the Białystok fish-ponds may reveal breeding Slavonian.

NAREW VALLEY

c. 53°00N 23°00E

This impressive 10-km-wide flooded valley (6.25 miles) along the River Narew is a myriad of meandering channels, backwaters, willow and alder thickets, reedbeds and meadows. Most of north-eastern Poland's typical birds occur, with numerous Marsh Harriers, both bitterns, Ferruginous Duck, Garganey, hundreds of pairs of both Spotted and Little Crakes, some Corncrakes, Crane, Ruff, Great Snipe, Black-tailed Godwit, Green Sandpiper and colonies of Common and Black Terns. This is also an excellent area for the white-spotted race of Bluethroat. Warblers are particularly well represented, with Grasshopper, Savi's, River, Reed, Marsh, Great Reed, Aquatic and Sedge. A good spot for Aquatic Warblers is the wet-meadows beyond the church in Waniewo. This small village has a Marshland Tourist Centre run by English-speaking conservationists who can organize boat trips through the wetland, arrange guides and are generally expert on all things local. Other birds in the Narew Valley include both storks, Montagu's Harrier, Penduline Tit and Thrush Nightingale.

CALENDAR

There is some spring passage of waders in April and early May but generally the area is at its best from mid-May to July.

SPECIES

◆ *Little Crake* Up to 250 pairs have been estimated.
◆ *Black Tern* Along with several other species its numbers have been drastically reduced by land reclamation over the last decade.
◆ *Savi's Warbler* Very common with singing males in every patch of reed in spring and summer.

ACCESS

The area is approximately 175 km (108 miles) north-east of Warsaw and 40 km (25 miles) westwards from Białystok. Take the E12 from Białystok to the Stare Jezewo junction and turn left heading on minor roads towards Sokoly. The second turning to the east from this minor road heads towards the Narew. A boat trip certainly gets one into the heart of this tranquil wetland but is not always the best way of seeing birds. Much of the valley is a Landscape Reserve and an IBA.

BIEBRZA MARSHES – SOUTHERN BASIN

53°14–53°30N 22°25–22°39E

This is a wonderful area of marshes, fens, wet-meadows, ox-bows, reedbeds and forests lying along the Biebrza River. The number and variety of breeding birds are remarkable, with Little Bittern, both storks, White-tailed, Short-toed and Lesser Spotted Eagles, Marsh, Hen and Montagu's Harriers, Spotted Crake, Corncrake, Crane, Ruff, Roller, Bluethroat, Aquatic Warbler and Scarlet Rosefinch just

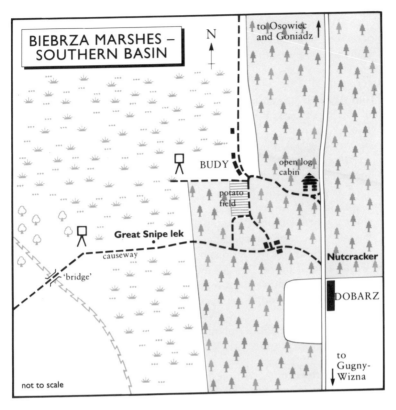

a selection. Thousands of ducks nest with more on spring passage. Yet, if there is one bird that most visitors come here for it is Great Snipe. The best way to see this is to visit the now well-known lek near Dobarz. This hamlet lies just north of Gugny on the road to Goniądz. A sandy track to the left leads through forest before becoming a causeway across open marsh with sedge and scrub. Half-way along this the birds can be heard and seen lekking to the right just before dusk. Snipe and Jack Snipe complete the trio with Woodcock, Aquatic and Grasshopper Warblers and Short-eared Owl also here. Nearby Budy is a White-tailed and Spotted Eagle area. Rollers, Crested Tits and Nutcrackers are to be found around Dobarz itself. South of here the marshes around Gugny are good for crakes and snipe and 3 km (2 miles) further on is another causeway to the right and a reserve for Aquatic Warblers. Between Laskowiec and a bridge over the Narew at Strekowa Gora are splendid wet-meadows with Ruff, Black-tailed Godwit and White-winged Black Tern. Across the valley, a cobbled road follows the river. Although one can be a shaking wreck after driving along it, excellent views over the whole southern basin are the reward. To the north, between Brzostowa and Mocarze, grebes, lekking Ruff and Common, Little, Black and more White-winged Black Terns are likely. Ortolan Buntings sing along the route. To the south the Biebrza meets the Narew near Wizna in a good area with Thrush Nightingale, Icterine and River Warblers, Penduline Tit and many birds already mentioned.

CALENDAR

From April to July. May and June are best for lekking Great Snipe and singing Aquatic Warblers.

SPECIES

- *Spotted Eagle* Although certainly around, not so straightforward as some observers suggest. Lesser Spotted Eagles can be easily mistaken for Spotteds by the over-eager.
- *Jack Snipe* Occasionally breeds.
- *Great Snipe* Now probably the most important area in Europe for this rare bird. Despite the sadly obvious trails into the lek and the encouragement of some local guides do not be tempted to disturb the displays of this mysterious bird.
- *White-winged Black Tern* All the mentioned sites should be visited as colonies may move from year to year according to water levels.
- *White-backed Woodpecker* Wet birch forests are the haunt of this species.
- *Aquatic Warbler* White ribbons on vegetation in the reserve at Gugny indicate a study site. Wait for males to climb a stalk to sing.

ACCESS

The largest town in the region, Łomza, is at the south-western tip of the area, approximately 150 km (93 miles) north-east of Warsaw along road 11. Being 30 km (18 miles) long and up to 12 km (7 miles) wide, this is a large area to work, but several convenient causeways in the east probe into the marshes and fens. The cobbled road on the western side north of Wizna is elevated and at times runs close to the river. Remember the Code of Conduct for Birdwatchers and resist the temptation to wade through breeding meadows. All the birds of the area can be found without leaving roads and tracks. An IBA.

BIEBRZA MARSHES – CENTRAL BASIN

53°30–53°42N 22°26–23°09E

The border of the two main basins of the Biebrza can be conveniently drawn along the road and railway line between Monki and Grajewo. As one would expect, the birdlife here is more or less as in the southern basin, although Spotted Eagles are more likely, there are more Ruffs and Corncrakes, and Black Grouse are easier to locate. If water levels are suitable, hundreds of White-winged Black Terns breed in meadows beyond the bridge north of Goniądz, which is also a good spot for viewing raptors. A car park near Osowiec at the southern tip of the area is convenient for a riverside exploration for grebes, crakes and marsh terns. Farther along road 669 towards Grajewo a ruined concrete bunker is another good vantage point over

One of Europe's rarest birds of prey, Spotted Eagle breeds in the Biebrza Marshes.

the flood-plain. Road 11 north from Grajewo to Augustów is the starting point for several good sites. Perhaps the most famous is Czerwone Bagno, the so-called Red Marsh, which is 12 km (7 miles) south-east of Rajgród. The south of the reserve is said to offer the best chance of Spotted Eagle. However, I have always found it a slightly disappointing, although certainly tranquil, place despite its dunes, birch woods and observation tower. The walk from the reserve barrier to the observation tower has all the typical woodland birds of the Biebrza marshes. Other birds here include Black Stork, Hen and Montagu's Harriers, Golden, Lesser Spotted and White-tailed Eagles and Crane. Lake Drestmo is *en route* and good for Red-necked Grebe, wildfowl and Black Kite. To the south of the road between Belda and Czerwone Bagno is an area of peatbogs, meadows and tiny hamlets amongst birch and conifer forest through which the River Elk flows. There are Corncrakes, Grasshopper Warblers, and several Black Grouse leks here. This excellent and wild area can also be worked from the south via Ruda.

CALENDAR
Spring and summer with overall May to mid-June probably the best period. Black Grouse lek in the early morning from March to June.
SPECIES
♦ *Spotted Eagle* The bridge over the Biebrza near Goniądz is a vantage point from which hunting birds can be seen.

- *Crane* Can be found anywhere between road 11 and the Red Marsh and river.
- *Whinchat* Common and widespread.
- *Corncrake* An impressive 1000 males are estimated to hold territories in the area.

ACCESS

Augustów, at the north of the area, is 250 km (155 miles) from Warsaw. The mentioned sites can be explored easily on foot via roads, paths and dykes. Entry into the Czerwone Bagno reserve is only by permit, available from the warden. Apply at his home (with Peacocks) which is on the left at the junction just before Tama on road 11. The right turn here heads for the reserve, passing through several hamlets. From the barrier, which should be opened upon production of the permit, there is a pleasant bird-lined walk of about 8 km (5 miles) to the dunes and observation tower. An IBA.

AUGUSTÓW LAKES

53°51N 23°00E

Augustów has a mixture of easily worked habitats such as parkland, is crossed by a useful river and canal system and is surrounded by extensive forests and large lakes. Lesser Spotted Eagle, Honey Buzzard, Goshawk, Black and Red Kites, Hobby and Black Stork can often be seen above the lakes without having to go on a major hike. The woodland has Black, White-backed and Middle Spotted Woodpeckers and the water and reeds have Red-necked Grebes, Little Bitterns, Red-breasted Mergansers, Goosanders, Goldeneyes and Great Reed, Marsh and Savi's Warblers among others. In spring, divers and all kinds of ducks use the lakes. There are Wrynecks, Icterine Warblers, Hawfinches and Thrush Nightingales in the town. The vast forests of Puszcza Augustowska begin just to the east and stretch to the border with Belorussia and beyond.

CALENDAR

April and May are good for spring passage and May to August for breeding birds.

SPECIES

- *Red Kite* Often at a rubbish dump to the south of the town off road 11.
- *Greenish Warbler* Worth keeping an eye and an ear open in parkland for this possibly under-recorded warbler.

ACCESS

Augustów is about 33 km (20 miles) south of Suwałki along road 11 in the very north-east corner of Poland. Access around most lakes is generally straightforward along paths. In the summer tourist season it is possible to take a boat trip through the region, which is a good way of covering a large area and seeing raptors but not always the easiest way to watch smaller birds. No IBAs are listed.

Mazurian Lakes

53°50N 21°00E

The whole of north-east Poland is one huge 'lake district' but with hundreds of waters of all sizes Mazuria is popularly given that title. Some lakes are enclosed by forests, marshes or reedbeds, most have islands and peninsulas, and many are linked by rivers and canals. There are no real birdwatching hot spots; the best policy is to explore the whole region: various grebes, ducks, White Stork, White-tailed Eagle, Red Kite, Crane and Thrush Nightingale are widespread. Lake Łuknajno (Swan Lake) near Mikołajki is perhaps the best-known site for birds as it is an ornithological reserve. As the name suggests, there should be no difficulty in finding Mute Swans here as well as Bittern, Red-crested Pochard, Marsh Harrier, Osprey and Black Tern. In addition, both kites, Lesser Spotted Eagle, Spotted and Little Crakes, Corncrake and Ortolan Bunting may also oblige. Thousands of ducks roost here in autumn. Lake Lanskie, in the west of the area 25 km (15 miles) south of Olsztyn, and the surrounding meadows and forests are good for Black Stork, Black Kite, Corncrake and Red-breasted Flycatcher. Lakes between Gizycko and Wegorzewo in the north have good reedbeds and several island bird reserves. The marshes and meadows along the valley of the River Czarna are good raptor areas, and forests throughout Mazuria have Black, Grey-headed and Middle Spotted Woodpeckers, Woodlark and Firecrest. As long as one avoids the obvious water-sport spots good birds will turn up throughout the whole of the Mazurian Lakes region.

CALENDAR
Spring and summer are the seasons to visit, with April and May best. Most of the lakes are frozen over in winter.

SPECIES
- *Osprey* With the highest number of breeding pairs this is the best area in Poland.
- *Red Kite* Can almost be described as common.
- *Red-crested Pochard* Lake Łuknajno is the favoured breeding site and hundreds occur in autumn.
- *Black Grouse* The Omulew Valley in the west of the lake district, to the south of Olsztyn, has several small leks.

ACCESS
Mragowo is at the centre of the region and is around 200 km (124 miles) north of Warsaw. Road 182 passes through Mragowo linking Olsztyn in the west and Elk in the east. This is a favourite summer holiday destination and so convenient roads and paths criss-cross the region. The Polish Tourist Board produces excellent detailed maps of the Mazurian Lake district indicating reserves and places to stay. Several reserves are dotted around but most birds can be seen outside the closed areas. There are several IBAs in the region.

THE CZECH REPUBLIC

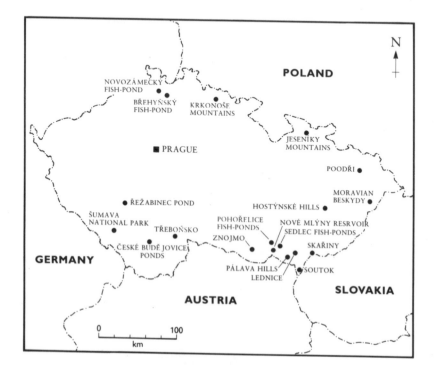

GENERAL INFORMATION

The Czech Republic comprises Bohemia, Moravia and part of Silesia. Despite having been behind the 'Iron Curtain' and thus in 'Eastern Europe', most of the country lies well to the west of Vienna. Although few birdwatchers visit this part of Europe, I have always found it a convenient and satisfying region to explore, with an organized tourist infrastructure, well-stocked shops and co-operative locals who are generally great lovers of the outdoors. Accommodation used to be a problem in some areas but now free enterprise has seen *zimmer frei* signs and small hotels sprouting up all around the country. German is the widest known second language. English is not generally spoken outside Prague and large hotels elsewhere. Credit cards and traveller's cheques are not widely accepted outside the capital and big hotels in the provinces, though this is changing rapidly. Prices are still reasonable, especially in comparison with neighbouring Germany and Austria. In general, accommodation is one's greatest expense. The unit of currency is the koruna, the Czech crown.

With a typical continental land-locked climate, the country has average winter temperatures of about 0 °C (32 °F). In mountainous areas it can drop well below that, with snow on the ground well into April and beyond. Summer temperatures can rise above 25 °C (77 °F) in July and August. South Moravia has an almost Mediterranean climate with milder weather than the rest of the country.

Free emergency treatment is available for foreigners upon production of a passport, though there may be a charge for medicines. Pharmacies in towns are well stocked and just about everything is obtainable in the larger Prague shops and hotels. Mosquito repellent may be needed in some marsh and fish-pond areas and ticks are a potential hazard in forests and woodlands. Tap water is officially safe, yet an increasing number of Czechs avoid drinking it. Thus, it is probably best to follow the local example.

The Czech Republic's former frontline status for the Warsaw Pact countries and its particularly hard-line leadership meant wide out-of-bounds border zones. These areas are often excellent for birds and are now generally open to the public; the tolerance of border guards to people brandishing telescopes and cameras is quite admirable. Permission is usually given to wander round fish-ponds and vineyards by the people working there if one is courteous. It is not necessary to know Czech, just to illustrate one's intentions by producing a guide like this. While exploring the countryside one is bound to meet ramblers and mushroom collectors. Czechs are probably the world champions at the latter; birdwatching has yet to take off.

IMPORTANCE FOR BIRDS

It has taken some time for the Czech Republic to be acknowledged as a place of any international importance for birds. However, the general opening up of this once hard-line communist state, a number of guided birdwatching tours to Bohemia and Moravia, and the activities of skilled local conservationists, have all contributed to the growing realization that this small state is an integral part of the European ornithological map. The globally threatened Red Kite has a healthy, stable population. White-tailed Eagle has been successfully reintroduced into Bohemia and has since returned to breed in Moravia. Corncrakes maintain a foothold, as does a small population of Great Bustards. Several species that are under pressure elsewhere in Europe, such as Black Stork, Black Kite and Black Grouse, also breed in good numbers. Indeed, the country is perhaps of greatest importance for its upland and forest birds: Hazelhen, Capercaillie, Eagle Owl, Pygmy Owl, Tengmalm's Owl (recently found to be the most common owl species in South Bohemia) and all nine European species of woodpecker are resident across the country. The lowlands' extensive fish-farms support populations of Little Bittern, Night Heron and Marsh Harrier and are important passage and wintering sites for wildfowl. Red-backed Shrikes, for example, are found in an almost surprising variety of places.

GETTING THERE

Both British Airways and Czech Airlines fly into Prague Ruzyně Airport daily. From Prague about ten domestic airports in the Czech Republic and Slovakia can be reached. Vienna Airport is an hour south of Moravia and can be a better arrival point for exploring both southern Moravia and parts of southern Bohemia. Prague is served by a good system of international trains from Germany, Austria and beyond. Driving in from Germany or Austria is convenient, with good roads and several new border crossings. A good transport system criss-crosses Bohemia and Moravia and, unlike most of the countries in this guide, it is feasible to birdwatch using public transport. However, major walks are necessary in some areas and it can be difficult to decipher timetables. Access is generally unrestricted in parks and reserves in the Czech Republic except National Nature Reserves and core areas of National Parks, when only public highways, marked trails and tourist paths may be followed.

CONSERVATION

Under the previous political system the availability of international ornithological literature was limited and debate on conservation matters in general discouraged. Now many who were silenced, and a new generation of conservationists, are making themselves known. The Czech Ornithological Society, which was mainly an organization composed of amateur and professional ornithologists working from museums and universities, has recently shifted towards establishing a more popular-based society. The COS can be contacted at Hornomecholupská 34, 100 10 Prague 10–Hostivar, The Czech Republic. Although in true eastern European fashion a complex and extensive system of protected areas, many of which are important for birds, was established by central government after World War II, political change seems to be benefiting birds and habitats in the country. An example is the swift declaration of National Parks in once closed, and thus inadvertently protected, border areas like Šumava.

HABITATS

Unlike the other countries of the region, which are usually characterized by a particular habitat type, the Czech Republic is a mosaic of upland forests and bogs, lowland fish-ponds and reservoirs and remnants of riverine forest in a largely agrarian landscape. Peat-bogs in the Krkonoše and Šumava Mountains are particularly imp-ortant for birds such as Capercaillie and Black Grouse. The largely coniferous forests of southern Bohemia support surprisingly large populations of Pygmy and Tengmalm's Owls. Fish-pond systems throughout Bohemia and South Moravia are an excellent example of how a landscape fashioned by man has become established as an important bird habitat in its own right. The fish-ponds of the Třeboň Basin, for example, support White-tailed Eagles, both storks, terns, crakes and innumerable warblers in a patchwork of ponds, lakes, forests and farmland. The riverine forest along the Morava and Dyje Rivers is a fine example of habitat which has sadly disappeared from most of the rest of Europe. It is perhaps ironic that this riverine forest, and the peatbogs and forests of Šumava, have only survived in the bird-rich state we find them today because of their former strategic position on the border between 'east' and 'west'.

SEASONS

SPRING

In my experience this is the best season to birdwatch in the Czech Republic. The weather can still be wintry in the hills well into April, but the country's special birds, its grouse, owls and woodpeckers, are easiest to find at this time. Fish-ponds are always worth a look in spring.

*Both treecreepers can be found throughout the Czech Republic
with Short-toed particularly common on the tree-lined dykes around
fish-ponds.*

SUMMER

Although the summer is quite short it is very pleasant in both the lowlands and uplands at this time of year. Early summer sees the arrival of storks, raptors and warblers as well as breeding resident birds. South Moravia is particularly pleasant both in terms of weather and birds.

AUTUMN

There is some wader and wildfowl passage on reservoirs and drained fish-ponds. There are many resident species, but this season is generally a quiet one for birds in the Czech Republic. The weather can be a little unpredictable, too.

WINTER

White-tailed Eagles and many species of waterfowl winter in southern Bohemia and southern Moravia although it can be pretty bleak and cold. The mountains are rather silent as regards birds, but busy with skiers. Snow lies on the ground well into spring in upland areas.

BIRDWATCHING SITES

KRKONOŠE MOUNTAINS

50°37–50°47N 15°23–15°53E

These are the so-called 'Giant Mountains' and perhaps the most scenic area of Bohemia, with timber chalets, high mountain meadows and a tundra-like zone. Certainly, this National Park is a popular recreational area for Czechs, attracting millions of ramblers and skiers every year. Krkonoše's peatbogs, alpine meadows and dense forests of spruce and pine all have their special birds. Black Stork, Red-breasted Flycatcher, Ring Ouzel, Crested Tit, Crossbill, Scarlet Rosefinch, Redpoll and Nutcracker can generally be found throughout the mountains. Perhaps the most special habitat here is peatbog; Black Grouse is one bird associated with these impressive places. Sadly, the region's forests have suffered badly from acid rain but extensive areas still hold Capercaillies and Eagle, Pygmy and Tengmalm's Owls, the last being the most widespread. There are also Three-toed, Grey-headed, Black, Middle Spotted and a few White-backed Woodpeckers. This is not the best site in the country for diurnal raptors, although Honey Buzzards are quite common and Hen Harrier, Lesser Spotted Eagle, Peregrine and Merlin are possible. Higher up an alpine zone has Alpine Accentors and Rock Pipits. The red-spotted race of Bluethroat is a Krkonoše speciality.

CALENDAR
The most sensible time to visit is probably June when all the summer birds have returned from winter quarters and any late snow has melted. Of course, an earlier visit is needed, from March to May, to see lekking grouse and active woodpeckers.

SPECIES
◆ *Black Grouse* Around 100 birds scattered in several leks.
◆ *Dotterel* Has declined drastically since World War II. Nowadays probably extinct as a breeding species.
◆ *Alpine Accentor* With around ten pairs this is an important site in the Czech Republic, with the most northerly breeding birds of the species in Europe.
◆ *Bluethroat* This is the only site in the country, and in contrast to the above species one of the most southerly in Europe, for the red-spotted race *svecica*.
◆ *Scarlet Rosefinch* Around 100 pairs and increasing.

ACCESS
Krkonoše nestles along the Polish border 130 km (81 miles) north-east of Prague via the E65. Border crossings with Poland lie just to the east and west of the range. There are several tourist centres as this is the main skiing area in the country. Harrachov, Špindlerův-Mlýn and Pec pod Sněžkou are good bases and have National Park information offices. A chair-lift runs from the last resort to the highest peak Sněžka at 1602 m (5256 ft). All of the National Park may be visited but only on marked paths in core areas (the so-called First Zones) which lie along the Polish border. An IBA.

BŘEHIŇSKÝ FISH-POND

50°34N 14°45E
This large pond is set in an area of diverse bird habitats. There is open water, large reedbeds, peat-bog, boggy forest and conifer plantations. If all these habitats are taken in on a spring visit then an impressive list can be chalked up. Birds include one or two pairs of breeding Cranes, Bittern, Little Bittern, White and Black Storks, Ferruginous Duck, White-tailed Eagle, Black Woodpecker, River Warbler, Collared Flycatcher, Crested Tit and Great Grey Shrike.

CALENDAR
Worth a visit at any time as there are always good birds about, whether they are wintering, passage or breeding species.

SPECIES
◆ *White-tailed Eagle* Can be seen in the area all year round.

ACCESS

The nearest settlement is Doksy, which is a famous spa 20 km (12.5 miles) south-east of Česká Lípa in northern Bohemia. Prague is only an hour or so to the south by road. Being a reserve, access is only via paths and roads, but being very wet underfoot the forests are in any case mostly impenetrable. Proposed as an IBA.

NOVOZÁMECKÝ FISH-POND

50°40N 14°30E

This is one of the very few places in the country where Cranes can be seen in summer. The pond is now almost totally covered in reed, and birds such as Bittern, Little Bittern, Spotted Crake, various 'reedy' warblers and Penduline Tit are specialities in summer. If adjacent meadows, peat-bogs, woodland and farmland are explored, Eagle Owl, Corncrake and Black Woodpecker, among others, can be added.

CALENDAR

Overall, best to visit in summer for breeding birds.

SPECIES

♦ *Crane* Along with the Břehiňský fish-pond (*see* above) this was one of the first breeding sites for the species in the Czech Republic. One or two pairs regularly nest.

ACCESS

The pond lies just off road 9 around 7 km (4.5 miles) south of Česká Lípa, and 70 km (45 miles) north of Prague. Being a National Nature Reserve, paths and roads must be kept to. An IBA.

ŘEŽABINEC POND

49°15N 14°06E

This South Bohemian fish-pond is one of many which also double as good areas for birds. It is a famous site locally, where many a Czech birder has started his career amidst much roasting of sausages. Large reedbeds, smaller ponds, a peat-bog to the south-west, meadows, surrounding farmland and adjacent forest mean plenty of variety in birdlife. Black-necked Grebe, Little Bittern, Garganey, Red-crested Pochard, Marsh Harrier, Goshawk, Spotted Crake, Black Tern, Penduline Tit and Savi's and Great Reed Warblers are all around in summer. On autumn passage in particular the pond is good for wildfowl and waders. Although not a rich raptor area, White-tailed Eagles and Hen Harriers are often here in winter.

CALENDAR

Worth a look at any season.

ACCESS

The historical town of Písek, which lies on the E49, is 8 km (5 miles) to the north-east. There is a marked nature trail and an almost permanent ringing camp where information can be obtained. An IBA.

ŠUMAVA NATIONAL PARK

48°40–49°20N 13°15–14°10E

This is a wonderful mountainous region which was depopulated and closed off under socialism as it lay along the border with Germany and Austria. Most of Šumava is covered in spruce, with some impressive primeval forest, but there are also deciduous areas, plantations, vast peatbogs, river and stream valleys and farmland. The primeval spruce forest on Mount Boubín, between Vimperk and Volary, can be a wet slog (it has rained every time I have been there) but it is also the place for Hazelhen, Capercaillie, Tengmalm's Owl, Black, Grey-headed, White-backed and Three-toed Wood-peckers, Ring Ouzel and in winter huge flocks of Bramblings. Follow the path around the protected area and good forest is on all sides. Mount Bobík, just to the south-east, has a similar collection of birds plus Black Stork and Red-breasted Flycatcher. Another excellent area is the flood-plain of the River Vltava which winds southwards for miles from Horní Vltavice. Specialities in summer here are Honey Buzzard, Lesser Spotted Eagle, Hen Harrier, Black Grouse at several leks, Corncrake, Great Grey and Red-backed Shrikes, Redpoll and Scarlet Rosefinch. Birds such as Woodlark, Goldcrest, Firecrest, Crested Tit and Nutcracker can be found

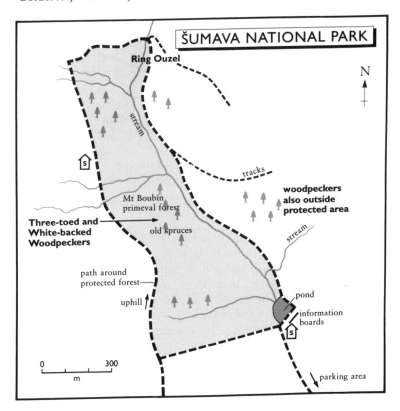

throughout Šumava. Pygmy and Tengmalm's Owls are quite wide-spread but the forest habitat is vast and they become increasingly elusive as the year progresses. The attractive sub-alpine meadows of Šumava are good spots to see feeding Ring Ouzels, Fieldfares and Redwings.

CALENDAR

The weather is the key to the timing of a visit. March and April are best for lekking grouse, owls and woodpeckers, although snow can still be on the ground in these months. From May onwards the weather improves and summer visitors such as Scarlet Rosefinch are present, but owls become more difficult as they cease calling.

SPECIES

- *Black Grouse* With up to 200 cocks this is an extremely important area for the species.
- *Tengmalm's Owl* A nest-box scheme has aided the study and probably the breeding of the species.
- *Ural Owl* Sightings are increasing and the species is now probably breeding in Šumava as a result of a reintroduction scheme in neighbouring Bavaria.
- *White-backed Woodpecker* Although concentrated in easily identified old forest, these birds can prove most elusive.
- *Three-toed Woodpecker* Quite common throughout Šumava but rather silent and not easy to observe.
- *Scarlet Rosefinch* Šumava is the best site in the Czech Republic for this species, though it is increasing in number across the country.

ACCESS

Vimperk, at the heart of the Šumava National Park, is 130 km (81 miles) south-west of Prague on road 4. Approaching from Germany cross the border at Strážný. Most of the National Park can be freely explored except for reserve areas which are signposted. It is forbidden and unnecessary to enter the primeval forest at Mount Boubín as it is enclosed by a convenient path. An IBA.

ČESKE BUDĚJOVICE PONDS

43°55N 14°25E

Česke Budějovice is famous for being the home of Budweiser beer. However, the environs of the town have a plentiful supply of that other South Bohemian liquid stalwart, the fish-pond. Ponds of all shapes and sizes, some with large reedbeds, lie in a mainly agricultural setting. The largest and most well known is the Dehtář Pond near the village of Dehtáre to the west of town, but the whole network is worth exploring. In summer breeding birds include Black-necked Grebe, Little Bittern, Spoonbill, Black and White Storks, Gadwall, Garganey, Red-crested Pochard, Marsh Harrier and River, Marsh and Icterine Warblers. There are a few Spotted Crakes, too. Woodland and farmland between and around the ponds offer such birds as Montagu's Harrier, sometimes Corncrake, Woodcocks, several woodpeckers, both treecreepers and Great Grey Shrike. But the area comes into its own in autumn when numerous passage species use the region. Black-necked and Red-necked Grebes, Spoonbills, Cranes, grey geese, ducks, Ospreys, both kites and various waders occur from August on. Wintering birds include Black-throated Diver, Smew, White-tailed Eagle and Hen Harrier. Give the region plenty of time, and in autumn try to locate recently drained ponds.

CALENDAR

May to July for breeding species. There is some spring passage but autumn is probably the best season. September and October are particularly good as many ponds are drained at this time.

SPECIES

- *Night Heron* No longer breeds but still occurs at the Dehtář Pond.
- *White-tailed Eagle* Several birds spend the winter in the area.
- *Crane* This is one of the few regular migration stop-overs in the Czech Republic.

ACCESS

Česke Budějovice is 150 km (93 miles) south of Prague on the E55. The border crossing with Austria at Dolni Dvořiště is 40 km (25 miles) to the south. The fish-ponds are scattered over a wide area to the north and west of the town. As fish-farming is an important industry in the area, access to most ponds is possible along metalled roads. Permission may be needed locally to visit some spots. The Dehtář Pond is an IBA.

TŘEBOŇSKO

49°02N 14°49E

All of the countries in this guide have bird-rich fish-pond systems but few can match this vast and famous complex of over 500 ponds created and linked by channels in the Middle Ages. Many ponds are surrounded by alder woods, reedbeds, marshes and peatbogs and some are enclosed by pine and spruce plantations. A particularly attractive and good birdwatching spot is the high dyke along the Roz̆mberk Pond to the north of Třeboň. As well as affording views over the water, the fine old oaks here are good for Short-toed Treecreeper, Wryneck, Middle Spotted Woodpecker and Collared Flycatcher. Also a little to the north the Velký Tisý Pond has Purple and Night Herons, White-tailed Eagle, Little Crake, Common Tern colonies, Grey-headed and Middle Spotted Woodpeckers, Bluethroat, Collared Flycatcher, Barred and Savi's Warblers, Penduline and Bearded Tits and Red-backed Shrike. Thousands of wildfowl pass through on migration, and Great White Egrets, Spoonbills and Ospreys regularly occur in spring and autumn. The various habitats of the Old River Reserve, the Stará Řka, to the east of Třeboň between

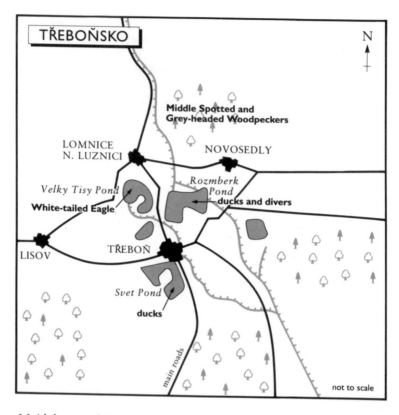

Majdalena and Stará Hlína, means a rich blend of birds. Bittern, Black Stork, Honey Buzzard, White-tailed Eagle, Green Sandpiper, Black Tern, Pygmy and Tengmalm's Owls, Nightjar and Black Woodpecker are all possible. The Svět Pond lies at the southern edge of Třeboň and is a good wildfowl site with Goldeneyes breeding in nest-boxes. On the far side of the pond an easy stroll through the parkland around a church usually produces several woodpeckers and Hawfinch. The town itself has White Stork, Serin and Black Redstart. To the south near Branná smaller roadside ponds are good for Black-necked Grebe, Gadwall, Garganey and Red-crested Pochard. Other birds at Třeboňsko are Hen and Montagu's Harriers, Woodcock, Woodlark, River, Barred and Icterine Warblers and Great Grey Shrike. The whole of Třeboňsko is a pleasant mosaic of water and woodland which should not be rushed.

CALENDAR

Worth a visit in almost any season. March and April are excellent for wildfowl, woodpeckers and calling owls in the surrounding forests. May and June have all the summer visitors in full song. In autumn many ponds are drained, attracting passage geese, ducks and waders.

SPECIES
- ◆ *Red-crested Pochard* In April smaller ponds have dozens of brightly coloured males and their mates, although few stay to breed.
- ◆ *White-tailed Eagle* A reintroduction project has boosted the population of this magnificent bird.
- ◆ *Collared Flycatcher* Common on the wooded dykes around the Rožmberk Pond and the River Lužnice.
- ◆ *Bluethroat* Around fifty pairs of the white-spotted race *cyanecula* breed, the best site being Velký Tisý.

ACCESS
The attractive old town of Třeboň is at the centre of the region and is 142 km (88 miles) south of Prague via the E55. České Budějovice is 24 km (15 miles) to the west and the Austrian border at Neu-Nagelberg 28 km (17 miles) to the south. Most ponds can be viewed from adjacent roads. An IBA.

ZNOJMO
48°47–48°51N 16°10–16°16E

This flat border area is now heavily farmed and, sadly, just a remnant of the extensive flood-plain and grassland habitat that once covered this region. However, as far as birds are concerned, it still has something to offer as the only place in the Czech Republic for

Although far from common in the rest of the country, Hoopoes are invariably encountered in summer in South Moravia.

Great Bustards and probably the last refuge of Stone Curlews in the country, too. Tawny Pipits also occur, and again, are rare birds for the country. Another bird, which is often associated with the grasslands and steppe further east but which is possible here, is Lesser Grey Shrike, although it is uncommon. Country roads through the area are lined with trees planted as wind-breaks and are always worth checking for shrikes and perching raptors. Stonechats, too, are roadside birds, and Hoopoes and Barred Warblers both occur. In winter, occasional Sakers, Rough-legged Buzzards, Hen Harriers and Great Grey Shrikes reside here and some years have invasions of Short-eared Owls.

CALENDAR

May and June are best for Stone Curlew, Tawny Pipit and other summer visitors. Great Bustard is resident, but perhaps easiest to locate in April or in the autumn. Winter is not so interesting although Great Bustards are around and there is always a raptor or two.

SPECIES

◆ *Stone Curlew* Now, sadly, very rare having suffered from unsuitable agricultural methods.
◆ *Great Bustard* Ten to twenty birds now remain and it is hoped that bringing the area under protection and implementing conservation measures may save and then increase this population.
◆ *Tawny Pipit* This is one of the very few places in the Czech Republic for this species.

ACCESS

The town of Znojmo lies just north of the Czech-Austrian border crossing at Hatě on the E59. As the crow flies, Znojmo is approximately 175 km (109 miles) from Prague and 75 km (46 miles) from Vienna. Most of the area is agricultural land and unprotected. Explore on minor roads and tracks between the town and Hrádek. Access should be unrestricted as long as one does not trespass into crops and private vineyards. An IBA.

POHOŘELICE FISH-PONDS

48°50–48°59N 16°30–16°34E

This set of three large fish-ponds with several smaller holding tanks, small islands and large reedbeds has a good selection of nesting birds and is also important during the passage of wildfowl. Both bitterns breed, along with Purple Heron, several pairs of Marsh Harriers, Great Reed Warbler, Bearded Tit and Greylag Goose. Water Rail and Spotted Crake are also here but more often heard than seen. This is also one of the few nesting sites of Ferruginous Duck and Red-crested Pochard in the region, although the latter are rare and the former much easier on passage when hundreds occur. Autumn in particular is good for passage Greylag and Bean Geese and the occasional White-tailed Eagle which sometimes lingers on through the winter. The surrounding area is not too exciting though White Storks nest in villages, a few Red-backed Shrikes are always on offer and a thorough search may turn up Grey-headed and Syrian Woodpeckers.

CALENDAR
April and May are good for spring passage with Osprey and parties of Black Terns regular. In summer there are both bitterns and crakes, and from October to March grey geese which can number thousands. Waders occur in the autumn when the ponds are drained.

SPECIES
◆ *Bittern* Rarely more than one pair.
◆ *Purple Heron* One of the few sites in the Czech Republic.
◆ *Marsh Harrier* Quite common in the summer.
◆ *Bean Goose* Up to 5000 in October and November.

ACCESS
Pohořelice is 24 km (15 miles) south of Brno on road 52. Starý Pond is just outside the village south of the road to Přibice with Vrkoč Pond behind. Novoveský Pond is right of the road south to Mikulov near Nová Ves. Roads and farm tracks pass near each pond. An IBA.

NOVÉ MLÝNY RESERVOIR

48°51–48°54N 16°36–16°39E

Nové Mlýny is an interesting case. One of communism's grand water-management schemes meant replacing a fine riverine forest with this huge wetland, which has become an important bird area as the only large body of water in the region. Now plans are afoot to reverse the overall process by lowering water levels on the middle section, draining the third section completely and leaving the first section as deep open water. As I write the reservoir is divided into three by two causeways, with the middle section being generally best for birds. White-tailed Eagles hunt over the whole area and can be seen in the dead trees of the third reservoir which are festooned with Cormorant nests. Common Tern and Black-headed Gull colonies usually have the odd pair of Mediterranean Gulls. A dyke on the northern shore of the middle reservoir gives views over the open water and adjacent woodland and marsh. Birds here include Purple Heron, White Stork, Ferruginous Duck, Marsh Harrier, Grey-headed and Middle Spotted Woodpeckers, Wryneck, Red-backed Shrike, Savi's Warbler and Penduline Tit. In spring and autumn Black-throated Diver, various grebes, Great White Egret, thousands of Bean and some White-fronted Geese, Red-crested Pochard, Osprey and Black Tern all pass through. Winter sees large numbers of geese, mainly Bean, various ducks and, if the weather is mild, Great White Egret.

CALENDAR
With a good selection of both breeding and wintering birds Nové Mlýny is worth a visit all year round. If the winter is not too harsh

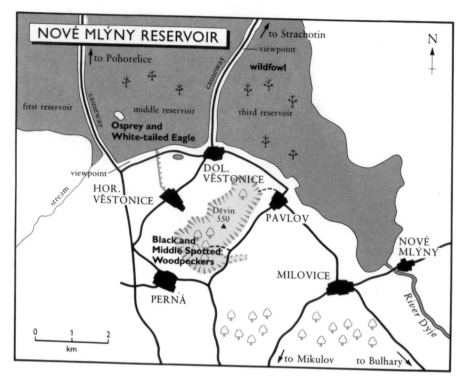

numerous wildfowl occur. From October to March for maximum numbers of geese.

SPECIES

♦ *Mediterranean Gull* A few pairs nest every year on the islands of the middle section of the reservoir.
♦ *White-tailed Eagle* Occurs all year with ten to fifteen in winter.
♦ *Smew* Occurs from October to early April.
♦ *Bluethroat* A few breed along the southern shores of the first and third sections of the reservoir.

ACCESS

The reservoir is around 40 km (25 miles) south of Brno along the E461 and 12 km (7 miles) north of the Austrian border at Mikulov on the same road. The two roads that cross the reservoir are good spots for viewing wildfowl, although parking possibilities are few. The road along the southern shore of the third section near Dolní Věstonice overlooks the Cormorant colonies. An IBA.

SEDLEC FISH-PONDS

48°43N 16°48E

These four large fish-ponds, which stretch eastwards from the village of Sedlec, are surrounded by good sized reedbeds, agricultural land and copses. Breeding birds include Little Bitterns, occasionally Purple Heron, Greylag Goose, Marsh Harrier, Savi's and Great

Reed Warblers and Bearded and Penduline Tits. There may also be Bluethroat. Bitterns occasionally nest and there are always Great White Egrets around but breeding has not been verified. White Storks nest in surrounding villages. During spring and autumn, wildfowl and waders pass through with thousands of Greylag, Bean and some White-fronted Geese, Wigeon, Teal, Shoveler and Red-crested Pochard. In autumn the ponds are drained to extract the fish, and the exposed mud and remaining pools attract many of the above birds plus gulls and waders such as Ruff. Vagrants are also possible at this time. Ospreys are regular in both spring and autumn and the ponds are also a regular wintering site for two or three White-tailed Eagles. The Nesyt Pond is the largest of the four and easily worked from a track which begins at the Sedlec level crossing and passes along the southern edge of the reedbeds. Higher ground, which gives way to vineyards, on the northern shores of the Nesyt and Hlohovecký Ponds, affords good views of the open water.

CALENDAR
Autumn is best, with October good for geese, ducks, waders and White-tailed Eagle. Check each pond at this time to find out which has been freshly drained.

SPECIES
◆ *Bearded Tit* With thirty to forty pairs this is a particularly good site for the country.
◆ *White-tailed Eagle* A regular wintering site with birds often perched in woodland around the ponds.
◆ *Red-crested Pochard* Hundreds on passage in March and April.
◆ *Syrian Woodpecker* Quite common throughout the area.

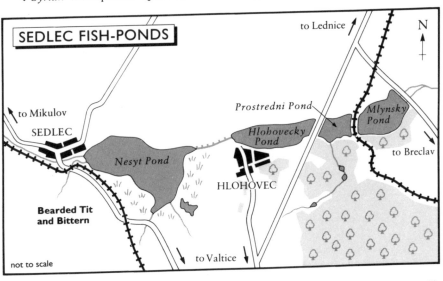

ACCESS

Sedlec lies approximately 50 km (31 miles) south of Brno on a minor road between Mikulov and Valtice. The ponds are just north of the border with Austria but the area is no longer 'sensitive'. Arriving from Austria cross the border at Mikulov. Tracks and roads skirt most sides of the ponds. Included in the Lednice IBA.

PÁLAVA HILLS
48°46–48°53N 16°37–16°45E

These scenic limestone hills are known locally for their unique flora but are also excellent for birds. Děvín Hill, above Pavlov and topped by a castle ruin, is the best area to explore. Its lower slopes are covered in vineyards and broad-leaved woodland with oak and hornbeam, then there is a scrub area, grassy steppe-like habitat and higher up rocky crags. Cuckoo, Hoopoe, Wryneck, Red-backed Shrike, Barred and Wood Warblers, Collared Flycatcher and Hawfinch are all quite common here in summer. Middle Spotted, Black and Grey-headed Woodpeckers are here all year and the wooded stretch of the nature trail on Děvín is as good a place as any to see them. Honey Buzzard and Eagle Owl are here, too, and in winter Wallcreepers often occur on the rock faces. Imperial Eagles are often seen here in spring but do not breed. Several other partly wooded limestone hillocks with similar birds to Děvín dot the area south of Pavlov to the chapel-topped Kopeček at the edge of Mikulov. The road from Pavlov to Bulhary passes good woodland with more woodpeckers, Goshawk and Black Kite. Villages around Pálava have White Stork, Black Redstart and Serin, with Syrian Woodpecker in orchards. Děvín is the highest hill in the range at 550 m (1804 ft) so these are fairly easy climbs.

CALENDAR

Worth a visit in winter if one is at nearby wetlands. April is good for woodpeckers, but Pálava is best for birds in late spring and summer.

SPECIES

◆ *Honey Buzzard* With around half-a-dozen pairs in a small area this is a key site.
◆ *Eagle Owl* Can often be heard on winter and spring nights as one returns from the wine cellars on the outskirts of Mikulov.
◆ *Middle Spotted Woodpecker* Try the woodland at the southern and western ends of Děvín.
◆ *Collared Flycatcher* Common in summer in the oak woods at Děvín.
◆ *Barred Warbler* Very common in the scrub areas of Pálava.

ACCESS

The hills lie 35 km (22 miles) south of Brno along the E461 between Mikulov and Pavlov. A border crossing with Austria lies at Mikulov. The Děvín Nature Trail, which can be joined at Dolní Věstonice or in vineyards just south of Pavlov, is a marked route around the best hill. To avoid further soil erosion, keep to paths! An IBA.

LEDNICE

48°43–48°48N 16°42–16°48E

For birdwatching in a stately setting there can be few places to rival the park, gardens and ponds of the Zámecký Chateau at Lednice. There are Spotted Flycatchers, Black Redstarts, Serins and Hawfinches and seven species of resident woodpeckers. Grey-headed, Green and Middle Spotted Woodpeckers are not too difficult to locate in the magnificent old trees, riddled with beetle larvae scars, and Black Woodpeckers often occur in the old oaks in the surrounding meadows and near the Dyje River at the far end of the park. There are also Wrynecks here in summer. A series of bridges and footpaths make wandering around the main pond straight-forward and getting good views of birds quite easy. The centre-piece at Lednice is an island colony of Night and Grey Herons, best viewed from the foot of the minaret at the far end of the park. Wildfowl include Gadwall, Garganey, Shoveler and Red-crested Pochard, particularly in spring. River and Icterine Warblers are also possible and there are Kingfishers on the feeder canal and the Dyje. Just across the road that skirts the western edge of the park is Pastvisko, a meadow, marsh and reedbed reserve with White Stork, Greylag Goose, Marsh Harrier, Savi's and Great Reed Warblers,

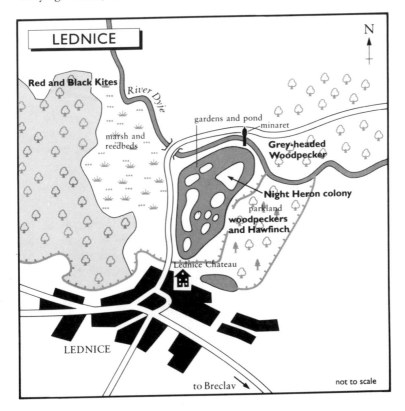

Bearded and Penduline Tits, and Black Tern on passage. Black Stork, Honey Buzzard and both kites often occur over the riverine forest behind the reserve.

CALENDAR

A rewarding place all year round. In winter various thrushes, Waxwings and Bramblings feed in the park. March and April are excellent for woodpeckers and ducks at Lednice, and May to August are best at Pastvisko for kites and warblers. In contrast to most of the areas in this book, there is the added bonus of a choice of two tea-shops in Lednice after a good day's birdwatching.

SPECIES

◆ *Great White Egret* Although breeding has not been confirmed, birds are present all year round at Pastvisko.

◆ *Night Heron* The main and only regular colony in the Czech Republic with over 200 pairs in some years.

◆ *Red-crested Pochard* Dozens of colourful males occur here in April before most move on to breed elsewhere.

◆ *Grey-headed Woodpecker* Trees by the path along the right-hand side of the pond are a regular haunt.

◆ *Red Kite* From the bridge over the river check the skies above the woodland beyond Pastvisko.

◆ *Hawfinch* Common and usually easy to see in the gardens and park of the chateau.

ACCESS

Lednice is 45 km (28 miles) south-east of Brno. Take the E65 motorway and the Podivín exit. Coming from Austria cross the border at Mikulov and then head east along a minor road for around 12 km (7 miles). The chateau park and gardens are open to the public. The reedbeds and marsh at Pastvisko are out of bounds but everything can be viewed adequately from the surrounding meadows and road. Part of the area is an IBA.

SOUTOK

48°37–48°44N 16°53–17°02E

Tucked away in an obscure corner of South Moravia along its borders with Austria and Slovakia, Soutok is an absolute gem. At the southern tip of the area the Dyje and Morava Rivers meet and the flood-plain between is a complex of riverine forest with old gnarled oaks, ashes and elms, willow and poplar plantations, ox-bow lakes, wet-meadows, temporary pools and channels. Whilst most habitat of this kind has disappeared across Europe, Soutok exists for two simple reasons: first, it was at the western edge of the Warsaw Pact countries, nestling up against Austria and closed to both the public and any development; second, it was kept as a game reserve. Indeed, it still is a hunting area mainly for Wild Boars and Red and Fallow Deer. Both Black and White Storks breed – the nests of the latter

Red Kites can be seen soaring over the woodland at Soutok throughout the year.

adorn wonderful old oaks in the wet-meadows. There is a good selection of woodpeckers: Middle Spotted are quite common, Black not too elusive and Grey-headed occurs although there are better sites for this species. Collared Flycatcher and Short-toed Treecreeper are two widespread specialities here and there are also River and Barred Warblers. Raptors include a few pairs each of Black and Red Kites and the impressive Saker. In spring the area is flooded and the meadows attract passage Osprey and White-tailed Eagle along with thousands of wildfowl, waders and storks.

CALENDAR
The best time to visit for birds is from April to July. In March and April woodpeckers are active and the first passage birds and storks arrive as the meadows are flooded. By mid-May flycatchers and migrant raptors have returned. In autumn some areas can be closed off for hunting.

SPECIES
- *White Stork* Around 25 pairs nest in loose colonies in the splendid old oaks.
- *Red Kite* A few birds will stay through the winter whereas others move on.
- *Collared Flycatcher* Quite common in this ideal flood-plain oak woodland habitat.

ACCESS

Bratislava is 65 km (40 miles) to the south and Brno 55 km to the north-west. Approach from Břeclav at the north of the area or take the road to Lanzhot and enter from there. Although parts of Soutok are protected, this is mainly a game reserve and can be closed off for hunting. Explore on foot on forestry roads and dykes as cars are not permitted. Soutok is a maze and detailed maps unavailable, so take a ball of string! An IBA.

SKAŘINY

c. 48°50N 17°00E

The River Morava has got to be one of the region's, if not Europe's, finest rivers for birds, lined as it is with stretches of that much-maligned habitat, the riverine forest. Skařiny is one such forest of old oaks, ash, poplar and elm where besides Black and Middle Spotted Woodpeckers, River and Wood Warblers, Short-toed Treecreepers and Collared Flycatchers, the main attraction is a mixed colony of Grey Herons and White Storks. Black Storks are also possible.

CALENDAR

From May to July when the colony is in full swing.

SPECIES

♦ Black Kite Also possible here from April through to August.

ACCESS

Skařiny is 5 km (3 miles) east of Mikulčice in South Moravia. Most of this distance must be walked. Brno is around 70 km (45 miles) to the north-west via the E65. In spring, the forest is regularly flooded, which is good for the trees, but can make access difficult. Nevertheless, if one is fascinated by groups of tree-nesting storks, as I am, then it is all worthwhile. Proposed as an IBA.

HOSTÝNSKÉ HILLS

c.49°25N 17°40E

Outside of local ornithological circles, little is known about the birdlife of these hills. Indeed, there are so many good uplands in the Czech Republic that the Hostýnské can easily be overlooked, but unlike other hill ranges in this book Hostýnské is relatively easy to explore on convenient roads and well-marked trails. Above all the forests here are good for White-backed Woodpecker with the western half of the range best. Black, Grey-headed and Middle Spotted Woodpeckers are also resident. Attractive stream valleys are good for Kingfisher, Dipper and Grey Wagtail. Red-breasted and Collared Flycatchers and Hawfinches are quite common in suitable woodland. Conifer plantations hold Firecrest, Crested Tit, Siskin, Crossbill and Nutcracker. There is also a chance of Hazelhen. By Czech standards this is not a particularly good raptor area but Goshawk and Honey Buzzard are quite common.

CALENDAR

March and April are best for woodpeckers, May and June for Red-breasted Flycatcher and other summer visitors. Although many good birds are resident, thick snow makes paths impassable in winter.

SPECIES

◆ *White-backed Woodpecker* An estimated twenty pairs breed in old stands of beech.

◆ *Red-breasted Flycatcher* Also found mainly in Hostýnské's beech forests.

ACCESS

The hills lie to the north of Zlín in central Moravia. Brno is around 90 km (56 miles) to the west. A road from Bystrice p. Hostýnem in the north-west to Jablunka in the east crosses the hills. This is a popular walking area and mostly of easy access on marked footpaths. Not listed as an IBA.

MORAVIAN BESKYDY

c. 49°35N 18°30E

This excellent upland region in the northern corner of the country is in many ways reminiscent of Šumava far to the west (*see* pages 51–2) with the exception that there are no large peatbogs here. There are, however, extensive spruce forests and three valuable areas of primeval beech and fir woodland, the National Nature Reserves at Mionší, Razula and Salajka, where much deadwood stands. The main attractions of the Moravian Beskydy are its forest birds, which include Black Stork, a few Capercaillies, Hazelhen, Pygmy, Teng-malm's, Eagle and Ural Owls and over a hundred pairs of White-backed Woodpeckers, making this surely one of Europe's best sites for this elusive bird. Three-toed Woodpeckers are also quite widespread in areas with spruce. High meadows are worth checking for Corncrake. Red-breasted and Collared Flycatchers, Firecrest, Ring Ouzel, Crested Tit, Nutcracker and Raven can be found throughout the mountains. Raptors include Honey Buzzard, Hen Harrier and a couple of pairs of Lesser Spotted Eagles.

CALENDAR

Snow can lie on the ground well into April, making an early spring visit difficult. From the end of April into May the owls and woodpeckers are still quite active and thus easier to track down. Mid-May onwards is good for flycatchers and other summer visitors.

SPECIES

◆ *Ural Owl* A few pairs regularly breed with more in good vole years. This species seems to be expanding its range westwards from Slovakia into the Czech Republic.

◆ *Ring Ouzel* One of the best sites in the country – it is very common.

◆ *Red-breasted Flycatcher* Common with hundreds of pairs in the beech forests here.

ACCESS

The Moravian Beskydy mountains lie in the north-east corner of the Czech Republic 35 km (22 miles) to the south of Ostrava. Approach them from Frenštát or Rožnov to the west of the range. The primeval forest reserves should not be entered and, indeed, there is no need, as all the key birds occur throughout the mountains. Proposed as an IBA.

POODŘI

49°25N 18°25E

Poodří is an area which is rich in bird habitats which are under threat throughout the Czech Republic, in particular wet-meadows which flood in early spring and later hold Spotted and Little Crakes and Corncrake. The core of the area is the River Odra and its ox-bows, meanders and tributaries where Red-necked and Black-necked Grebes, Black Stork, Little Bittern, Marsh Harrier, Black Grouse, Middle Spotted and Grey-headed Woodpeckers, River, Icterine and Barred Warblers, Collared Flycatcher and Penduline Tit all breed. There are also fish-ponds, reedbeds, copses, broadleaved forest, farmland and hills in the east. But this is not a totally scenic region, being also very industrial and dotted with coal mines, however, as is often the case, this does not deter the birds. In spring and autumn

Apart from Třeboňsko, Poodři is the only other regular breeding site for Goldeneye in the Czech Republic.

there is good passage of waders, terns and warblers through Poodří. The area around Libavá, at the heart of the region, was until very recently a huge military base and is rumoured to be very good for birds.

CALENDAR
This is a place worth checking out at any time of year.
SPECIES
- *Goldeneye* Apart from the Třeboň Basin this is the only place in the Czech Republic where this species regularly breeds.
- *Penduline Tit* Common and widespread throughout the area.
ACCESS
In the north-east of the country, the area lies between Šternberk to the west, on road 46, and Odry to the east, on road 47. Several minor roads link villages dotted about the area. The city of Ostrava is 40 km (28 miles) to the north-east via road 47. Enquire locally before exploring the former military areas around Libavá. Proposed as an IBA.

JESENÍKY MOUNTAINS
*c.*50°07N 17°15E
This is the second highest mountain range in the Czech Republic after Krkonoše (*see* pages 48–9) and the birds are, of course, similar with Alpine and forest species like Hazelhen, Capercaillie, Eagle and Tengmalm's Owls, Grey-headed, Black and Three-toed Woodpeckers, Red-breasted Flycatcher, Crested Tit, Ring Ouzel, Alpine Accentor and Nutcracker being the lure. The mountains are blanketed in conifer forests with some areas of beech where White-backed Woodpeckers might occur, peat-bogs with Black Grouse, Redpoll and Scarlet Rosefinch, pastures, rushing stream valleys and bleak moors. The highest peak is Mt Praděd at 1492 m (5850 feet), where moorland sometimes hosts Dotterels. Unfortunately, Jeseníky is one of the country's uplands most seriously affected by acid rain.

CALENDAR
Best to visit in late spring and summer when the weather is milder and breeding birds are present.
SPECIES
- *Dotterel* Possibly breeding in the Praděd Reserve.
ACCESS
Situated in northern Moravia, this is a busy winter-sports centre which means that there are convenient chair-lifts to the high peaks. Šumperk on road 44, about 220 km (140 miles) east of Prague, is the gateway to the mountains and there are famous spa towns at Karlova Studánka and Janské Lézně. A system of trails, which in reserves such as Praděd must be kept to, is marked on a locally obtainable map. Proposed as an IBA.

SLOVAKIA

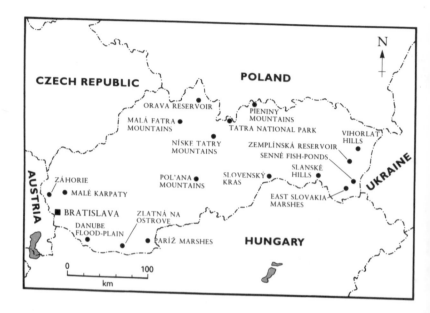

GENERAL INFORMATION

Slovakia is a small country stretching from its capital Bratislava on the Austrian border in the west to the Ukraine in the east. Most of Slovakia's best birdwatching areas lie in the east and thus are a little out of the way. A thorough tour round Slovàkia will prove most rewarding but it may be more practical to add some days in eastern Slovakia to a visit to eastern Hungary or southern Poland. One thing is sure, this is a part of Europe that few birdwatchers have bothered to explore and thus new ground is lying in wait for the intrepid. The places mentioned in this book are all within easy reach of towns with hotels. Very reasonable prices can be expected unless one stays in skiing resorts. Credit cards are more or less useless and traveller's cheques only accepted in large hotels and banks. The unit of currency is the koruna, the Slovak Crown.

The climate varies tremendously between the lowlands along the Danube and in the east and the high peaks of Slovakia's impressive mountains. Winter temperatures often fall below 0 °C (32 °F) throughout Slovakia and in summer about 25 °C (77 °F) can be expected. High ground has snow well into the spring and, indeed, the weather can change for the worst in the mountains at almost any time.

Free medical aid is apparently available for foreign citizens, with charges for some medicines. Pharmacies outside major towns are basic and thus medicaments should be taken. Mosquito repellent may be needed along parts of the Danube and other rivers. Tap water is said to be unsafe in some areas, but as bottled mineral water is inexpensive and widely available, this potential problem is effectively solved.

English is not widely spoken outside tourist offices and major hotels. German is more useful. Polish and Hungarian are spoken in regions where these ethnic groups occur.

Rambling, climbing, fishing, hunting and other 'country' pursuits are common amongst Slovaks. Birdwatching in the western sense is a rare hobby but nevertheless one which is understood.

IMPORTANCE FOR BIRDS

Slovakia's importance to European bird populations is mainly due to its numerous hill and mountain ranges. Raptors are well represented with important populations of two globally threatened species, Red Kite and Imperial Eagle, a Lesser Spotted Eagle population of hundreds of pairs and some Sakers. Corncrakes breed mainly in upland meadows and Great Bustards hang on in agricultural land in the Danube flood-plain. Europe's rarest owls and woodpeckers inhabit Slovakia's vast forests in mostly unknown but seemingly large numbers. Ural Owls breed in several hill ranges in good vole years, and a general increase and westward expansion of this species's range is apparent. Hazelhens are said to be common in some forests. The alpine habitat of the higher mountain ranges supports key populations of Golden Eagles and Wallcreepers. The remaining wetlands of eastern Slovakia are important migration stop-overs for Cranes, geese and waders and have small but significant breeding populations of Bittern, White Stork, Montagu's Harrier, Whiskered Tern and occasionally White-winged Black Tern. Recently two other globally threatened species, Pygmy Cormorant and Aquatic Warbler, as well as Short-toed Lark, which is threatened in Europe, have also bred.

GETTING THERE

At present no direct scheduled flights from Britain reach Slovakia. There are daily flights from Prague to various places in Slovakia and in view of the distances on quite slow roads from west to east a flight should perhaps be considered. As I write, both Czech Airlines and Slov-Air operate services between the larger cities. Vienna Airport is less than an hour's drive from Bratislava, the Slovak capital, and the Hungarian capital Budapest is even nearer to the best sites in the east, so these may be worth considering as bases or as departure points for a hire-car. An alternative may be a direct charter flight to the High Tatras on a skiing package tour. Once in the country, a car is really the only way to travel, as although public transport can be quite good and inexpensive, it wastes valuable birdwatching time and will not get one into the heart of the best areas. In Slovakia, access is generally unrestricted in parks and reserves with the exception of State Nature Reserves where public roads and marked trails and tourist paths must be kept to. It is worth remembering that if one sets off on a walk with a local warden or guide one should count on covering double the mileage that is mentioned at the outset. (To be fair to my Slovak friends, this goes for all of the countries in this guide!)

CONSERVATION

As with the Czech Republic, Slovakia has a tradition of conservationists working from institutions such as universities, forestry departments and regional museums. The protection of raptors is particularly well established, with a network of dedicated volunteers guarding nests and monitoring populations. The Society for the Protection of Birds in Slovakia (SPBS) is a recently established nongovernmental organization which is developing into a popular membership-based body. Besides bird conservation its activities include public awareness and publicity campaigns.

The Slovak Ornithological Society (SOS) is more of a scientific organization. A BirdLife International section has been established and there are various nature and ornithological clubs. Because of a lack of people on the ground and the perpetual problem of funds, much remains to be discovered in terms of bird studies. The lack of a popular consciousness in favour of nature conservation seems to be borne out by the continuing saga of the Danube Dam scheme where there is apparently widespread public support for a project rejected by the majority of the general public on the other side of the border.

HABITATS

Slovakia is, above all, a land of high mountains. The snowy peaks of the High Tatras with their Marmots and Chamois are not the full story, however, as a belt of other alpine and subalpine mountain ranges dominate the country's landscape. There are also numerous foothills and limestone karst ranges with scrub and semi-steppe. Not surprisingly this is all good habitat for raptors. The forests which blanket these ranges are living places for owls and woodpeckers of largely unknown numbers. Upland meadows are a refuge for Corncrakes, and hunting grounds for Sakers and Imperial Eagles. Some riverine forest habitat survives along the Danube in the west of Slovakia and along stretches of smaller rivers in the far east of the country. As with all the countries in this book, Slovakia has its share of fish-ponds which provide important wetland habitat. Grasslands and steppe have largely disappeared courtesy of the plough, but there are remnants along the Danube and in the south-east corner of Slovakia, and these form important habitat for White Storks, Lesser Grey Shrikes and other lowland species. Agricultural land dominates the Danube flood-plain but is by no means birdless with, for example, White-tailed Eagles recently breeding and woodpeckers and warblers widespread.

SEASONS

SPRING

Many of the best birdwatching areas in Slovakia are in uplands which lie under snow well into April and often beyond. Yet, some of the best birds, particularly grouse, owls and woodpeckers, are easier to find in this season. Wetlands along the Danube and in the east are worth visiting in April for wildfowl and wader passage. Fish-ponds in the very east of the country are excellent at this time of year.

SUMMER

For the best combination of Slovakia's special birds and suitable weather this is the time of year to visit. As is usually the case in this part of Europe the optimum period is mid-May and early June, whether in the mountains or along river valleys. July and August are far from silent months in the Tatras but do not expect to be alone up there.

AUTUMN

This is a fairly quiet season for birds in Slovakia. Many good species are, of course, resident but less active and thus more difficult to find. There is some Crane, wader and wildfowl passage through the very east of the country and the Danube is always worth checking out, although the situation here varies from year to year.

WINTER

The mountains are certainly picturesque and a haven for skiers at this time of year, but are perhaps a little too quiet as regards birds to make a special trip worthwhile. Lowlands and wetlands can also experience harsh weather, forcing geese and ducks to move on as lakes freeze over. But if one is already in the country there are enough resident species to warrant excursions.

BIRDWATCHING SITES

DANUBE FLOOD-PLAIN

47°45–48°12N 17°00–18°45E

This large area of riverine woodland, plantations, backwaters, marshes, meadows and agricultural land lies along the Danube as it flows east from Bratislava. Once an impressive maze of habitats, the dam at Gabčíkovo has cast a shadow over the area's future. There are some good woodland areas between the Slovak capital and Šamorín; beyond here the river forms the border with Hungary. Common birds in the general region are Cormorant, White Stork, Kingfisher, Middle Spotted Woodpecker, River and Icterine Warblers, Penduline Tit, Short-toed Treecreeper and Golden Oriole. In suitable spots there are Little Bittern, Night Heron, Black Stork, Ferruginous Duck, Collared Flycatcher and Barred Warbler. Raptors include Honey Buzzard, Goshawk, Black Kite, Marsh and Montagu's Harriers and White-tailed Eagle. Other birds which are possible, but certainly not widespread, are Bittern, Purple Heron, Great White and Little Egrets, marsh terns, Savi's Warbler and Bearded Tit. A spot worth trying for many of the last-named is the Číčov Reserve between the village of the same name and Klúčovec. Riverside woodlands are particularly good for songbirds and woodpeckers with Black, Grey-headed and Syrian all present. The Danube itself is in some years an important refuge for passage and wintering geese and ducks, though sometimes birds choose the marshes and ox-bows of the area to roost. With some sites on the flood-plain now facing an uncertain future, this is an area for a general exploration.

CALENDAR

Without doubt spring and summer are the seasons to visit, though autumn and winter can be interesting on the Danube proper with grebes and ducks sometimes in good numbers.

SPECIES

◆ *Black Kite* Some pairs scattered along the river.
◆ *Icterine Warbler* Quite common in summer.
◆ *Penduline Tit* Common all year round.

ACCESS

The area stretches from Bratislava eastwards along the Malý Dunaj (Small Danube arm) and south-eastwards along the Danube proper. There are many villages and minor roads and raised dykes give access to wetlands and the riverside. Road 63 crosses the area. For a time police and officials near the dam were sensitive about visitors with optical equipment and this may still be the case. Part of an IBA.

ZLATNÁ NA OSTROVE

47°45N 17°55E

The main attraction of this largely agricultural region is that it is the only site for Great Bustards in Slovakia. Around 25–40 birds remain in a flat area stretching from the small town of Zlatná na Ostrove in the east to Zemianska Olča in the west. The River Danube forms the southern edge of the area. Some grassland remains but is not necessarily the place to find the birds, which are often present in fields of lucerne, rape and other crops. Other birds include White Stork, Buzzard, Marsh Harrier, a few Red-footed Falcons, Quail, Short-eared Owl, Tawny Pipit, Stonechat and Red-backed Shrike. Rough-legged Buzzards, Hen Harriers and Great Grey Shrikes occur in winter. A minor road runs from the outskirts of Zlatná near the Drop Restaurant (*drop* means 'Great Bustard' in Slovak) to the Danube. Here the river is lined with woodland and a dyke where River and Icterine Warblers, Penduline Tit, Short-toed Treecreeper and Golden Oriole are possible. The river itself is worth looking at in winter for grebes and ducks, although at the time of writing it is unclear how the new dam at nearby Gabčíkovo is affecting water levels and the river's wildlife. In any event, this is a large area which needs time.

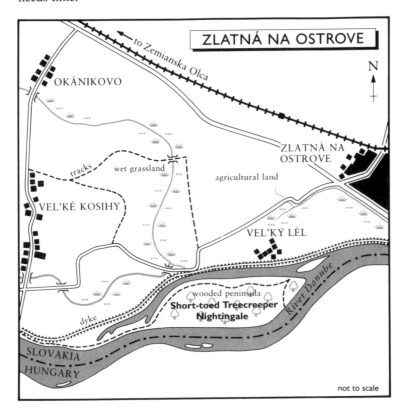

CALENDAR

The Great Bustards are resident all year round, but early in the year, April or May, is perhaps best for tracking them down. Alternatively, tie in a winter visit with an exploration of the Danube.

SPECIES

- *Great Bustard* Sadly, this is now one of the small isolated populations that dot Central and Eastern Europe, the nearest viable flocks being far to the south-east in Hungary.
- *Tawny Pipit* Although the species is not common here the area is still one of the best in Slovakia.
- *Serin* Common in and around settlements.
- *Short-toed Treecreeper* Much more likely than its near relative in the woods along the Danube.

ACCESS

The general area lies 85 km (53 miles) south-east of Bratislava along road 63 which cuts right across the region. Zlatná na Ostrove is 12 km (7 miles) west of Komárno. Some of the area is a State Nature Reserve. The best bet is to explore by branching out from the main road on to minor roads, farm tracks and dykes. An IBA.

PARÍŽ MARSHES

47°52N 18°30E

This is a relatively small wetland with reedbeds and peatbog pools tucked away in a little-explored corner of the country between the River Hron and the Danube. Its main claim to fame is that this is *the* Slovak site for Moustached Warbler, although there are only a few pairs. Yet it would not be a total surprise if a thorough survey of the whole region were to reveal more sites for this often overlooked species. There are other warblers, too, with Grasshopper, Savi's, River, Reed, Marsh, Great Reed and Sedge completing the set. Other reed-dwelling birds at Paríž are Bittern, Little Bittern, Purple Heron, Marsh Harrier, Spotted and Little Crakes and Bluethroat. Black-necked Grebe, Garganey, Ferruginous Duck and Black Tern also breed. White Storks adorn village rooftops and telegraph poles with their nests, and feed in the wetland. Surrounding agricultural land and wet-meadows may still hold some Corncrakes and Quails. Redshank, Black-tailed Godwit and Red-backed Shrike are more likely. Patches of woodland along the two rivers are usually good for the occasional woodpecker, Icterine Warbler, Penduline Tit and Short-toed Treecreeper. Although this is not the hottest spot for birds in Slovakia it is a fine remnant of what once must have been a tremendous wetland chain along the Danube.

CALENDAR

May and June are best, with all the warblers and crakes present, although there is some wader passage through the area in spring and autumn.

SPECIES
◆ *Moustached Warbler* This is one of the very few known breeding
sites in Slovakia for this species and, as mentioned elsewhere, a late
March or April visit is best before other warblers arrive and make
things more complicated.

ACCESS
Situated just to the north of the small village of Gbelce which is 35
km (22 miles) south-east of Nové Zámky. There are border crossings
into Hungary at Štúrovo 18 km (11 miles) to the east, by ferry across
the Danube, and at Szob, by road, 12 km (7 miles) farther on. As a
State Nature Reserve the area can only be visited on public roads and
paths. Part of a larger IBA.

MALÉ KARPATY
48°10–48°45N 17°07–17°50E

This 100-km-long range of karst mountains in the Carpathian chain
begins in the south-west corner of Slovakia. The mountains are mostly
covered in beech forests with clearings, meadows, rocky areas, and
vineyards and orchards on the southern slopes. This is an important
area for raptors; Goshawk, Honey Buzzard, Short-toed and Imperial
Eagles, Hobby, Saker and Peregrine are all possible. In addition, more
than a dozen pairs of Eagle Owls are scattered through the hills.
Woodpeckers, too, are well represented with Black, Grey-headed,
Syrian and Middle Spotted all widespread and the extensive stands of
old beech make this good White-backed Woodpecker country. A
couple of pairs of Rock Thrushes breed every year and Rock Bunting
may also be around. Bee-eaters can be seen in the very south of the
range. Red-breasted and Collared Flycatchers are both here along
with some Pied. One or two villages have nesting White Stork, and
Black Stork breeds in the hills proper. Other birds found throughout
the region are Wryneck, Nightjar, Woodlark, Red-backed Shrike,
Barred Warbler, Stonechat, Black Redstart, Golden Oriole, Serin and
Raven. The warmer southern slopes of the range are generally more
productive, especially for hunting raptors.

CALENDAR
Weather permitting, the earlier in the year the better for woodpeckers
but overall visit from mid-May onwards to guarantee that all the
summer visitors have returned.

SPECIES
◆ *Honey Buzzard* By far the most common of the larger raptors
mentioned.
◆ *Rock Bunting* Though I have not heard of any records, parts of the
Malé Karpaty certainly seem ideal for this often overlooked bird.

ACCESS
The capital of Slovakia, Bratislava, sits at the southern tip of the
range. The foothills rise in the city itself. Vienna is 60 km (37 miles)

to the west. Nové Mesto nad Váhom marks the northern tip of the range and the convenient road 61 skirts the south-eastern side of the mountains linking this town with Bratislava. There are numerous villages in the Malé Karpaty connected by minor roads which allow access into the forests. Proposed as an IBA.

ZÁHORIE

48°30'N 17°00'E

The flood-plain of the River Morava here on the Austrian border is a bird-rich blend of meadows, marshes, peatbogs, ponds, reedbeds, pine, oak and poplar forest and wet willow woodland. Over the border is the better known WWF Marchegg Reserve, but that is only a remnant and here is the real thing. Indeed, those well-watched Austrian White Storks always flew the few hundred metres into Slovakia to feed at Záhorie when for 'security' reasons the area was out of bounds to all but locals. Both storks breed here in loose woodland colonies. Common birds include Little Bittern, Kingfisher, Middle Spotted Woodpecker, River and Barred Warblers, Collared Flycatcher, Penduline Tit and Red-backed Shrike. Although not quite as common, Bittern, Black Tern, Grey-headed and Black Woodpeckers, Spotted and Little Crakes, Corncrake, Short-eared Owl and Bearded Tit are all here, too. Raptors such as Honey Buzzard, Red and Black Kites, Marsh and Montagu's Harriers and Saker have all benefited from being in this once-closed area. Osprey and White-tailed and Short-toed Eagles also occur, especially in spring. At the centre of the area, near Jakubov, are fish-ponds with large reedbeds and breeding Black-necked Grebe, Gadwall, Garganey and various warblers. This is also a good migration stop-over for wildfowl. On the other side of the E65 motorway north of Malacky is a drier area of sand dunes and pine forest which is worth exploring for Nightjar, perhaps Roller, Hoopoe, Woodlark, Tawny Pipit and Lesser Grey Shrike. Záhorie is another of those wonderful border areas for birds.

CALENDAR

All kinds of birds, in addition to the above-mentioned, use the area on spring migration. By the end of May all the summer visitors are back. Winter excepted, Záhorie is worth at visit at any time.

SPECIES

♦ *Spotted Crake* The most common crake here with around 35 pairs.
♦ *Middle Spotted Woodpecker* Probably the most common woodpecker with an estimated 250 pairs.
♦ *Short-toed Treecreeper* The only treecreeper to breed here, which perhaps makes visual identification somewhat more straightforward!

ACCESS

Záhorie lies between the Austrian border, formed by the River Morava, and the busy E65. Bratislava is about 20 km (12 miles) to the south. A minor road which can now be freely taken links three villages in the area, Vysoká pri Morave, Záhorská Ves and Jakubov. A Protected Landscape Area, it is mostly open, although the very nature of the flood-plain makes it a little difficult to work. An IBA.

POL'ANA MOUNTAINS

c.48°33N 19°10E

Not quite as high as most Slovakian mountain ranges, and just a little further to the south, the Pol'ana range combines pseudo-alpine species with birds associated with lower altitudes. Thus, Middle Spotted Woodpecker and Lesser Grey Shrike are here almost alongside Three-toed Woodpecker and Ring Ouzel. Imperial Eagles, too, often occur. As the area is mostly forested, owls, woodpeckers, flycatchers and finches form the main attractions. Open areas of pasture, rocky scrub and meadow have Corncrake and Barred Warbler, and are hunting areas for the birds of prey.

CALENDAR

From mid-April through to August for breeding birds.

SPECIES

◆ *White-backed Woodpecker* In some areas this is said to be the most common woodpecker species.

◆ *Hazelhen* The most common grouse species here.

ACCESS

One step down from the Níske Tatry, and situated in the Western Carpathians, these mountains are some of the least touristed in Slovakia. Zvolen is the gateway to the area. Proposed as an IBA.

NÍZKE TATRY MOUNTAINS

48°48–49°04N 19°06–20°18E

One should not let the name Nízke Tatry (Low Tatras) lull one into thinking that this is an area for a casual bird walk. In true spectacular Slovak fashion, this is often 2000-metre-plus (6500-ft) high country, blanketed in forest and dotted with tarns, deep valleys, limestone cliffs and weird rock formations. The alpine zone has Ring Ouzel, Rock Pipit, Alpine Accentor and Wallcreeper. Lower down, almost never-ending coniferous forests have Hazelhen, Capercaillie, Pygmy and Tengmalm's Owls, Black and Three-toed Woodpeckers, Crossbill, Siskin and Nutcracker. Lower down still, beech takes over and Black Stork, Grey-headed and White-backed Woodpeckers, Red-breasted Flycatcher and Hawfinch come into play. Open areas of pasture, and forest edges have Black Grouse, Corncrake, Nightjar, Woodlark and Redwing. Lesser Spotted Eagle is probably the most common large raptor.

CALENDAR

Summer, from June to August, is the season to visit.

SPECIES

◆ *Hazelhen* With up to 400 pairs, this could be *the* place!

ACCESS

Stretching for 80 km (50 miles) between Banská Bystrica and Spisská Nová Ves, this is a vast area to explore. Road 66 skirts the south and the E50 the north of the range. Marked trails, chair lifts and cablecars facilitate exploration. Partly a National Park and IBA.

MALÁ FATRA MOUNTAINS

49°07–49°15N 18°53–19°13E

The Malá Fatra (Little Fatra) Mountains form an impressive range of high peaks with deep river valleys, cliffs, gorges, pastures and forests of oak, beech, pine, spruce and dwarf pine at various altitudes. Hazelhen are common, and there are Black Grouse and Capercaillie, Pygmy and Tengmalm's Owls and typical alpine species such as Three-toed Woodpecker, Ring Ouzel, Rock Pipit, Alpine Accentor, Wallcreeper and Nutcracker. Not surprisingly with the the amount of beech forest, woodpeckers such as Grey-headed, Black and White-backed are relatively common. Do remember, however, that this is a vast, wild region totally unsuited to a quick visit. Plan for a birding trek rather than a quick clean-up of species.

Besides the numerous natural rock faces, resort buildings and ski-stations in Slovakia's mountains are often good places to look for Wallcreeper.

CALENDAR

Everything depends on the weather. The owls are easiest in early spring, but the range is often impenetrable then. Overall, summer is perhaps safest and best.

SPECIES

◆ *Red-breasted Flycatcher* Quite widespread, but elusive once males stop singing in mid-summer.

◆ *Nutcracker* When nesting, usually in April, it can be very elusive, but is otherwise easily encountered.

ACCESS

The E50, which runs through Zilina and Martin, cuts through the mountains. Ski-lifts reach the high peaks and marked trails are divided into degrees of difficulty. A good map, often available locally, is essential. Partly a National Park and an IBA.

ORAVA RESERVOIR

49°24'N 19°33'E

This huge man-made reservoir lying near the border with Poland is situated on a flyway through the Western Carpathians and thus is very interesting in spring and autumn when divers, egrets, herons, waders and such birds of prey as Osprey and White-tailed Eagle move through. Habitats around the water include sand and pebble beaches (frequented by tourists throughout the summer), wet alder, birch and willow woodlands, pine forest, meadows, bogs, reedbeds and farmland. Both storks, Lesser Spotted Eagle, Red-backed Shrike and Scarlet Rosefinch should all be picked up on a summer's day. A trek through nearby forests and meadows could add Hazelhen, Black Grouse, Spotted Crake, Corncrake and Grey-headed and Black Woodpeckers, although the going can be wet to say the least.

CALENDAR

April–May for spring passage and all summer for breeding birds in the surrounding area. September–November for autumn passage. The reservoir itself is busy with boats and fishermen in high summer.

SPECIES

◆ *Corncrake* In summer, easily heard in nearby meadows, but not so easy to pinpoint, as is often the case.

ACCESS

The reservoir is just to the north-west of the main E77 as it enters Poland. Mostly accessible, although the going underfoot once one is away from roads or paths can be a problem. An IBA.

TATRA NATIONAL PARK

49°05–49°18N 19°35–20°20

Not surprisingly, the habitats and birds of these famous mountains are similar to those in the Polish National Park of the same name just over the border. This is an equally popular holiday destination for rambling, climbing and winter sports fans, too. The National Park covers the High and Belanské Tatry ranges which reach 2655 m (8710 ft) at Gerlachovský Štít. Lower down, around settlements, there are mixed woodlands and scenic valleys with birds such as Corncrake, Woodlark, Collared and Red-breasted Flycatchers, Dipper, Firecrest, and Grey-headed, Black, Middle Spotted and some White-backed Woodpeckers. As the mountains rise, this sub-mountain level soon changes to vast pine and spruce forests and open meadows with Black Grouse, Capercaillie, Hazelhen (the last quite common), Eagle, Pygmy and Tengmalm's Owls, perhaps Ural Owl, Three-toed Woodpecker, Crested Tit, Ring Ouzel, Scarlet Rosefinch, Raven and Nutcracker. Finally there are the impressive rocky massifs of the alpine zone, dotted with isolated tarns, sheer rock walls, rugged cliffs and innumerable boulders. These are home to Water Pipits, Alpine Accentors, Redpolls, Wallcreepers and, in summer, hordes of walkers. Some preparation and proper clothing are needed as this is an area to be reckoned with once one is away from tourist centres. Raptors in the Tatras include Lesser Spotted and Golden Eagles and mammals such as Brown Bear, Lynx, Marmots and Chamois are possible, too.

CALENDAR
Much depends on the weather, which is unpredictable. From the end of May most areas are accessible on foot, but the main trails can be choked with ramblers and climbers. Rain and snow storms can descend without warning throughout the summer. Winter here is quiet for birds and full of skiers.

SPECIES
◆ *Hazelhen* The easiest of the three grouse species present.
◆ *Capercaillie* One of Slovakia's best sites with over 100 cock birds estimated.
◆ *Pygmy Owl* There are certainly easier places in the region to see this species, though in April and May almost any clearing in coniferous woodland here could have a calling male.
◆ *Three-toed Woodpecker* Around 100 pairs estimated.

ACCESS
The National Park lies just to the north and north-east of Poprad, which is the major town in the region and has an airport. There is a border crossing with the Polish Tatras at Lysǎ Pol'ana to the north. A road runs through the mountains connecting Štrbské Pleso, Starý Smokovec, Tatranská Lomnica and numerous resort villages, all good starting points for walks on marked trails. Cable-cars and chair-lifts from Tatranská Lomnica and other resorts run to the high peaks. The mountains are covered in clear trails, some of which are only open from July to October, but the good, locally obtainable, map is still essential. As with many upland areas it is important to keep to the marked paths as erosion is a major problem. An IBA.

PIENINY MOUNTAINS

49°22–49°26N 20°25–20°30E

This is a fine Slovakian upland region on the Polish border, with all the birds one would expect. Habitats include pine and beech forests, limestone crags and cliffs, stony screes, meadows, large plantations and arable land. Peregrine and Lesser Spotted and Golden Eagles are here. Eagle, Ural, Pygmy and Tengmalm's Owls are also possible, but need some effort if not up-to-date local knowledge. A good range of woodpeckers includes White-backed and Three-toed, the former in beech woods and the latter in spruce woodland. Red-breasted and Collared Flycatchers can be found in broad-leaved woodland. Away from the forest, Wallcreeper and Rock Thrush are said to breed, but there is an awful lot of suitable ground to cover. More common birds include Black Woodpecker, Woodlark, Ring Ouzel, Redwing, Crossbill, Scarlet Rosefinch and Nutcracker.

CALENDAR

This is a busy hiking and climbing area in summer, which means plenty of facilities, but some disturbance. Weather permitting, the earlier in the year the better for birdwatching.

SPECIES

◆ *Scarlet Rosefinch* Arrives later than most other migrants, often in early June.

ACCESS

North-east of the Tatras, the area, some of which is a National Park, can be reached via road 67 and then minor roads. An IBA.

SLOVENSKÝ KRAS

48°30–48°41N 20°25–20°55E

This picturesque area forms one whole limestone karst region with the Aggtelek National Park in neighbouring Hungary. The centrepiece here is the State Nature Reserve of Zádielska Dolina, a scenic limestone gorge in the east near Zádielske Dvorníky. As well as being outstanding for flowers, this area of rocky plateaux, stream valleys, meadows, oak woodland and scrub-steppe dotted with junipers has several birds difficult elsewhere in Slovakia. This is the best site in the country for Rock Bunting and Rock Thrush, Hazelhen are widespread and Saker are possible. Other raptors are Goshawk, Honey Buzzard, and Short-toed, Lesser Spotted and Imperial Eagles; the valley around Hrhov is a good area. Ural, Eagle, Pygmy and Tengmalm's Owls are all possible though the last two species are far from common here. Rollers still hang on, but this colourful species has declined badly here as throughout Slovakia. Nightjar, Collared and Red-breasted Flycatchers, Wryneck and Lesser Grey and Red-backed Shrikes are faring rather better. If one covers all the habitats of Slovenský Kras, it is technically possible to pick up every European species of woodpecker. White Stork, Turtle Dove, Hoopoe,

Woodlark, Barred Warbler, Golden Oriole, Tree Sparrow and Hawfinch are all quite common birds.

CALENDAR

Worth a visit at any time of year, as many good birds are resident. May is the best month with the perfect combination of spring and summer activity, although the area is particularly beautiful and still good in June and July.

SPECIES

◆ *Rock Bunting* This is not only the best site, but also the only reliable one in Slovakia.

◆ *Ural Owl* In some years almost common but this is a species notorious for its fluctuations in population.

◆ *Syrian Woodpecker* Unlike Great Spotted, which is also here, it does not occur in woodland proper, rather around villages.

ACCESS

Slovenský Kras lies just to the south and east of Roznava. The E571 runs through the area and is the starting point for tracks and minor roads. Being a State Nature Reserve the 4-km-long Zádielska Dolina can only be worked from the road which passes through it and along marked tourist paths. An IBA.

SLANSKÉ HILLS

48°15–49°00N 21°00–21°30E

The Slanské Hills are excellent for raptors and relatively easy to explore. The range stretches roughly from Presov in the north to the Hungarian border in the south, and continues as the Zemplén Hills in Hungary. There are broad-leaved forests, scrub and open areas with Honey Buzzard, Goshawk, Short-toed, Booted, Lesser Spotted, Golden and Imperial Eagles and Saker. Eagle and Ural Owls are both resident and there is a selection of woodpeckers. The woods along the main Kosice Secovce road are good for Middle Spotted, Grey-headed and Black Woodpeckers. The deciduous forests here hold many of the hill's typical species. White-backed Woodpeckers are also said to breed. Birds of forest edges and open areas include Nightjar, Hoopoe, Wryneck, Woodlark, Tree Pipit, Barred Warbler and Red-backed Shrike. Several stream valleys head from the hills to the Hornád and Olsava Rivers and these are likely spots for Kingfisher, Nightingale, Grey Wagtail and Dipper. Corncrakes are possible in these valleys, too.

CALENDAR

Without doubt the time to visit is in spring and summer. At the end of April migrant raptors such as Lesser Spotted Eagles and Honey Buzzards have returned and by mid-May Red-breasted and Collared Flycatchers are singing in the forests. Having said that, the owls, woodpeckers and even Hazelhens are possible all year round.

SPECIES

◆ *Red-breasted Flycatcher* The beech forests of Slanské are worth exploring from May to July for singing males.

◆ *Ural Owl* Traditionally a stronghold for this species.

◆ *Syrian Woodpecker* Possible in the town park in Kosice.

ACCESS

The region is best visited from Kosice which lies 15 km (9 miles) to the west. Roads from Kosice cross the hills to Trebisov and Secovce (E50) in the south and from Presov to Vranov nad Toplou in the north. If approaching from Hungary, cross the border at Tornyosnémeti. Parts of the range are strictly protected and can only be explored along roads and marked paths. In addition local ornithologists and foresters guard the nesting sites of certain species and are with some justification wary about unknown visitors. An IBA.

VIHORLAT HILLS

48°48–48°57N 22°00–22°20E

The Vihorlat Hills are mainly covered in thick broad-leaved forests of oak and beech with some conifer plantations and are tucked away in the extreme east of Slovakia on the border with the Ukraine. Certain core areas are reserves but interesting birds can be found just about anywhere. The heart of the hills is heavily forested, but there are clearings, patches of scrub, some rocky areas and occasional small

Golden Eagles are possible in almost every mountain range in eastern Slovakia.

lakes. This is good raptor country with, for example, Short-toed and Imperial Eagles. The latter is more likely to be encountered in the south of the range. There is also a chance of Golden Eagle. Ural Owls are always present, in some years in good numbers, although a bit of luck is needed. Eagle and Pygmy Owls both occur. Booted Eagle is possible though Lesser Spotted Eagle, Goshawk and Honey Buzzard are more common. Hazelhens seem to like stream valleys lined with thick undercover although they can be elusive. Dipper and Grey Wagtail are easier to observe. Some of the Vihorlat's beech woods are quite impressive and are good for Red-breasted Flycatcher. Grey-headed, Middle Spotted and Black Woodpeckers are widespread. Older and dead stands of woodland are the haunt of White-backed Woodpeckers. Black Storks nest in the hills and White Storks in villages lower down. Typical Vihorlat woodlands surround Morské Oko, a small lake in a picturesque and central setting, and can be explored on clearly sign-posted and marked trails in all directions. These hills are also the home of wolves, wild cats and Lynx, although with hunting a popular pastime they keep a low profile.

CALENDAR
April sees migratory raptors such as Lesser Spotted and Short-toed Eagles returning to breed and woodpeckers quite active. By May most species are back for the summer, the weather is more reliable and thus this is probably the best time to visit.
SPECIES
♦ *Lesser Spotted Eagle* The eagle most likely to be seen on a brief visit.
♦ *Hazelhen* Apparently widespread but not easy to observe.
♦ *Ural Owl* The Vihorlat is a traditional stronghold but this delightful owl is notorious for its fluctuations in numbers.
♦ *White-backed Woodpecker* Said to be common in suitable woodland here.
ACCESS
The Vihorlat Hills can be explored from Michalovce, a town with a surprisingly large hotel but little else to recommend it, which lies to the south-west of the range. Morské Oko is a short but uphill walk from a convenient car park with information boards (in Slovak) 7 km (4 miles) north of Remetské Hamre. The Okna stream follows most of the route. Alternatively, a tougher trek from Zemplínské Hamre to the north reaches the same destination. Good woodland also lies just to the south of Humenné in the north-west of the hills. An IBA.

ZEMPLÍNSKÁ RESERVOIR
48°46–48°50N 21°55–22°05E
This man-made reservoir is the largest body of water in eastern Slovakia and offers a contrast to birdwatching in most of the surrounding area which is invariably montane. Indeed, the reservoir

lies along the southern foot of the Vihorlat Hills. In summer most of the northern shore is a holiday resort with campsites; hence few birds of interest are found on the water nearby. The eastern end of the lake, however, is set aside as a reserve where hunting and water sports are forbidden. Large numbers of ducks sometimes winter, along with the occasional Slavonian Grebe and diver or two. At the beginning and end of summer herons and storks rest here on passage. Autumn passage in particular can be exciting with the chance of Lesser White-fronted Geese, parties of Cranes and various waders. At the very eastern end of the reservoir between the villages of Kusín and Jovsa, are two reed-fringed ponds where in summer Black-necked Grebe, Bittern, Little Bittern, Gadwall, Garganey, Ferruginous Duck and Spotted Crake are all possible. Some of these birds can also be found on the quieter and less accessible southern shore of the reservoir proper. Suitable habitat hereabouts offers the chance to separate Nightingale and Thrush Nightingale, as both breed. Great Reed Warblers can be found all around the reservoir. Black Redstart, Serin and Syrian Woodpecker are around the holiday resorts. Roadside quarries between Vinné and Kaluza are worth checking for Eagle Owl and Rock Thrush.

CALENDAR
Although a good selection of birds can be picked up in and around the reservoir in spring and summer, autumn is perhaps the best time to visit. September sees both White and Black Storks, Night and

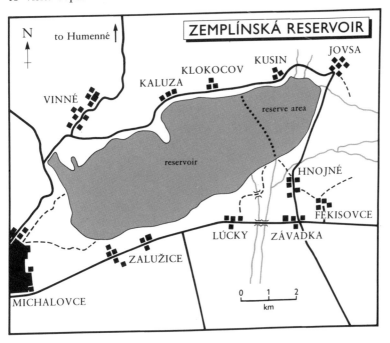

Squacco Herons and Great White Egrets passing through. In October large numbers of Cranes and grey geese stop here as they move south along the eastern flyway.

SPECIES

◆ *Great Snipe* Regularly recorded on passage.
◆ *Lesser White-fronted Goose* The best period is from the end of September into October.
◆ *Rock Thrush* The quarries on the northern shore are a regular site for this declining migratory species.

ACCESS

Zemplínska Reservoir is just to the east of Michalovce. The best route for access to the waterside is along the northern shore from the town through several villages to Kusín. Just outside Kusín is a camping resort from where the reservoir can be scanned. Another good vantage point is from the waterside church in the same village. Access to the waterside along the southern shore is more difficult because of settlements and roadside ditches. However, at the very eastern end of the reservoir, between Hnojné and Jovsa, the road runs alongside the dyke overlooking the protected area. Permission is not needed to view the water from the shore. Partly an IBA.

SENNÉ FISH-PONDS

48°42N 22°05E

This is one of Slovakia's most famed sites for birds, with a reputation for rarities as well as a collection of breeding species seldom found elsewhere in the country. There is one main pond (a reserve) north of the complex, with open water, stands of reed and two islets with willow scrub, and around twenty other ponds of various sizes used for fish-farming. There is a Cormorant colony on the reserve pond in dead trees and other vegetation on and around the water. To the immediate west of the protected area is a patch of wet grassland with Corncrake, Black-tailed Godwit and Short-eared Owl. The ponds have Bittern, Little Bittern, Purple Heron, Spoonbill, Spotted Crake, Black-winged Stilt, Black and Whiskered Terns and Savi's Warbler. Ducks include Gadwall, Garganey, Teal, Shoveler and Ferruginous Duck. Pygmy Cormorants have bred. When one adds another occasionally breeding bird, Aquatic Warbler, one can see why local ornithologists are so proud of Senné. White Storks nest in the villages around the complex and feed in the agricultural land. The surrounding area is good for Montagu's Harrier, Red-footed Falcon, Hobby and Buzzard among the raptors, as well as Tawny Pipit, Whinchat, Marsh Warbler and Red-backed and Lesser Grey Shrikes. The working ponds should not be neglected, as many key birds can be found here. A canal forming the western border of the complex, is followed by a convenient dyke from which much can be seen. Autumn sees Black and White Storks, Crane and waders stopping over on passage; vagrants have included Marsh Sandpiper and White Pelican.

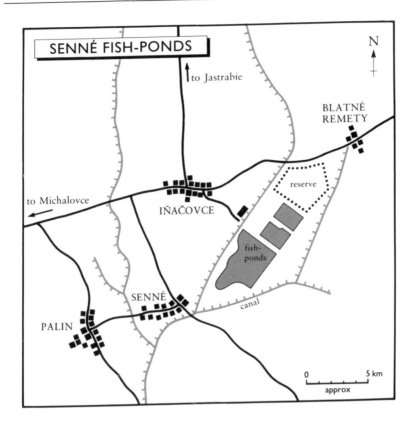

SENNÉ FISH-PONDS

to Jastrabie

N

BLATNÉ REMETY

reserve

to Michalovce

IŇAČOVCE

fish-ponds

SENNÉ

canal

PALIN

0   5 km

approx

CALENDAR

There is something of interest at Senné almost all year round with good numbers of birds on spring and autumn passage, Cranes in October, wintering wildfowl and always the chance of a rarity. All of the breeding birds are present from May to July, with the migration of storks beginning again in August. Autumn also traditionally sees the fish-ponds drained to harvest the fish, which usually attracts birds to the exposed mud.

SPECIES

- *Great White Egret* Some birds present all year round.
- *Pygmy Cormorant* The first breeding record for Slovakia was here in 1992.
- *Black-winged Stilt* The only regular site in the country.
- *Ruff* Often tens of thousands in the spring with some staying on to breed.

ACCESS

The area lies 25 km (15 miles) north-east of Trebisov and 13 km (8 miles) south-east of Michalovce in the extreme south-east corner of Slovakia. Access to the fish-ponds can be difficult as the dirt roads and tracks quickly turn to mud after rain and at the best of times need a four-wheel-drive vehicle. Approach from Inacovce on a metalled road to the fish-farm buildings which lie at the centre of the complex. Then explore on foot, after asking permission from the staff. From the buildings walk north-eastwards along the canal to the reserve section which can be viewed from the canal dyke. Alternatively, approach on foot from Blatné Remety to the north-east of the ponds. An IBA.

EAST SLOVAKIA MARSHES
48°21–48°48N 21°40–22°15E

Most of what was once a vast flood-plain of several small rivers winding through this little visited corner of Europe, from the hills in the north and from the Ukraine in the east, has been converted to agricultural land. However, remnants of marsh, ox-bow lakes and riverine forest do remain and hold some typical eastern European birds. Black Stork, Black Kite, Nightingale and Thrush Nightingale, River Warbler, Short-toed Treecreeper and Golden Oriole are all birds of the riverine woodlands. The Uh at Pavlovce nad-Uhom, the Laborec near Oborin, the Latorica north of Leles and the Bodrog at Pavlovo all have stretches of forest. A series of wet-woodlands of mainly willow and poplar near Zatín are typical of the region. Black, Green, Grey-headed, Great Spotted and Syrian Woodpeckers are all possible in such places. An ox-bow lake and wet-meadows to the north of the same village hold Little Bittern, Ferruginous Duck, Little Crake, Corncrake, Kingfisher and Lesser Grey Shrike. Near the Hungarian border just outside Streda nad Bodrogom, where the main road to Královsky Chlmec is flanked by an arm of the River Bodrog and a railway line, is Tajba Marsh. In addition to most of the above

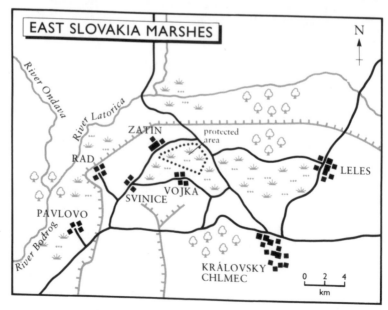

birds, there are Red-footed Falcons, the occasional Bluethroat, Bee-eaters, Penduline Tits and Red-backed Shrikes here and healthy numbers of mosquitoes. White Storks nest in loose colonies on telegraph poles and chimneys in several villages, and this region is also one of the few places in Slovakia where Whiskered and White-winged Black Terns are possible in summer.

CALENDAR

To get the best out of the area, visit in May or June when the nightingales and warblers are in full song, White Storks are in the villages and Corncrakes are calling. The region can look impressive in spring and autumn when the rivers occasionally flood a wide area.

SPECIES

◆ *Red-footed Falcon* The border area with Hungary is one of the few regular sites in Slovakia for this species.

◆ *Montagu's Harrier* One of the best regions in Slovakia for this species, too.

◆ *River Warbler* Quite common and widespread and not necessarily along the rivers.

◆ *Little Egret* Another bird which is rare in Slovakia and has a foothold here.

ACCESS

The area nestles into the very south-east corner of Slovakia about 20 km (12 miles) south-east of Trebisov. Bordered by Hungary to the south and the Ukraine to the east, it is best to take care where one is walking, although it is hard to imagine any serious trouble with border guards these days. Several nature reserves dot the area and permission to enter may be required. As many stretches of forest and marsh are just as good for birds as the reserves, it is perhaps better to explore the whole area taking note of notice boards. A useful track passing through a good area around the River Latorica runs from Bol' to Oborín. An IBA.

HUNGARY

On the map: UKRAINE, SLOVAKIA, AUSTRIA, CROATIA, YUGOSLAVIA, ROMANIA

AGGTELEK, ZEMPLÉN HILLS, BODROGKÖZ, BÜKK HILLS, TISZADOB, SZIGETKÖZ, PILIS AND BUDA HILLS, BÖRZSÖNY HILLS, DANUBE BEND, LAKE TISZA, HORTOBÁGY, HANSÁG, LAKE FERTŐ, LAKE TATA, VÉRTES HILLS, BUDAPEST, ÓCSA, MIDDLE RIVER TISZA, SÁRRÉT, LAKE VELENCE AND DINNYÉS MARSHES, BIHARUGRA FISH-PONDS, TIHANY, LAKE BALATON, KISKUNSÁG SALT-LAKES, KIS-BALATON, LAKE PÉTERI, KARDOSKÚT, BORONKA, TOLNA, SZEGED FISH-PONDS

N

0 100 km

GENERAL INFORMATION

O f all the former socialist countries of central and eastern Europe, Hungary is generally regarded as the most advanced in terms of standards of living and tourist facilities. Yet this is really only true of the capital, Budapest, which can match, and even surpass, western European capitals in many things, including hotel prices and car-hire rates! Once one gets into the countryside, especially east of the Danube, things change. In some areas, including those which birdwatchers will want to explore, accommodation can be limited in both availability and standard. However, this is more than compensated for by the fact that Hungarian birdwatching is usually five-star. Compared with Britain, for example, prices are still low for most things, although not so ridiculously cheap as they used to be in the socialist era. Credit cards should not be relied upon outside Budapest, tourist offices and larger hotels elsewhere. The unit of currency is the forint.

Hungary is a land-locked country with a continental climate, which varies greatly from season to season. In July and August temperatures can rise above 30 °C (86 °F). The coldest month is

January when below 0 °C (32 °F) is the norm, though it can be much colder than this on the flat windswept plain and in the higher hills.

A bilateral agreement means that emergency health care is free for British passport-holders. Every town has a well-stocked pharmacy but supplies of mosquito repellent should be brought along. Ticks can be a problem in woodland areas. Officially, tap water is safe but with bottled mineral water available everywhere I recommend drinking that, although one or two brands are an acquired taste.

English is usually spoken by at least one member of staff in hotels and restaurants, but the main tourism language, for the moment, remains German. Visiting birdwatchers are usually eagerly helped by local people. Except where signs clearly indicate that entry is forbidden, into a reserve or private fish-farm for example, it is acceptable to wander just about anywhere. Of course, the usual codes of conduct should be practised.

IMPORTANCE FOR BIRDS

With about 1000 birds, Hungary has a crucial population of Great Bustards. This population is all the more important when one considers the fact that the European range of this majestic species has drastically decreased, to the point of near extinction in neighbouring countries. In addition to this high-profile bird, Hungary has significant breeding populations of four other globally threatened species, namely Imperial Eagle, White-tailed Eagle, Corncrake and Aquatic Warbler. One of Europe's most enigmatic birds, the Saker, has a stronghold, and there is Europe's largest population of Great White Egrets. Hungary is also of great importance as a migration stop-over for two other rare species, Slender-billed Curlew and the Lesser White-fronted Goose, and for thousands of Cranes and other migratory species in the autumn. Despite the ravages of post-war agricultural policy, when large tracts of grassland and marsh were converted into farmland, the country still holds good numbers of breeding lowland species such as Red-footed Falcon, Lesser Grey Shrike and Marsh Harrier. Large populations of Bitterns, Night Herons, Spoonbills and incalculable numbers of *Locustella* and *Acrocephalus* warblers also make Hungary an important country for wetland birds.

GETTING THERE

It is almost inevitable that one will pass through the capital, Budapest. There are two flights a day into the city by Malév (Hungarian Airlines) and British Airways from London. All of the major European carriers also fly into the capital. Flight bargains seem few and far between. Budapest is also linked to all parts of Europe by rail and is a good base from which to head farther on into the Balkans. The daily connection from London Victoria takes 28 hours. A regular express bus service also runs from Munich and Vienna. By far the best way to birdwatch in Hungary, however, is to drive. A car is essential in order to get the most out of a visit as, although there is a good transport system and most sites can be reached by bus or train, once there a great deal of walking is often necessary. Locally obtainable detailed maps to most areas are excellent.

CONSERVATION

Hungary has a great tradition of nature conservation and birds have always been studied and watched. Although hunting is another tradition there is no 'culture' of shooting non-game birds as in the Mediterranean. Hungary has signed all the major international convention documents and has a long-standing network of reserves and protected areas. The Hungarian Ornithological and Nature Conservation Society (MME) is active in all fields of bird conservation and protection and has a growing membership. For information and membership details write to: MME, 1121 Budapest, Költö utca 21, Hungary. Records and unusual sightings should be sent to the Nomenclature Standing Committee (NAB), c/o the MME.

HABITATS

From an international point of view Hungary is significant for a unique kind of habitat, the *puszta*. This lowland steppe-grassland, inadvertently created by the felling and burning of woodlands over the centuries, has become a crucial habitat for many threatened birds. Great Bustard, Stone Curlews, Short-toed Lark, Tawny Pipit, Red-footed Falcon and Lesser Grey Shrike are all typical *puszta* birds. Several rare raptors also hunt over the various *puszta* areas, which are scattered across Hungary from the Austrian border to the Hortobágy, the largest being east of the Danube. Hungarian wetlands include salt-lakes, marshes, flood-plain forests along the Danube, Bodrog and Tisza Rivers and fish-ponds. The last are found throughout the country, with sometimes large reedbeds and are almost always excellent places for birds. They are also important wintering areas for wildfowl. Although not a mountainous country, Hungary has a belt of wooded hills running roughly along its northern border. The broad-leaved woodland and karst habitat here supports many species including rare raptors, owls, woodpeckers and flycatchers. Most of Hungary is agricultural land which, in general, is bad for birds although some species do well, especially where traditional farming methods are practised. Great Bustards, for example, often nest and feed in lucerne and other crops. Vineyards, allotments and smallholdings are also often good habitats.

Seasons

SPRING

March is peak time for woodpecker activity in the woodlands of the north. From mid-April onwards migratory birds of prey begin to arrive in their territories. Moustached Warbler is the first 'reed' warbler to arrive and is easiest to track down from mid-March into April. In May, Great Bustards are in full display. Reedbeds are good places for passage songbirds.

SUMMER

Bee-eaters and Rollers have all returned by the first week of June. Red-footed Falcons are well into their struggle to displace Rooks from nests in copses on the Great Plain and there is much noisy activity around heron and egret colonies across the country. August sees an influx of Long-legged Buzzards. The *puszta* is bone-dry in July and August and care should be taken as fires quickly take hold.

AUTUMN

September sees the first Cranes and Dotterels arriving on the Hortobágy. White Storks move south in groups, soon followed by Black Storks. The *puszta* hosts an influx of raptors. In October, Lesser White-fronted Geese appear on the Hortobágy and tens of thousands of Cranes pass through the east of the country. In September and October one or two Slender-billed Curlews regularly occur. October is generally a good time for vagrants.

WINTER

Large numbers of wildfowl roost on the Danube, Lakes Balaton, Tata, Velence and larger fish-ponds if the winter is not too hard. Parties of Lapland Buntings and Twites invade the puszta. Great Bustards congregate in flocks and Rough-legged Buzzards roam the country. White-tailed Eagles congregate on fish-ponds. Great Grey Shrikes and Hen Harriers from farther north appear along with huge flocks of Rooks. It can be bitterly cold on the open *puszta* and in the higher hills.

BIRDWATCHING SITES

LAKE FERTÖ

47°35–47°38N 16°37–16°40E

This shallow saline lake is the first of several which dot the Hungarian countryside. Most of Fertö lies in Austria and is perhaps familiar as the Neusiedler See. However, the Hungarian section of the lake has been exploited less for tourism and has vast reedbeds several kilometres wide in places, a result of having been right on the border between 'east' and 'west'. Bittern, Little Bittern, Great White Egret, Purple Heron and Spoonbill all found this no-man's land ideal for breeding and still do. Moustached, Savi's and Great Reed Warblers are all common. Ducks include Shoveler and Ferruginous Duck. A minor road skirts the lake from Fertórákos through Balf to Hidegség, and being high up gives panoramic views. There is a lake-side resort after Fertórákos which is fed by a road running through reedbeds, from which reed-dwelling birds can be observed without having to enter the strict reserve. Farther east, the village of Fertód is dominated by the Eszterházy Chateau. The gardens hold Icterine Warbler, Black Redstart and Green, Great Spotted and Syrian Woodpeckers. From Fertód a road heads north to Fertóújlak right on the Austrian border (it is a sign of the times that this road can be taken; I was turned back in 1989) where a salt-marsh is good for Black-tailed Godwit, Curlew and Kentish Plover. Before one gets this far, the grassland to the left has a reputation for turning up surprises, but you should remember to stick to the roads and paths. An old frontier watch-tower here is now used as a hide. Damp thickets *en route* are good for River Warbler, Nightingale and Golden Oriole.

CALENDAR

Reedbeds are generally best from April to June, although Moustached Warblers often stay around well into October. White Storks breed in villages in the area and occur in groups around the lake, along with some Black Storks, in August before migrating south. Autumn brings tens of thousands of grey geese to the lake on passage with some staying on to winter. Bean Geese are the most numerous. Hen Harriers and Rough-legged Buzzards occur from October through to March.

SPECIES

♦ *Bittern* Often easy to see in cold weather when they venture out into the open.

♦ *Spoonbill* Around twenty pairs breed and up to 100 in autumn.

- *Moustached Warbler* As far as I know no one has surveyed this species here, though the amount of suitable habitat available surely means a large population.
- *Great Reed Warbler* Probably the most common 'reed' warbler, certainly the loudest.
- *Short-eared Owl* Groups of up to ten possible in autumn on grasslands near the lake.

ACCESS

Lake Fertö is 210 km (130 miles) west of Budapest and about an hour by car from Vienna, crossing the border at Klingenbach-Sopron. Now a National Park, the lake and surrounding area are crossed by a network of paths and cycle routes. New border crossings with Austria have been opened, making exploration from there easier, but permission is needed for most of the best areas. Write in advance to: Fertö National Park, Sopron, Károlymagaslati u.4, 9400, Hungary. An IBA.

HANSÁG

47°45N 17°15E

Although it arguably cannot compete with sites in the east of Hungary since it has been heavily exploited, the Hanság is still a fine birding area. A mosaic region of meadows, alder, willow and poplar woods, reedbeds and farmland, it holds Great White Egret, Purple Heron, both storks, Black Kite, Marsh and Montagu's Harriers, some Corncrakes, Black Tern, Black Woodpecker, Bluethroat, Barred, Moustached and Savi's Warblers, Red-backed and Lesser Grey Shrikes and a few Great Bustards. A reserve with a ringing camp at Lake Fehér (Fehér-tó) near the village of the same name is good for Bittern, Penduline Tit and other reed-dwelling birds.

CALENDAR

Spring and summer are the seasons to visit.

SPECIES

- *Montagu's Harrier* The Hanság is a particularly good region for this species.

ACCESS

The area lies between Mosonmagyaróvár to the north and Csorna and Kapuvár to the south, in the north-west corner of Hungary near the Austrian border. Road 86 cuts across the Hanság. Access around protected areas is by paths and tracks only. An IBA.

SZIGETKÖZ

c.47°45N 17°30E

In the very north-west of Hungary, between Mosonmagyaróvár and Györ, the two branches of the Danube are flanked by a myriad of channels, ox-bow lakes, wooded islets, wet-meadows and farmland. The 'old' Danube branch forms the border with Slovakia

Although Icterine Warbler is widespread in Hungary's parks, copses and plantations, riverine woodlands like Szigetköz are particularly good for this species.

here and corresponds to the Danube Flood Plain site there. Not surprisingly, the birds at Szigetköz are similar. Great White Egret, Purple and Night Herons, Black and White Storks, Ferruginous Duck, Honey Buzzard, Goshawks, Black Kite, Marsh and Montagu's Harriers, Black and Syrian Woodpeckers, Nightingale, Bee-eater, Penduline Tit and Icterine Warbler are among the attractions in summer. Winter sees large numbers of wildfowl. The future of Szigetköz hangs in the balance because of the Gabcikovo dam project.

CALENDAR
From April to August is best overall for breeding birds.
SPECIES
♦ *Icterine Warbler* Very common here.
♦ *Short-toed Treecreeper* Also very common.
ACCESS
Between Dunakiliti and Nagybajcs the 'old' Danube can be difficult to work as it is a border area and a complex wetland. Several minor roads link villages lying between road 1 and the border. Austria is just a few miles to the west. Proposed as an IBA.

continued on page 105

BIAŁOWIEŻA FOREST, POLAND

Lesser Spotted
Eagle

Booted Eagle

Greenish
Warbler

White-backed
Woodpecker

Three-toed
Woodpecker

Collared Flycatcher

Hazelhen

Red-breasted Flycatcher

Corncrake

Thrush Nightingale

Nutcracker

Pygmy Owl

Black Woodpecker

Grey-headed Woodpecker

Redwing

Crested Tit

Ring Ouzel

Tengmalm's Owl

Capercaillie

Black Grouse

VIHORLAT HILLS, SLOVAKIA

Black Stork

Imperial Eagle

Raven

Honey Buzzard

Eagle Owl

Ural Owl

Golden Oriole

Red-backed
Shrike

Hawfinch

Barred Warbler

Little Egret

Great White Egret

Black Tern

Spoonbill

Bearded Tit

Penduline Tit

Savi's Warbler

Great Reed
Warbler

Bluethroat

Moustached
Warbler

Saker

Montagu's Harrier

Marsh Harrier

Roller

White Stork

Red-footed Falcon

Stone Curlew

Great Bustard

Tawny Pipit

Short-toed Lark

Dalmatian Pelican

White Pelican

Pygmy Cormorant

Ferruginous Duck

Glossy Ibis

Ruddy Shelduck

Night Heron

Little Crake

Squacco Heron

Spotted Crake

DOBRUDJA, ROMANIA

Peregrine

Rough-legged
Buzzard

White-tailed
Eagle

Red-breasted Goose

White-fronted
Goose

Black-necked Grebe

White-headed Duck

Lesser White-
fronted Goose

Smew

Red-crested
Pochard

LAKE ATANASSOVO, BULGARIA

Sandwich
Tern

Gull-billed
Tern

Whiskered
Tern

Collared
Pratincole

Black-headed
Bunting

Little
Bittern

Purple Heron

Mediterranean Gull

Slender-billed
Gull

Black-winged Stilt

LAKE TATA

47°39N 18°18E

With a motorway nearby, the town of Tata on three sides and a resort along one shore, Lake Tata may seem an unlikely place for birds, yet it is of international importance for wildfowl. The lake is fed by a warm stream which prevents it from totally freezing over, and thousands of geese and ducks find it an ideal roost in winter. Numbers vary, but up to 10,000 Bean Geese winter, and more use the lake at the end of the season on their way north. Greylag and White-fronted Geese also occur. Autumn is generally less interesting in terms of numbers but rarities such as Red-breasted Goose are more frequent then. The lake is also one of the few places west of the Danube where I have seen Crane. Pochard, Garganey, Teal, Goldeneye and Tufted Duck also winter and pass through. The lake also functions as a fish-farm, and in autumn the shallow water is drained leaving expanses of exposed mud. The surrounding area is predominantly agricultural land, to which the geese fly to feed by day. Dawn fly-out can be quite spectacular if one is in place before the sun comes up. Wildfowl watching at Tata in winter is often supplemented by Waxwings, Hawfinches, Bramblings and various woodpeckers in the adjoining park and in woodland at the lake's southern end.

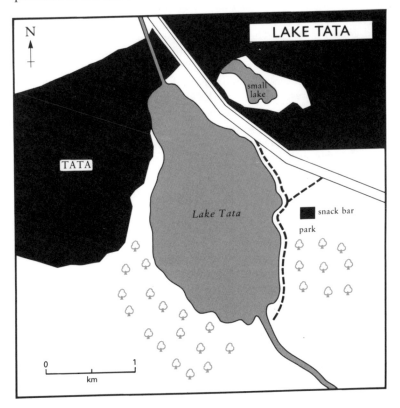

CALENDAR

Although Syrian and Grey-headed Woodpeckers are present all year, and a small reedbed has Great Reed and Sedge Warblers, summer does not offer very much by Hungarian standards. Lake Tata is best from October to February when wildfowl numbers can be impressive.

SPECIES

♦ *Bean Goose* Maximum numbers usually in February.

♦ *Garganey* Several hundred on autumn and spring passage.

♦ *Grey-headed Woodpecker* Often in trees near the snack-bars on the eastern shore.

ACCESS

Tata lies just north of the M1, 70 km (43 miles) west of Budapest. The lake is a Nature Conservation Area, but no permission is required to birdwatch as long as one keeps to the shore. A convenient path runs along the eastern edge of the lake and is a good vantage point. An IBA.

VÉRTES HILLS

47°43N 18°54E

These wooded limestone hills are excellent for raptors with Honey Buzzard, Short-toed and Imperial Eagles, Goshawk and Saker all present. Several open and rocky areas at the southern edge of the range between Csákvár and Csákberény are favoured hunting areas and good for views. There are also Montagu's and Marsh Harriers here. The mixed woodland covering much of the hills supports Black, Middle Spotted and Grey-headed Woodpeckers. I have only seen Syrian Woodpeckers in orchards and allotments around villages; never in the forest itself. From the village of Csókakó at the western end of the range, an easy walk begins at the foot of a castle ruin and passes through beech woods with Middle Spotted Woodpecker, Collared and Red-breasted Flycatchers and Hawfinch. A pleasant walk by vineyards between Csókakó and Csákberény along the very southern edge of the hills should produce Honey Buzzard, Raven and Bee-eater in summer. Areas that have regenerated after felling are good for Barred Warbler and Woodlark. Red-backed Shrike, Nightingale and Tree Pipit are just about everywhere and quarries near the mining settlement of Gant hold Black Redstart and, occasionally, Rock Thrush. The forests are notorious for ticks.

CALENDAR

The best time to visit is from May to July when all the summer birds are in place. Winter has its attractions, with Imperial Eagles resident and Hen Harriers and Great Grey Shrikes replacing their respective summer relatives.

SPECIES

♦ *Imperial Eagle* Areas with Susliks' holes are often the best places to see hunting birds.

◆ *Black Woodpecker* The presence of Stock Doves, which depend on Black Woodpeckers for nesting holes, means that you are in a good area for this species.

◆ *Collared Flycatcher* Females in particular should be carefully checked as Pied Flycatchers also occur.

ACCESS
Csákvár, at the foot of the Vértes, is 25 km (15 miles) north of Székesfehérvár. From Budapest take the M1 west to the Bicske exit and the minor roads. From Székesfehérvár take road 81 northwards to Mór turning off at Söréd. Military exercises take place here from time to time but are usually well sign-posted. With the exception of two inner areas the hills can be explored at will on a series of good paths. Most of the range is a Landscape Protection Reserve. An IBA.

SÁRRÉT

47°08N 18°15E
This is an under-birded area of peatbogs, reed-fringed canals, pools, acacia and willow copses, meadows and farmland against an industrial backdrop of slag heaps and smoking factories. Do not, however, be put off, there are Ferruginous Duck, Marsh and Montagu's Harriers, Spotted and perhaps Baillon's Crakes, Short-eared Owl, Tawny Pipit, Red-backed and Lesser Grey Shrikes, Penduline Tit and Barred Warbler amongst others. In winter, birds of prey such as Buzzard and Rough-legged Buzzard, Hen Harrier, Merlin and Great Grey Shrike move in. Planned habitat reconstruction promises to attract even more species.

CALENDAR
May to August for breeding birds and winter for hunting raptors, which can be numerous.

SPECIES
◆ *Great Bustard* Traditionally one of Transdanubia's best sites. A few birds may still be hanging on.

ACCESS
Situated about 20 km (12.5 miles) west of Székesfehérvár to the south of Várpalota. A minor road south from road 8 to Nádasdladány skirts the area. An IBA.

KIS-BALATON

46°40'N 17°14'E
There are, in fact, two Kis-Balatons; Old and New. The first is a vast area of reed, sedge, willow and small ponds which is totally impenetrable except along closed-off dykes which require a permit and guide. The second area is a water-storage reservoir and somewhat easier to work, although excellent dyke roads which criss-cross the water also require permits. A range of habitats in the Kis-Balaton region guarantees a good variety of birds. White-tailed

Eagles breed, Marsh Harriers are common and there are a few pairs of Montagu's Harriers in surrounding meadows. Great White and Little Egrets, Spoonbill, Whiskered and Black Terns and Marsh and Great Reed Warblers can be seen around Kányavári Island, which has two observation towers and lies just north of Balatonmagyorod. There is more vegetation at this end of the lake, as well as such birds as Squacco Heron and Black-necked Grebe. Ducks include Garganey, Ferruginous Duck and a few Red-crested Pochard. Another good vantage point is a causeway across the water beyond Zalavár. Just south of Zalavár, on the way to Balatonmagyarod, the road crosses the River Zala which can be followed from here for a way through Old Kis-Balaton in the direction of Lake Balaton proper. This is a good area for Night Heron, Kingfisher and Penduline Tit amongst others. White Stork pairs nest in surrounding villages.

CALENDAR

There are birds here all year round. Spring brings occasional Ospreys and singing Moustached Warblers in April and a return passage of waders and summer visitors throughout May. The end of summer sees parties of White Storks and waders on their way south. Winter has White-tailed Eagle, Hen Harrier, Penduline Tit, Greylag and Bean Geese. For variety Kis-Balaton is perhaps best from April to August.

SPECIES

◆ *Night Heron* An important site with up to 200 pairs.
◆ *Great White Egret* Mild winters see dozens staying on.
◆ *Squacco Heron* Entry into the reserve proper is necessary to get good views.
◆ *White-tailed Eagle* Kis-Balaton is a hunting area for breeding birds with more in winter.
◆ *Whiskered Tern* The most common marsh tern here.

ACCESS

Kis-Balaton is 10 km (6 miles) south of Keszthely at the south-west end of Lake Balaton. A permit is needed to get to the heart of the Kis-Balaton Landscape Protection Reserve. However, I suggest dropping into the ringing camp of the MME at Fenékpuszta, on the road to Keszthely just north of the junction with road 76, near where the River Zala leaves Kis-Balaton and enters Lake Balaton. The camp leaders can often arrange visits and are a good source of information. Leave a donation in the collection box! An IBA.

LAKE BALATON

46°50N 17°40E

Balaton is the largest lake in central Europe and in summer a busy resort, although quiet corners with reedbeds do have Ferruginous Duck, Marsh Harrier, Kingfisher, Moustached, Great Reed and Savi's Warblers, Bluethroat and Bearded and Penduline Tits. The lake is best for birds in winter when the occasional diver, grebes, rafts of ducks, grey geese and gulls occur. Good watching places include Paloznak Bay, near the village of the same name, Bázsa Bay on the west of Tihany Peninsula (*see* below), Keszthely Bay at the west end of the lake, and the point where the River Zala enters it. In harsh winters, the lake freezes and few birds stay. In autumn, there is some passage of Teal, Garganey and Shoveler among others.

CALENDAR

The summer tourist season ends in August, and autumn passage occurs from September. The lake is usually ice-free from October to December, with January generally the harshest period.

SPECIES

◆ *Bean Goose* Up to 1000 can roost in winter.

ACCESS

Being 77 km (50 miles) long, Lake Balaton has a lot of shore to cover, most of which is accessible. The M7 reaches the lake directly from Budapest. A proposed IBA.

TIHANY

46°55N 17°50E

Lake Balaton is the major summer resort in Hungary and, although a wintering ground for wildfowl, of little interest for birdwatchers when wind-surfers and swimmers take over. Yet, there are good sites for birds around the lake and Tihany, an attractive village and resort on a peninsula on the northern shore, is one of the best with two small lakes, orchards, vineyards and woodland within a compact area. Woods beyond Sajkod on the western shore have Nightingale, Golden Oriole, and Tawny and Scops Owls. The better lake, Külső-tó (Outer Lake) is mostly covered in reed, and is home to Little Bittern, Purple Heron, Garganey, Gadwall, Ferruginous Duck, Marsh Harrier, Great Reed and Savi's Warblers and Penduline Tit. Approach on tracks from the direction of Gödrös. Belső-tó (Inner Lake) is used for angling and usually is not very exciting. At the south of the peninsula a sandy, scrubby area can be a good spot for Nightjar and Red-backed Shrike. Vineyards and other open areas at the heart of the peninsula have Hoopoe, Stonechat, Crested Lark and, in some years, Red-footed Falcon. Black Redstarts are common in Tihany and other villages. Lake Balaton can be scanned from the peninsula, and in autumn and winter when the tourist season has ended grebes, ducks and gulls can be interesting. The bay at the eastern foot of the peninsula near Balatonfüred is usually good for Scaup, Goldeneye, Long-tailed Duck and Smew.

CALENDAR

Visit from May to August, or October–March for wintering birds on the lake which can be shrouded in fog and occasionally freezes over.

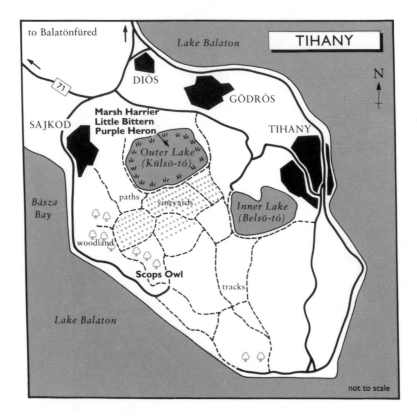

SPECIES

- *Scops Owl* The orchards and woodland here are a regular site for a few pairs of this uncommon Hungarian breeder.
- *Purple Heron* There should be no problem in seeing this species in summer at the 'Outer Lake'.
- *Red-backed Shrike* The range of habitats in which this species can be seen in Hungary is quite remarkable and Tihany is no exception.

ACCESS

The Tihany Peninsula is 126 km (78 miles) from Budapest by the M7 and then road 71 along the northern shore of Lake Balaton. Balatonfüred is a busy summer resort at the foot of the peninsula. Tracks and footpaths criss-cross the area from roads on both sides of Tihany. No permits are needed, but vineyards should be explored only with the permission of locals. A road along the western shore is closed to cars at Sajkod lido but can be followed on foot.

LAKE VELENCE AND DINNYÉS MARSHES

47°10N 18°32E

Most of the western end of the lake is covered in reed where Savi's, Moustached, Sedge, Reed and Great Reed Warblers all breed. Great White Egret, Purple Heron and Spoonbill also nest in the safety of the reedbed which is a bird reserve. Marsh Harriers are numerous. Spotted and Little Crakes are also here, but will require some luck to see. On the northern shore a small peninsula is the departure point for ferries in summer and is a good vantage point. There is also a *csarda* (traditional restaurant) here, from where I have often seen Bitterns moving around the reed edge; this is also a good spot for Moustached Warbler. At the south-west tip of the lake Dinnyés railway station has resident Crested Larks. There are Bluethroat and Penduline Tit in the bushes around a fish-farm opposite, which is also a good place for Night Heron, Little Bittern and Black Tern. White Storks nest in the village. Indeed, there is a great deal of movement between the lake, fish-farm and marsh. In addition to the above birds the Dinnyés Marshes have Red-necked and Black-necked Grebes, Ferruginous Duck and Bearded Tit. From October until the first hard frosts thousands of grey geese, mostly Bean, roost here along with ducks and Curlew. Most of the southern and eastern shore of Lake Velence is a busy summer resort and not really recommended unless one wants to observe Hungarians at play.

CALENDAR
An excellent place all year round, but probably at its best from April to June when warblers and other summer visitors are active. Autumn has its attractions with passage Ruff and other waders at Dinnyés and the arrival of the geese. If it is mild, some thousands of geese overwinter along with ducks, Great White Egret, Hen Harrier, Great Grey Shrike and Long-eared Owl, which roost in acacia copses.

SPECIES
◆ *Little Bittern* Quite common all around the lake but usually only seen in flight.
◆ *Great White Egret* Some regularly overwinter.
◆ *Ferruginous Duck* Can be seen just about anywhere and some occasionally overwinter.
◆ *Moustached Warbler* The rarest of the warblers and best tracked down from mid-March to April as it is the first to arrive back from wintering areas and can be heard singing without competition from Sedges and Great Reeds. Even the poorest imitation of its song can entice the species out from the reeds.

ACCESS
Just 50 km (31 miles) south-west of Budapest along the M7, or take road 70 which follows the south shore. By train, Dinnyés is on the Budapest–Székesfehérvár line. The reedbeds must not be entered, and a permit is needed to walk around Dinnyés Marshes as both are Nature Conservation Areas. Write to the Ministry of Environment and Regional Policy, Budapest 1121, Költó u. 21, Hungary. Much can be seen in the area without having to enter the reserves and the fish-farm staff at Dinnyés usually allow one to explore the ponds. An IBA.

Ócsa

47°15N 19°15E

Habitats such as meadows, peatbogs, ponds, alder and willow woods and reeds make up this mosaic area which is an easy day trip from the capital. Common birds here such as River Warbler, Nightingale and Marsh Harrier are usually easy to see from roadsides. White and Black Storks nest and occur in groups in the autumn. Reedbeds hold Spotted and Little Crakes, Little Bittern, Savi's and Great Reed Warblers and Great White Egret. An observation tower at the Ócsa ringing camp, a good source of information, is as good a place as any to get views. The camp is on the right of a minor road just before one enters the village coming from Alsónémedi. Ferruginous Ducks are quite common. Baillon's Crakes, however, are now only rarely encountered here because of the gradual drainage of their bog and marsh habitat. Wet-meadows near the village of Bugyi have Corncrake, Redshank and Black-tailed Godwit and patches of drier grassland have Lesser Grey Shrike, Montagu's Harrier, Roller and sometimes Short-eared Owl. There is also the chance of Saker in the neighbourhood. Rather more common are Red-backed Shrikes which in summer seem to be everywhere. Although generally derided, poplar plantations along the road to Dabas are not without their birds;

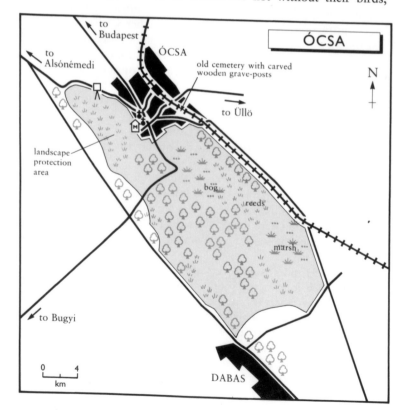

Black Woodpecker, Golden Oriole and even River Warbler inhabit such places. Ócsa village itself has Syrian Woodpecker, Serin, Black Redstart and nesting White Stork. One drawback at Ócsa can be the hordes of mosquitoes, so come prepared.

CALENDAR
Mosquitoes apart, summer is the best birdwatching time here. Bittern, Great White Egret, Hen and Marsh Harriers and Saker sometimes winter and can be seen well at this time of year. During August and September both storks can be seen in the area.

SPECIES
◆ *Saker* Electricity pylons in the area should be checked as these are favourite roosts.
◆ *River Warbler* Seems to go with the worst mosquito areas.
◆ *Roller* Sadly, on the decline here as elsewhere in Hungary.
◆ *Syrian Woodpecker* The village graveyard is as good as anywhere.

ACCESS
Ócsa is 20 km (12 miles) south-east of Budapest between the M5 and road 50. Much of the area is a Landscape Protection Reserve and permits are needed to enter some areas. Write to Bercsényi utca 4, Ócsa, which is a village museum and reserve headquarters, or drop in and staff may be able to organize a guided tour on the spot. Alternatively, leaders of the ringing camp located just outside the village may also be able to arrange entry into restricted areas. An IBA.

PILIS AND BUDA HILLS
*c.*47°30–47°47 18°30–19°03E
These fine hills offer excellent birdwatching within easy reach of the capital, indeed even in it. There are large forests of beech, hornbeam and oak, open meadows, scrub, stream valleys, limestone crags, vineyards, orchards and allotments. Widespread birds include Black, Grey-headed and Middle Spotted Woodpeckers, Wryneck, Woodlark, Tree Pipit, Red-backed Shrike, Barred Warbler, Short-toed Treecreeper, Hawfinch, Serin and Golden Oriole. Suitable woodland has Collared Flycatcher, and some parts of the Pilis have Red-breasted Flycatcher. A useful walk with many of the above, as well as Grey Wagtail and Dipper (the latter far from common in Hungary), starts from the village of Visegrád on the Danube Bend and follows a stream up into the hills. Raptors in the Pilis include Short-toed Eagle, Goshawk, Honey Buzzard, and there is a chance of Saker. Black Kites are possible along the Danube, and some White Storks nest in villages. Black Stork and Raven both breed in the hills but the former is elusive. The south of the Pilis merges into the Buda Hills roughly along road 10. Quarries along this route occasionally hold Rock Thrush and Rock Bunting. There are Bee-eaters here, too. The Buda Hills from Normafa to János Hill are a favourite walking spot but are also good for woodpeckers and other woodland species.

CALENDAR

March and April are best for woodpeckers, although they can be found all year. In May flycatchers and raptors return. Fine weekends can be a little crowded in some places on the Danube Bend.

SPECIES

◆ *Syrian Woodpecker* Parks, gardens and orchards throughout the area. Try the parkland on Gellért Hill and Castle Hill in Budapest, although beware, as Great Spotted Woodpeckers also occur here.
◆ *Collared Flycatcher* The oak woods around János Hill, the highest point in Budapest, are as good a place as any.
◆ *Hawfinch* Common in any woodland with beech and hornbeam.
◆ *Raven* Often around Visegrád Castle, which overlooks the Danube.

ACCESS

The Pilis Hills nestle in the Danube Bend just to the north of Budapest. Take road 11 north along the river or road 10 which skirts the south of the hills. Most of the area can be freely explored and is well covered by paths. The Buda Hills lie in the west of the city. Normafa can be reached by the 21 bus from Moszkva tér to the terminus where Middle Spotted Woodpecker should be waiting. The Pilis Hills are an IBA.

DANUBE BEND

47°29–47°47N 19°05–18°44E

The River Danube passes through one of its most scenic stretches between the historic town of Esztergom and Budapest. Temporary sandbanks and several islands, including the huge Szentendre Island, dot and split the river at various points. In summer, the river can be busy with tourist traffic, but riverside woodland and Szentendre Island are still good for woodpeckers and warblers. In winter, however, the river itself becomes an important wildfowl area. Grey geese, Teal, Pintail, Tufted Duck, Pochard, Common and Velvet Scoters, Goldeneye, Goosander and Smew can all be seen here. Slavonian Grebe and divers also turn up, and White-tailed Eagle winter. Syrian Woodpecker, Great Grey Shrike, Brambling and Hawfinch are usually by the river in winter, too.

CALENDAR

The best time for wildfowl is from October through to February, although in extremely cold winters most birds move on elsewhere.

SPECIES

◆ *Velvet Scoter* Usually found on the stretch between Vác and Göd.

ACCESS

Road 2, north of Budapest, passes close to the river between Göd and Vác, and road 11, on the opposite bank near Visegrád, is often useful. Another convenient area is by road 12, between Nagymaros and Verőcemaros. Proposed as an IBA.

BÖRZSÖNY HILLS

47°55N 18°55E

Covered in mixed woodland interspersed with open meadows and rocky crags, the Börzsöny Hills contain a good selection of raptors, woodpeckers and songbirds. If time is limited, this is the nearest area to Budapest for White-backed Woodpecker. I have always found this much sought-after species in older stands of beech, such as on the southern slopes of the highest hill, Csóványos. Approach with a walking map from Diósjenó on the eastern edge of the hills. *En route* Wryneck, Grey Wagtail and Firecrest should be encountered. Black and Grey-headed Woodpeckers can be found throughout the hills. Middle Spotted Woodpeckers are found in broad-leaved forest along with Collared Flycatchers. Amongst the raptors, Honey Buzzard, Short-toed, Lesser Spotted and Imperial Eagles and Saker are all possible. Open areas near a popular rambling and picnic spot called Királyrét, which can be reached by road or rack railway from Verócemáros in the Danube valley below, are hunting grounds for these species. Woodlark, Barred Warbler and Red-backed Shrike are other birds here. Villages have nesting White Stork, Black Redstart and Serin. In true Hungarian fashion, the lower slopes of the hills are covered in weekend houses with their vineyards, allotments and gardens. Birds around these include Bee-eater, Hoopoe, Syrian Woodpecker and Golden Oriole.

Although Bee-eater has declined in Hungary, it is still locally common in summer around the Börzsöny Hills.

CALENDAR

The best time to birdwatch here is from the end of April to June. The best time for tracking down woodpeckers is from February to April when they are drumming and calling. Imperial Eagles sometimes occur in winter but, generally the hills and forests are rather silent except for parties of tits and treecreepers at this time of year.

SPECIES

◆ *White-backed Woodpecker* Once young have fledged in May this species becomes very difficult.

◆ *Hazelhen* Sightings have become very rare and thus any reports will be most welcome.

◆ *Short-toed Treecreeper* In the Danube valley this species is generally found lower down, with Treecreeper in the woodland higher up. Beware, they do overlap.

ACCESS

The hills are 50 km (31 miles) north of Budapest on road 2. For Diósjenó carry on farther north, for Királyrét take road 12 along the southern edge of the range. Most of the hills are a Landscape Protection Reserve but can be explored on well-marked paths. An IBA.

BÜKK HILLS

48°10N 20°30E

Eight species of woodpecker and four eagles inhabit the forests, vineyards and clearings of these hills. There is the largest population of White-backed Woodpeckers in Hungary and Middle Spotted are also common. Wooded steppe areas are dotted across the southern slopes of the Bükk east of Eger and are good for observing raptors which in summer soar out from the forest to hunt. Lesser Spotted Eagles are most likely, but there are also Imperial, Short-toed and Booted Eagles and Saker. These open areas of scrub also hold Barred Warbler and Red-backed Shrike. Farther into the hills north of Eger are limestone quarries and crags which can be searched for Rock Thrush and Rock Bunting (indeed, the centre of the hills is a limestone plateau). Vast vineyards sprawl around Eger (the home of Bulls Blood), from where a scenic road winds through the hills via Répáshuta to Miskolc. From this road, excursions can be made in all directions on an extensive system of footpaths. Birds that should be encountered without too much difficulty are Wryneck, Woodlark, Tree Pipit, Collared Flycatcher, Raven and Hawfinch. Red-breasted Flycatchers also breed. The oak, hornbeam and beech forests of the Bükk Hills are large and should be given plenty of time.

CALENDAR

Summer is best, as winter can be pretty quiet in the Bükk, as in most Hungarian ranges. April is best for woodpeckers and is also when species such as Saker and Imperial Eagle return from the plain to breed. By the middle of May most migrant songbirds have returned.

SPECIES

◆ *Lesser Spotted Eagle* Present from mid-April to mid-September.

◆ *Middle Spotted Woodpecker* Most common in beech and oak forest of which there is plenty.

◆ *Red-breasted Flycatcher* Unlike the examples in most field guides, males here often have little or no red on the breast.

ACCESS

Eger, which is a good base, is 130 km (81 miles) north-east of Budapest by road. Most of the Bükk is a National Park which is crossed by marked nature trails and footpaths. Further information can be obtained from the National Park Directorate, 3304 Eger, Sánc u.6. Hungary. An IBA.

AGGTELEK

48°27N 20°32E

Nicely tucked away in a quiet corner of the country, Aggtelek is well worth the trip. Most of the typical birds of Hungary's hill ranges are here, along with one or two specialities. Lightly wooded karst hillsides are home to Woodlark, Red-backed Shrike and Rock Bunting. The slopes above the lake at Aggtelek village are a good place to start. Short-toed Eagle and Honey Buzzard are also found hereabouts. One of the best areas for Lesser Spotted and Imperial Eagles is farther east along the road between Bódvaszilas and Tornanádaska on the border with Slovakia. Hazelhens have disappeared from many of Hungary's forests but seem to have held on at Aggtelek. Valleys worth exploring for this difficult species run north from the main road between Szin and Szinpetri. Manual cutting of meadows in this same area has benefited Corncrake. Aggtelek's many open patches of scrub are good for Barred Warbler. From the pleasant village of Jósvafó, marked footpaths heading north enter thicker forested areas with Black and Middle Spotted Woodpeckers, more chances of Hazelhen and Black Stork. There are some White-backed Woodpeckers, too. This is also Ural Owl country, although numbers fluctuate from year to year. Dipper, Kingfisher and Grey Wagtail are around the pond near the Jósvafó cave entrance.

CALENDAR

A winter visit might produce residents like Ural Owl, Rock Bunting and woodpeckers, but a lot of snow can lie on the ground here making exploration difficult. The best time is from April to August.

SPECIES

◆ *Hazelhen* This is now a rare bird in Hungary and I would be interested to hear of any sightings.

◆ *Ural Owl* Some years see 'invasions' and some years produce no reports. Early in the year from February to April is the best bet.

◆ *Rock Bunting* In its Hungarian stronghold here.

ACCESS
The Aggtelek National Park is 240 km (149 miles) north-east of Budapest and 60 km (37 miles) north of Miskolc. The northern edge of the park is formed by the border with Slovakia. Almost the whole National Park can be explored on paths and roads. An IBA.

ZEMPLÉN HILLS
48°14N 21°25E
These are the best hills in Hungary for raptors, although it must be said that they do not give up their secrets lightly. There are dense conifer forests, oak, hornbeam and beech woodland, scrubby clearings, wooded steppe areas and hillsides blanketed in vineyards. Birds differ, of course, according to each habitat, although some, like Buzzard, Black Woodpecker and Red-backed Shrike, are not too choosy. Special birds in the Zemplén are Ural and Eagle Owls, both of which are more likely to be found early in the year when they are calling, and Imperial and Golden Eagles. All these birds are easiest to see in their hunting areas, that is to say the western slopes and open clearings and meadows of the hills. A regular site for Lesser Spotted Eagle is the road between Fony and Regéc. White Storks nest in villages throughout the Zemplén and some Black Storks nest in more remote inner areas. Songbirds include Red-breasted and Collared Flycatchers in broad-leaved woodland, with Woodlark, Barred Warbler and Hawfinch widespread. Grey-headed and Black Woodpeckers are quite common but White-backed Woodpeckers, as usual, are difficult, requiring some hiking up into old beech stands. The valley of the River Hernád runs along the western edge of the hills and is good for Bee-eater, Lesser Grey Shrike, hunting raptors and, in winter, Great Grey Shrike, Merlin and Rough-legged Buzzard.

CALENDAR
There are good birds at all seasons, with resident woodpeckers, owls and Imperial Eagle. Summer is more productive overall when the full complement of raptors and passerines have returned to breed.
SPECIES
◆ *Imperial Eagle* Get yourself into position at around 11 a.m. on a summer's day in any open area and wait.
◆ *Booted Eagle* Mainly a woodland hunter, it is the most difficult of the raptors to find.
◆ *Ural Owl* Always present, but perhaps easier to find in winter when it often hunts during the day.
◆ *Hawfinch* On a good day here one can become almost blasé about this species.
ACCESS
The Zemplén Hills lie to the north of Szerencs, which is 35 km (22 miles) east of Miskolc on road 37. Most of the hills are a Landscape Protection Reserve but are of relatively free access and

in good Hungarian style crossed by well-marked footpaths. Several of the quarries are protected; others are working and entry is forbidden. An IBA.

BODROGKÖZ

48°15N 21°25E

The River Bodrog flows into the Tisza at the wine centre of Tokaj and just to the north and east of town, between the two rivers, lies a vast flood-plain of wet-meadows, ox-bow lakes, marshes, riverine forest and copses. Occasionally, the rivers flood the whole area, which then becomes a tree-dotted wetland, but usually Bodrogköz can be explored on foot. Birds found along the two rivers and around backwaters include Little Bittern, Squacco Heron, Great White and Little Egrets, Black Stork, Ferruginous Duck, Whiskered and Black Terns and Kingfisher. Tokaj and the villages along the Bodrog have numerous rooftop-nesting White Storks which feed in Bodrogköz. This is also a good raptor area with Honey Buzzard, Black Kite, Short-toed Eagle and Marsh and Montagu's Harriers all on the cards in summer. I have also seen Lesser Spotted Eagles heading here to hunt from the nearby hills and Eagle Owls apparently do the same. The impressive and extensive meadows have Corncrake, Black-tailed Godwit, Short-eared Owl and Grasshopper Warbler. River Warblers

Although common at Bodrogköz, River Warbler is notoriously difficult to see when it is breeding.

are widespread and both nightingale species are here to tackle. This is not always the easiest place to explore but it is worth the effort.

CALENDAR
Summer is best, from May on, when the Corncrakes and River Warblers are in full cry. Flocks of both storks occur in September and parties of Cranes occur in October. White-tailed Eagle, Hen Harrier and Short-eared Owl winter.

SPECIES
◆ *Corncrake* With around 100 pairs this is the best site in Hungary for this threatened species.
◆ *River Warbler* Usually not too difficult to see in May before they breed as males often rattle away from the top of bushes.
◆ *Thrush Nightingale* Certainly here, but their close relatives are more common. Elements of the songs of both species can be heard from individual birds.

ACCESS
Tokaj is 223 km (138 miles) from Budapest via Miskolc. Ferries of various shapes and sizes cross the Bodrog at Tokaj, Bodrogszegi and Olaszliszka on the north-west side of the area. The Tisza can be crossed at Timár and Balsa to the south. All of these routes lead into the area which can then be explored on foot via dykes and farm tracks. Much of the area is a Landscape Protection Reserve. An IBA.

TISZADOB
48°00N 21°10E
This is one of a series of flood-plain forest areas on the upper reaches of the River Tisza in north-east Hungary. Sadly, during the twentieth century much of the Tisza has been regulated and its forests felled and replaced with poplar plantations. At a place like Tiszadob, one can only wonder at what the birdlife must have been like. Besides the river itself, there are ox-bow lakes, meadows and some old oak forest. There is a colony of Night Heron, Little Egret and a few Purple Herons. White Storks are common throughout the whole region. Raptors include Marsh Harrier and Black Kite. From May onwards the meadows are a good area for calling Corncrakes, and the woodland has Black Woodpecker, Roller, Nightingale, Golden Oriole and perhaps Black Stork. Ferruginous Duck, Whiskered and Black Terns, Kingfisher and Penduline Tit can be found on the main dead branch of the river. There is an interesting collection of warblers here with Grasshopper, River, Reed, Marsh, Great Reed and Sedge all occurring and inviting comparison.

CALENDAR
The best time to visit is from May to August. The first migrants return at the end of April, with Corncrakes and most songbirds in

mid-May. Migrating White Storks congregate in the meadows in September. Winter is pretty quiet.

SPECIES

◆ *Night Heron* One of several colonies along this stretch of the Tisza is here.

◆ *Black Kite* Tiszadob is a typical site for the species.

◆ *Corncrake* Although difficult to see, several pairs inhabit the meadows.

◆ *Thrush Nightingale* If this species breeds here, this is probably the farthest south it gets along the Tisza.

ACCESS

As the crow flies Tiszadob is 12 km (7 miles) north of Tiszaújváros (marked on some maps by its former name of Leninváros) in the north-east of the country. Approach from Tiszaluc to the north-west or from Tiszavasvári which is 15 km (9 miles) to the east along a minor road. The area is a Nature Reserve but can be worked by following a convenient dyke at the edge of the village. An IBA.

HORTOBÁGY

47°37N 21°05E

This is one of Europe's great bird areas, but it is also another site which tries to keep its secrets. There can be tens of thousands of Cranes roosting here in autumn, and yet without detailed knowledge you will see only a few small flocks flying overhead. The birdlife here is so rich, however, that even a casual drive along road 33 in summer will turn up Great White Egret, Spoonbill, White Stork, Marsh and Montagu's Harriers and Red-footed Falcon. The Hortobágy can be roughly divided into three basic habitats: *puszta*, fish-ponds and marshes. The *puszta* is essentially grassland-steppe with, in summer, Montagu's Harrier, Stone Curlew, Short-eared Owl, Roller, Lesser Grey Shrike, Short-toed Lark and Tawny Pipit. Hungary's national bird, the Great Bustard, is resident. Winter on the *puszta* sees Rough-legged Buzzard and flocks of Lapland and Snow Buntings. In general the *pusztas* to the north of road 33 can be explored freely and those in the south of the National Park are out of bounds. Fish-ponds are dotted all over and have different birds, depending upon water quality, depth and function. In summer there are Red-necked and Black-necked Grebes, Purple, Squacco and Night Herons, Great White and Little Egrets, both bitterns, Spoonbill, various ducks, Little Crake, Whiskered Tern, Savi's and Moustached Warblers, Bluethroat and hordes of Bearded Tit, to name only a few. Hortobágy-halastó, to the north of road 33 just before Hortobágy village, is the best system, with a thatched hide at its centre and all of the above birds as well as a few Pygmy Cormorants and Glossy Ibis. In winter these same ponds can hold thousands of wildfowl and several White-tailed Eagles. The marshes of the Hortobágy are the most problematic habitat to visit being by nature difficult to explore, and the best places are out of bounds. There are some accessible spots, in particular by road 33 near Tiszafüredkócs and near Ohat. Squacco Heron, Black and White-winged Black Terns and Ferruginous Duck are likely birds here in summer. Baillon's Crakes breed on the Hortobágy but in totally inaccessible marshes. Although I have seen Aquatic Warbler elsewhere on the Hortobágy, most of the population resides in closed areas which can be visited only with the warden. Besides the three main habitats mentioned there are numerous patches of reed, acacia copses, temporary marsh and canal banks on the Hortobágy, all of which have good birds. An excellent place for birds and the most birdwatched area in Hungary, many rarities and vagrants have been found on the Hortobágy.

CALENDAR
Excellent at any time of year. Spring sees thousands of waders on passage and the arrival of breeding birds. Summer can be spectacular. In September there is an influx of both storks and such raptors as Saker, Long-legged Buzzard and Imperial Eagle. October heralds the arrival of huge numbers of Cranes and geese. Mild winters have raptors and wildfowl. In hard winters it can be very bleak.

SPECIES
◆ *Lesser White-fronted Goose* Some hundreds usually occur from September to November, roosting on fish-ponds.
◆ *Saker* August and September are particularly good months on any stretch of *puszta* for this spectacular bird.
◆ *Red-footed Falcon* Around 400 pairs nest in numerous colonies and isolated trees right across the region.
◆ *Crane* Probably the most important stop-over in Europe for these birds with tens of thousands roosting in October and November.
◆ *Aquatic Warbler* The 200 pairs here constitute the only known breeding population in Hungary.
◆ *Collared Pratincole* Although not common, they are often seen as they drink at marsh edges or near cattle troughs.

ACCESS
The Hortobágy, much of which is a National Park, lies between Tiszafüred and Debrecen in the far east of the country around 200 km (124 miles) from Budapest. Hortobágy village is at the centre of the region, 35 km (22 miles) west of Debrecen. Road 33 crosses the area and is the starting-point for many key sites. Strictly protected areas are usually signposted in several languages and wardened, so do not be tempted to enter without permission. An IBA.

LAKE TISZA
c.47°35N 20°30E
This huge man-made wetland, skirted by the Tisza to the east, consists of three parts. The southernmost, between Kisköre and Abádszalok, is a resort, and of least birdwatching interest, although there are camp

sites. The middle section, north of here to road 33, is apparently set aside for anglers but does have some good bird spots, notably woodland along the River Tisza south of Tiszafüred. The third section of the lake, to the north of the road between Poroszló and Tiszafüred, is a bird reserve and the place to visit. Just out of Poroszló, the road bends and crosses the lake on a causeway it shares with a railway line. The lake is visible on both sides here, but do not be tempted to stop at the roadside as this is a dangerous stretch. Rather, take a left turn across the railway line on to a metalled road which follows the dyke northwards. There is a pump-house after about 100 m from where the water can be scanned for ducks. The bushes lining the waterside are good for Nightingale, Penduline Tit, Great Reed Warbler and Golden Oriole. White-tailed Eagle and Black Kite occur, and Ospreys pass through in spring and autumn. A Cormorant colony in dead trees out in the lake can be viewed from farther along the dyke. Some pairs of Pygmy Cormorants breed here, too, along with Night and Squacco Herons. Other birds here include Great White Egret, Little Bittern and Black Tern. The forests along the River Tisza and the eastern shores of the lake are difficult to work and, in any case, are infested with mosquitoes for much of the year; however, Black Kite and Black Stork can be seen soaring here.

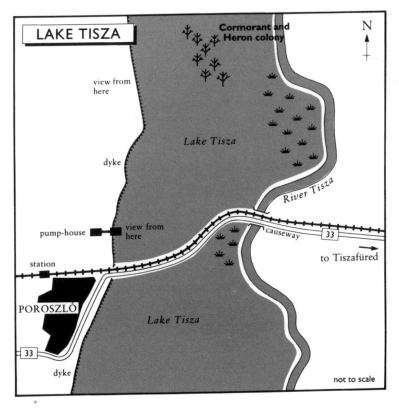

CALENDAR
There is something of interest in all seasons at Lake Tisza. May and June are best for breeding birds, August and September for passage storks and raptors, and winter often sees several White-tailed Eagles visiting the lake along with good numbers of ducks and geese. Once again, this all depends on the weather.

SPECIES
♦ *Pygmy Cormorant* One of the few Hungarian sites for this species which has recently returned to breed.
♦ *Black Kite* Far from common in Hungary, but often seen above the riverine forest along the River Tisza.
♦ *Olivaceous Warbler* Scarce and probably at the northern limit of its range here.

ACCESS
Lake Tisza lies along the River Tisza just to the west of Tiszafüred which is 155 km (96 miles) east of Budapest. Boats are forbidden in the Bird Reserve (though someone should tell the locals!) and in any case are not necessary as everything can usually be seen from the dyke road, but bring a telescope. An IBA.

MIDDLE RIVER TISZA
47°10N 20°10E
The whole length of the River Tisza is littered with good birds. The middle section, north and south of Szolnok, is lined by huge dykes which can mostly be walked and make observations easier over the top of what is often impenetrable woodland dotted with swampy mosquito-infested backwaters and ox-bow lakes. Little Bittern, Night Heron, Little Egret, both storks, White-tailed Eagle, Black Kite, Black Woodpecker, Roller, Lesser Grey Shrike and Barred, Icterine and Olivaceous Warblers are among the attractions.

CALENDAR
Best from May through to August for breeding birds.

SPECIES
♦ *Olivaceous Warbler* This species is expanding north along Hungary's rivers, and is more common than other literature might suggest.

ACCESS
Szolnok, at the heart of the area, is 100 km (60 miles) from Budapest via the busy road 4. Mostly a Landscape Protection Reserve, but accessible along dykes, roads and fishermen's tracks. An IBA.

BIHARUGRA FISH-PONDS
46°58N 21°35E
This excellent fish-pond complex is in a far-flung corner of the country but is certainly worth the extra mileage. There are large and small fish-ponds, huge reedbeds, marsh, *puszta* and meadows in a

A typical bird of the pusztas of eastern Hungary, Lesser Grey Shrike will often hunt from roadside wires.

wild mosaic area. Ducks include Gadwall, Garganey and Ferruginous Duck with many more on passage. Reed-dwelling birds, too, are numerous with both bitterns, Great White Egret, Purple Heron, Marsh Harrier and Little Crake. All the usual warblers are here as well as Bluethroat and Bearded and Penduline Tits. Besides the water birds most of the typical Hungarian plain species are also in the vicinity with Red-footed Falcon, Lesser Grey Shrike and some Great Bustards. Long-eared Owls breed and roost communally in nearby copses in winter. Biharugra is on the eastern flyway, one stop down from the Hortobágy, and thus is an important spot particularly for Ruff in spring, White and Black Storks in September and thousands of wildfowl in October and November.

CALENDAR

March and April see good wildfowl and wader passage and the arrival of Moustached Warbler. May and June are good for breeding birds. Autumn and winter often have grey geese, Merlin, Rough-legged Buzzard, Hen Harrier and White-tailed Eagle.

SPECIES

◆ *Purple Heron* Seems to be the most common member of the heron family in summer.

◆ *Moustached Warbler* Could be quite common in the vast reedbeds, but is usually the most difficult of the warblers to observe in summer.

◆ *Savi's Warbler* Also common, but unlike Moustached sings exposed at the top of reeds and is easy to pinpoint.
◆ *Lesser Grey Shrike* An excellent site for this species with several pairs in the area around the ponds.

ACCESS

The ponds lie on the Hungarian-Romanian border near the village of Biharugra in Békés County. The historic town of Gyula, where there is a border crossing, is 45 km (28 miles) to the south. Despite the general easing of border tensions in the region, the Hungarian-Romanian frontier remains an awkward one. I recall once flushing an embarrassed conscript, complete with rifle, out of the reeds. Carry your passport at all times and respect warning signs and officials, although it would be surprising if anything serious were to happen nowadays. An IBA.

KARDOSKÚT

46°30N 20°28E

This relatively small area, comprising a shallow salt-lake, reedbeds, *puszta* and farmland, is a major stop-over for migrating wildfowl, waders and, in particular, Crane. In recent years, the number of birds passing through has declined, but this is still a very worthwhile place to visit if one is in the south-east of the country. From August onwards, ducks pass through. From the end of September until the first frosts occur in November, Crane and grey geese roost here. Remember that goose flocks in eastern Hungary are always worth checking for Red-breasted and Lesser White-front. This is a favourite site for local birders, who over the years have recorded such rarities as Slender-billed Curlew and Pallid Harrier. Breeding birds in the area include Bittern, Great Bustard, Kentish Plover, Black-tailed Godwit and sometimes Black-headed Wagtail.

CALENDAR

Worth a visit at almost any time of year, but can be pretty bleak in winter. Overall, late summer until the onset of winter is perhaps best.

SPECIES

◆ *Crane* A decline in numbers of birds in October here coincides with an increase farther north on the Hortobágy.
◆ *Short-toed Lark* Kardoskút was a traditional Hungarian stronghold, but numbers now fluctuate greatly.

ACCESS

Kardoskút village is 7 km (4.5 miles) south of Orosháza and 5 km (3.25 miles) east of the site. The salt-lake is protected and needs a permit but, along with the surrounding *puszta*, can be worked easily from farm tracks and the road which skirts the north of the area. An IBA.

SZEGED FISH-PONDS

46°15N 20°10E

This is another typical Hungarian lowland site with fish-ponds, reedbeds, salt-marsh and patches of *puszta* all side by side. Bittern, Little Bittern, Night, Squacco and Purple Herons, Great White and Little Egrets, Spoonbill and sometimes Glossy Ibis all find the area ideal. A Black-headed Gull colony with some Common Terns and Mediterranean Gulls, on an island in one of the ponds, can be scanned from a convenient platform. Coming north from Szeged, turn right near a cemetery, just before the road to Sándorfalva, onto a road which winds through fields to a small car park by the platform. Marsh, Savi's, Great Reed and Moustached Warblers are here, too. Several dykes pass between the ponds and through thick reedbeds, and are a good way of getting close to warblers, although you should check with the fish-farm workers first. A minor road from the E5 to Sándorfalva skirts the north of the area and is good for many of the above, as well as Avocet, Black-tailed Godwit, Kentish Plover and Red-backed and Lesser Grey Shrikes. The last-named are often on wires here, which are also always worth checking in this part of the country for Red-footed Falcon and Roller. To the east of the complex, riverine forest along the Tisza offers the chance of Black Stork and Olivaceous Warbler. To the north of Lake Fehér, salt-lakes near Kistelek are a regular site for Black-winged Stilt. All in all the area just to the north of Szeged is one of the best in Hungary.

CALENDAR

From March to May large numbers of waders pass through. May and June are good for warblers. August and September for return passage of egrets and storks. October and November have large numbers of geese and Cranes. White-tailed Eagle and ducks winter if the lakes do not freeze over.

SPECIES

◆ *Little Egret* Several pairs breed and many more occur on autumn passage.

◆ *Mediterranean Gull* The most reliable site in the country for this rare breeder.

◆ *Kentish Plover* The salt-marsh half-way along the minor road to Sándorfalva is a good spot in summer.

◆ *Ruff* Spring passage, particularly April, sees thousands using the general area.

◆ *Moustached Warbler* The first of the family to arrive, in early April, when it has the reeds almost to itself and is much easier to locate.

ACCESS

Szeged is 171 km (106 miles) south-east of Budapest along the E5. Lake Fehér (Fehér-tó) is just to the north of the city. The afore-mentioned observation platform and surrounding roads are of free access making entry into the strict reserve unnecessary. An IBA.

LAKE PÉTERI

46°37N 19°52E

This excellent reserve is typical of many in Hungary, being formerly a salt-lake and today a collection of lakes functioning as a fish-farm. All the usual birds breed: Purple, Squacco and Night Herons, Little and Great White Egrets, Spoonbill and White Stork. The dyke that divides the two largest lakes and leads to an observation tower is lined with reeds and bushes good for Marsh, Reed and Great Reed Warblers, Penduline Tit and Water Rail. Large reedbeds here have Savi's and Moustached Warblers, Bearded Tit and Marsh Harrier. On a spring or summer day all the main species can often be seen from this well-placed tower. The copses and plantations around the reserve are worth checking for Icterine Warbler, Nightingale, Golden Oriole and Red-backed Shrike. These same woods can host various passage passerines in spring and at the end of summer. Ducks can be plentiful in spring and Gadwall, Garganey and Ferruginous Duck breed. Raptors in the area include Red-footed Falcon and Hobby. Winter often sees a White-tailed Eagle or two. Breeding waders include Avocet and Black-tailed Godwit, although when a pond is drained to harvest the fish, usually in autumn, more waders are attracted.

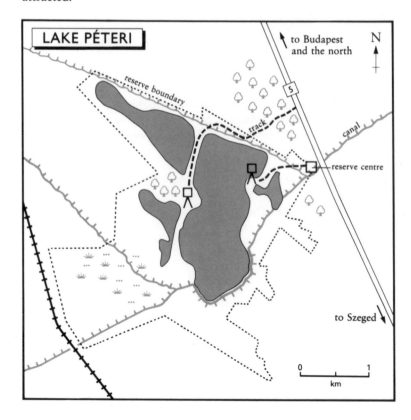

CALENDAR
Best from April to June for singing warblers and the heron colony, but always worth a visit with good passage and many species resident.

SPECIES
◆ *Ferruginous Duck* Quite common here and possible all year.
◆ *Little Crake* Apparently quite common but, as with most crakes, more often heard than seen.
◆ *Penduline Tit* A common resident, with small bands roving through the reeds in winter.

ACCESS
In the Kiskunság region 12 km (7 miles) south of Kiskunfélegyháza. The E5, from Kecskemét to Szeged runs by the reserve which is obscured by poplar plantations. Look for a white-painted lodge on the right as you head south. Lake Péteri is a Bird Reserve, which works as a fish-farm, but can be explored on paths and dykes. An IBA.

KISKUNSÁG SALT-LAKES

46°49N 19°15E

The Kiskunság is a flat region between the Danube and the Tisza to the south of Budapest. Most of the Kiskunság is good for birds and birdwatching, but perhaps the most unique site is a group of salt-lakes at the heart of the region to the west of Kecskemét. Four shallow lakes which periodically dry up, expanses of *puszta*, reedbeds, marsh and scattered woodland all form part of the Kiskunság National Park. Spoonbill, Avocet, Kentish Plover, Black-tailed Godwit and odd Collared Pratincoles breed. In spring and autumn Curlew, Ruff and Spotted Redshank pass through. The reedbeds host Marsh Harrier, Great White Egret, Bittern, Purple Heron, Bearded Tit and Savi's, Great Reed and probably Moustached Warblers amongst others. This is also a good site for Ferruginous Duck and Garganey. Kelemen Szék, the largest of the lakes, has some Mediterranean Gulls in its Black-headed colony and also Black and Whiskered Terns. There is an observation tower, although permission is needed. Roadside birds include Red-footed Falcon, Roller and Lesser Grey Shrike which perch above the *puszta* on telegraph wires. A useful walk begins across the road from a *csarda* (a kind of rustic Hungarian restaurant) on road 52 along a canal to the west of Kelemen Szék where Night Heron, Little Bittern and Penduline Tit should be seen. There are also Tawny Pipits and Great Bustards hereabouts. The road between the villages of Szabadszállás and Fülöpszállás and road 52, which cuts through the area, are both good vantage points.

CALENDAR
Spring passage sees waders around the lakes and on the wet *puszta*. Egrets and herons also pass through with April perhaps the best month. From May to August all the typical *puszta* species such as Red-footed Falcon and Lesser Grey Shrike are in place and so this is

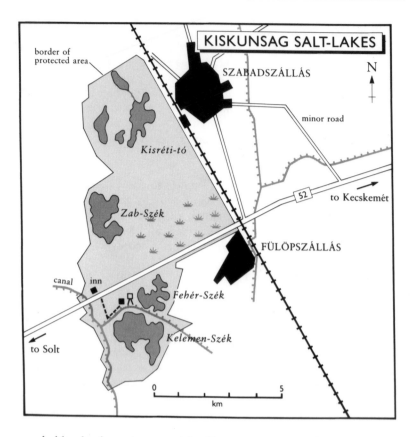

probably the best time to visit. However, autumn does see good numbers of grey geese and an influx of raptors.

SPECIES

◆ *Roller* The road to the east of Fülöpszállás is a regular haunt.

◆ *Ferruginous Duck* Check the reed-fringed canals crossing the area.

◆ *Bean Goose* Up to 10,000 possible in October and November.

◆ *Spoonbill* Kisrét is usually best for this species.

ACCESS

The salt-lakes lie 30 km (19 miles) to the west of Kecskemét along road 52 to Solt. Permission is needed to approach the lakes, so write to the Kiskunság National Park, 6001, Kecskemét, Liszt F. utca 19, Hungary. The towpath and roads mentioned above and tracks outside the reserve will produce most of the key species. An IBA.

TOLNA

46°25N 18°48E

Except for a few dedicated locals, this attractive county has few birders. Rolling hills, sandy semi-steppe, meadows, wet-woodlands, fish-ponds, orchards and vineyards all add up to a rich diversity of species. Hillsides around Szekszárd are good places for Scops Owl.

Typical birds of the grasslands north of the town of Tolna are Bee-eater, Hoopoe, Blue-headed Wagtail, Lesser Grey Shrike, Nightjars and Whinchat. Suitable places have Savi's, Grasshopper, Marsh and Great Reed Warblers. Little Egret and Night Heron can be found along the River Sió and at Gemenc, a riverine forest reserve along the Danube, with, in addition, White-tailed Eagle, Black Kite and Roller. Birds around settlements include White Stork, Barn Owl, Black Redstart and Serin.

CALENDAR
From May through to August for summer visitors.
SPECIES
◆ *Scops Owl* Tolna remains a stronghold while many seemingly suitable habitats around the country are unoccupied.
ACCESS
Tolna county lies in the south of Hungary to the west of the Danube and is bisected by road 6 from Budapest. With the exception of private vineyards and orchards most areas can be explored freely, although you should keep to the paths in the nature reserves. Gemenc is an IBA.

BORONKA
*c.*46°36N 17°25E
These fish-ponds are unique in two resects: first, they are quite different in character from most Hungarian fish-ponds being enclosed by forests; second, they have been bought by conservationists who manage them for wildlife. Resident birds include White-tailed Eagle, Great White Egret and Black Woodpecker. In summer, they are joined by Ferruginous Duck, Black and White Storks, Spoonbill, Purple Heron, Little Bittern, Spotted and Little Crakes and various warblers. Good numbers of ducks and some waders pass through in spring and autumn.

CALENDAR
Worth a visit at almost any time of year.
SPECIES
◆ *White-tailed Eagle* This is the speciality here: its healthy population is partly due to conservation work including nest erection.
ACCESS
The Boronka Reserve lies to the south of Lake Balaton between Marcali and Nagybajom, which is about 25 km (15.5 miles) west of Kaposvár. For visiting details contact Somogy Természetvédelmi Szervezet, 7400 Kaposvár, Szt Imre utca 14, Hungary. Proposed as an IBA.

ROMANIA

GENERAL INFORMATION

Romania is a challenge for visiting birdwatchers. It has some of the best birds and least-known bird areas in Europe, opportunities to make discoveries, arguably Europe's greatest wetland, stunning mountain scenery and innumerable 'adventures' in store. But it can be a difficult country to travel in, and everything that could conceivably be needed on a birdwatching holiday should be taken along. Although the new era of eastern European politics is upon us, one can perhaps be forgiven for thinking that word has not yet fully got round to everyone in Romania. Having said that, I have never had to contend with more than slightly frustrating, or amusing, problems when exploring the spectacular Romanian countryside, either during or since the previous regime. Romania is still very poor and although there has been a visible increase in goods for sale many basics are still often lacking. By any standards prices for almost everything are very low, although hotels and tourist centres can be overpriced. Credit cards are of little use away from large hotels. The unit of currency is the lei.

The hottest time of the year is from June to August, with average daytime temperatures often above 30 °C (86 °F) on the Black Sea coast and possibly even higher in the very south. In January and February temperatures often drop to well below 0 °C (32 °F). After watching Red-breasted Geese in Dobrudja in January and February, I can say that icy winds add a considerable chill factor.

Emergency medical aid is free for British citizens but most medicines are difficult to obtain. Animals, certainly foxes and dogs, should be avoided as, although slight, there *is* a risk of rabies. A remedy for diarrhoea should be taken along, and after walks through woodland one should check for ticks.

Many Romanians speak some (often a lot of) French, and often another language such as German or Hungarian as well. Because of the Latin connection with Romanian I have always found that rusty Italian goes a long way. In hotels and other places frequented by foreigners there are always English-speaking staff. Although times have changed and visiting birdwatchers are no longer viewed as potential spies, old habits die hard and pointing optical equipment in the direction of airports, large bridges and border areas is not advisable. In my experience most of the Romanian countryside can be explored at will so long as the normal courtesies are practised. Most Romanians are familiar with the concept of birdwatching as a hobby.

IMPORTANCE FOR BIRDS

Romania is blessed with a number of bird species that are decidedly rare vagrants to most of the rest of Europe. Ruddy Shelduck, Pallid Harrier, Black-winged Pratincole, Marsh Sandpiper, Paddyfield Warbler and Pied Wheatear, although certainly not common, are all birds that breed on the important coastal plain of Dobrudja. Even Rose-coloured Starlings occasionally nest. However, in addition to such biogeographic novelties, Romania also has important pop-ulations of the globally threatened Dalmatian Pelicans and Pygmy Cormorants, the largest number of nesting White Pelicans in Europe and in some winters hosts what may be almost the entire world population of Red-breasted Geese and some Lesser White-fronted Geese. The much-maligned White-headed Duck also winters and may still breed. The Danube Delta is home to a who's who of birds that are threatened across their ranges, and the importance of this incredible wetland for both breeding and migratory birds cannot be stressed too highly. Transylvania, and in particular the Carpathians, are known to have large populations of Hazelhens and Capercaillies and, until detailed surveys are carried out, one can only speculate on the numbers of owls, woodpeckers and passerines residing there.

Imperial Eagle and Corncrake also breed in unknown, but seemingly good, numbers in the uplands, and Lesser Kestrel and Levant Sparrowhawk, both threatened across Europe, inhabit parts of the coastal plain.

GETTING THERE

Scheduled flights into Bucharest used to be an adventure in themselves, but nowadays things are a little more relaxed upon arrival. There are now daily flights by British carriers and Tarom (Romanian Airlines) from London Heathrow and Stansted, and other European airlines have now started flying into provincial airports. From Bucharest, the Black Sea coast, the Danube Delta and various ranges in the Carpathians can all be reached by car in half a day. An alternative way of exploring Dobrudja and the Black Sea is to take a beach package tour to a resort such as Mamaia, flying into Constanta from London Gatwick or Manchester. A skiing package to Poiana Braşov, for example, will place you in good mountain habitat. Two-centre beach and mountain holidays are on offer, and could in theory prove very rewarding for birdwatchers. The advantages of joining package tours to Romania are that for the price of a scheduled flight, hotel and board are included, eliminating the hassle and inflated prices of making accommodation arrangements upon arrival. Check the brochures in any high-street travel agent. Being on a package tour also means not having to apply individually for a visa (which at the time of writing is still necessary). However one gets into the country, a car will be needed to explore once there, although I have worked Dobrudja by train and on foot. Car-hire is now available at airports and in all cities. I have found driving from Hungary a good way of exploring Transylvania, avoiding Bucharest altogether. Although the petrol situation has improved tremendously, play safe and refuel whenever the opportunity arises. Public transport is not really recommended.

CONSERVATION

Almost as soon as Ceausescu had been removed, a small group of independent conservationists founded the Romanian Ornithological Society (SOR), something which had been impossible under his regime. After only a few years the dedicated staff of the SOR have made great strides. They have concentrated their work on young people and on developing their growing membership. For information on any aspect of Romania's avifauna and details of international membership write to: SOR, 3400 Cluj, Str Republicii 48, Romania.

The Danube Delta seems to have also been granted a reprieve by political change. The worst development schemes have been

The Crested Lark is one of the most familiar birds to be seen along Romania's roadsides.

abandoned and international conservationists are now working closely with the Romanian authorities to safeguard this crucial and spectacular wetland. The whole delta, stretches of the Danube Valley and the adjacent lagoons, now comprise one huge Biosphere Reserve, the largest wetland reserve in Europe. A Danube Delta Institute has also been established. In the last couple of years great progress has been made in the quest to save this the most wonderful of Europe's wetlands.

HABITATS

Although most birdwatchers probably think of the Danube Delta and the Black Sea coast when Romania is mentioned, the country is in fact a land of mountains. Over two-thirds of Romania is covered by alpine, subalpine, montane and hilly habitat. Much of this is wooded, and some is wild forest. The Carpathians dominate, and support mostly unknown populations of birds. The frequency with which Brown Bears, Wolves and even Lynx are encountered does seem to suggest, however, that Romania's uplands are very rich in prey. Impressive gorges are also very much part of the landscape and are often good places for birds. Of course, wetlands cannot be ignored and the Danube Delta is quite rightly regarded as Romania's, and arguably Europe's, greatest bird area, with the largest reedbeds in the world. The Black Sea coast, particularly its string of lagoons, is also renowned for its breeding and wintering bird habitats. Agricultural land can also be good habitat, because of inefficient farming techniques. Wheatears and larks, for example, thrive in some areas, but at the same time some species have suffered, particularly shrikes, warblers and buntings, because of the large-scale removal of trees and scrub. However, even the apparently endless and birdless fields of winter wheat in Dobrudja come into their own as often the world's main wintering ground for Red-breasted Geese. As well as these major habitats, fish-ponds, reservoirs, orchards, vineyards and scrub all provide important living places for birds and should not be overlooked *en route* to the main sites.

SEASONS

SPRING
From April to mid-May, the wetlands along the Black Sea are alive with passage birds. A trip to the Danube Delta can be problematic as boats are difficult to arrange before the summer tourist season. The mountains of the interior have lekking grouse and calling owls and woodpeckers but many areas remain under snow and are inaccessible throughout the season.

SUMMER
A visit to any part of the country is rewarding in June, July or August. The weather and range of breeding birds are excellent both on the coast and in the mountains. The Danube Delta and Black Sea lagoons are always impressive but in summer are quite amazing.

AUTUMN
Although Romania's forests and mountains are not at their best, the Black Sea coast more than compensates with a rich blend of passage birds using the delta, lakes, lagoons and steppe in late August and September. The list of birds that pass through eastern Romania in this season is remarkable. The weather, too, is at its best.

WINTER
The Black Sea sites and the adjacent Dobrudja Plain offer some of the best winter birdwatching in Europe. So long as the temperature does not drop too low, Red-breasted and White-fronted Geese are numerous. Around half a million grebes, ducks and geese have been counted in some winters. Inland, things are rather quiet as lakes and reservoirs freeze over.

BIRDWATCHING SITES

DANUBE DELTA
44°25–45°28N 28°45–29°40E

This is Europe's most spectacular wetland and should be on every birdwatcher's list of places to visit. The birdlife here is tremendous with, in summer, thousands of White Pelicans, Pygmy Cormorant, Little Bittern, Purple, Squacco and Night Herons, Little and Great White Egrets, Spoonbill, Glossy Ibis and various wildfowl – Ferruginous Duck being common. Warblers such as Grasshopper, Savi's, River, Great Reed and Moustached are everywhere, but can be difficult to watch owing to the vastness of the reedbeds and the need to birdwatch from boats. Paddyfield and Cetti's Warblers are here, too, although they are not so widespread. Almost any patch of trees can be checked for Olivaceous Warbler and several woodpecker species. Raptors are somewhat easier from boats, with Black Kite, Osprey, White-tailed and Lesser Spotted Eagles, Marsh Harrier, Saker, Hobby and Red-footed Falcon all possible. Terns include Gull-

Marsh Sandpipers are regular on passage through the Danube delta and some breed in eastern Romania.

billed, Sandwich, Black, White-winged Black and Whiskered. Spotted, Little and Baillon's Crakes all breed but like the warblers can be elusive. Indeed, this raises the main problem for birdwatchers here, getting one's feet on to traversable dry land for those species that are difficult to watch from the water. Besides the many open lakes, channels, backwaters, floating islands of vegetation and the vast reedbeds, the delta does have some terra firma: sand dunes, dykes, agricultural land and wooded islands occasionally provide welcome opportunities to set up one's telescope. Caraorman is one accessible village on a huge *grind* (Romanian for sand-dune system), deep in the delta south of Crisan. This is a good site for waders including Marsh Sandpiper, Stone Curlew, shrikes and larks. The coastal strip south of Sulina is another walking area, especially good for terns and gulls. There are also forests and steppe on a vast *grind* around Letea in the north-east of the delta, which is a White-tailed Eagle area. Perhaps the bird most visitors come to the delta to see, however, is Dalmatian Pelican. Sadly, numbers have declined drastically, but a few days here usually produces some soaring overhead. In winter most of the delta's birds change but there is still good birdwatching, the main attraction being rafts of swans and ducks with attendant White-tailed Eagles.

CALENDAR

Summer, from May to August, is the best time to visit when the full complement of breeding birds and the local boatmen are both on hand. Winter can be pretty bleak here: the delta proper freezes and access is thus difficult. At such times the lagoons to the south should be visited, and, if one persists, the wildfowl numbers will be impressive. In mild winters Cetti's and Moustached Warblers may stay on, although there is a daunting amount of habitat to search.

SPECIES

- *Dalmatian Pelican* Lacul Rosu south of Sulina, Lacul Rosca in the north of the delta and the area to the south of Sfintu Gheorghe are usual haunts.
- *Glossy Ibis* Although apparently still common and widespread, its numbers have in fact declined badly.
- *Saker* Now very rare with perhaps only a couple of pairs.
- *Whiskered Tern* The most common marsh tern in the delta.
- *White-headed Duck* May breed in the delta but records are few and far between.
- *Lesser White-fronted Goose* Some usually amongst larger flocks of other geese in autumn and winter.
- *Gull-billed Tern* Try the beach on the Black Sea coast mid-way between Sulina and Sfintu Gheorghe.
- *Roller* Common throughout the delta in summer, usually seen perching on wires along the river and canal banks.
- *Bluethroat* Breeds in small numbers in areas with dense reedbeds.

ACCESS

The delta is in the eastern corner of Romania on the border with the Ukraine. Indeed, part lies in the Ukraine. Bucharest is around 290 km (180 miles) to the south-west along road 22a to Slobozia and road 2a (E60). The port of Tulcea is the gateway to the delta. From here, scheduled passenger boats ply the main three channels and the tourist office offers boat excursions. These methods of travel will get one into the delta proper and provide views of the larger and more common birds, but to really work the area one needs to hire a private boat or join an organized birdwatching expedition. Fishermen in delta villages can often be hired to guide visitors to more remote areas, but exploring independently needs plenty of patience and *ciubuc* (the Romanian equivalent of *baksheesh*), and not necessarily in that order. Permission, obtainable from the Danube Delta Biosphere Reserve Administration in Tulcea, is needed to visit several strictly protected areas. An IBA.

TULCEA

45°13N 28°36E

As this is the main point of entry for the Danube Delta, most visitors inevitably pass through or spend a night in this now rather shabby port. However, some time in and around the town can prove very rewarding as many of the delta's birds also reside around here. If one flies to Tulcea, the birds begin upon arrival at the airport, with perhaps Quail, both Red-backed and Lesser Grey Shrikes and Black-headed Wagtail. A useful spot is the hill topped by the *Independentei* monument at the north of town. From here there are views over the Tulcea branch of the Danube, *Bratul Tulcea*, for gulls. More importantly, looking across the marshes to the east may produce White Stork, Little Egret, Squacco Heron, Little Bittern, Spoonbill, Glossy Ibis and Ferruginous Duck. This is sometimes a good wader site, too. The marshes can also be watched from the minor road out of town towards Nufaru; locals usually let one cross their land for closer views. Farther along the road is another good, high vantage point over the marshes. This is also a good area for Bee-eater and Hoopoe. Syrian Woodpecker, Wryneck, Crested Lark and Red-backed Shrike are on the hill itself.

CALENDAR

There is always something in the vicinity of the town, although it is probably at its best from April through to August. From October to February, White-fronted and Red-breasted Geese flocks are often in the general area.

SPECIES

◆ *Yellow-legged Gull* Common in and around the port.
◆ *Bee-eater* Scattered pairs nest in the hillside along the Nufaru road.
◆ *Roller* Possible on the outskirts of town.

ACCESS

Tulcea is 281 km (175 miles) north-east of Bucharest and 125 km (78 miles) north of Constanţa. Internal flights connect Tulcea with the capital. Most of the area around the town can be freely explored, although gardens and allotments should, of course, only be entered with permission. Not listed as an IBA.

MĂCIN HILLS
45°12N 28°15E

These bare, rugged hills are amongst the oldest in Europe. In summer, birds of prey which hunt over the arid stony slopes, steppe and agricultural land of the region are the main attraction. Short-toed and Lesser Spotted Eagles, Levant Sparrowhawk and Montagu's Harrier are definitely here. Long-legged Buzzard seems likely and Saker and Pallid Harrier may also occur. Typical roadside birds include such colourful delights as Roller, Bee-eater, Hoopoe and Ortolan Bunting, all of which are quite common.

CALENDAR

From April to August

SPECIES

♦ *Buteo species* Care should be taken with any *Buteo* as Buzzards here are often very reddish, there are *B.b. vulpinus* about, and many tails seem unbarred, making Long-leggeds far from simple.

ACCESS

The hills lie about 40 km (25 miles) to the west of Tulcea. A minor road which runs between roads 22 and 22a passes through Horia and Cerna before reaching Măcin, and skirts the western edge of the range. Not listed as an IBA.

RAZELM LAGOON
44°50N 29°00E

This vast, slightly brackish lake, which nestles into the south of the Danube Delta, is almost totally cut off from the Black Sea by the huge sandbar of Grindul Cosna. Although full of good birds, Razelm keeps its secrets to itself. Grindul Cosna and Popina Island are isolated, and virtually impossible, yet, by lagoon-watching from the shore and exploring the numerous fish-ponds and farmland around Razelm, one will be able to see most birds. The bay south of Sarinasuf is a particularly good spot for wintering swans, geese and ducks. Geese fly between the fields along the northern shore and the lagoon. Similarly, the western shore around Sarichioi has large fields of winter wheat and thus flocks of Red-breasted Geese in most years. In summer, birds that can usually be seen around Razelm without much effort include Black-necked and Red-necked Grebes, White Pelican, Squacco Heron, Glossy Ibis, White Stork, Black Kite, Hobby, Black-winged Stilt, Mediterranean Gull, Whiskered Tern, Bee-eater,

Although the Pallid Harrier is certainly rare, some pairs have bred in Dobrudja.

Roller, Crested, Short-toed and Calandra Larks, Tawny Pipit and Lesser Grey Shrike. Besides these there are other less common but regular species such as Slender-billed Gull, Gull-billed Tern and Ruddy Shelduck. Although adjacent to the Danube delta, onto which it is often tagged as an afterthought, Razelm lagoon is a quite separate entity, and a very large area deserving plenty of time.

CALENDAR
The lagoon and surrounding habitats hold good birds almost all year round. This is an important site for wildfowl from October to March, April sees considerable passage of waders and in summer all the key birds of the Romanian coast occur.

SPECIES
◆ *White-fronted Goose* Huge numbers are possible in winter, with the birds roosting on sandbars and in shallow parts of the lagoon.
◆ *Ruddy Shelduck* A few pairs are said to breed on Popina Island.
◆ *Pallid Harrier* Scattered steppes along the western shore of the lagoon are worth visiting for this rare breeder.

ACCESS
Tulcea is around 25 km (15 miles) to the north and Babadag 12 km (7 miles) to the west. road 222 north from Unirea links the villages on the western shore with access to the water near Martie, Sarichioi

and Sabangia. To the north road 222c passes through Iazurile, Colina and Sarinasuf. Once away from roads it is a case of walking where one can. Exploring the seaward side of the lagoon is almost impossible and, without local knowledge, probably unwise. An IBA.

BABADAG
44°53N 28°44E

Babadag is a good base from which to explore the northern part of Dobrudja. Besides Lake Babadag, with its typical Romanian wetland birds, there are fish-ponds north of town, areas of grassland and crops, stony steppe, rolling hills and deciduous woodland. Of course, many of the birds here are the same as in the nearby wetlands, but Babadag offers some additional species. Above all, this is a rich raptor area. Short-toed, Booted, Imperial and Lesser Spotted Eagles all breed, and more pass through in autumn. There are Levant Sparrowhawk, Honey and Long-legged Buzzards, Saker, Red-footed Falcon and Lesser Kestrel. There is a chance of Pallid Harrier, too, which would certainly round off a very impressive list. The best areas for most of these birds are to the west and north-west of town. To the east of Lake Babadag, a ruined castle at Enisala gives views over the whole impressive area. Birds around here include Syrian Woodpecker, Calandra and Short-toed Larks, Tawny Pipit, Lesser Grey Shrike, Bee-eater, Roller, Hoopoe and Black-headed Bunting. The main road south from Babadag to Constanţa crosses the Babadag Hills, where

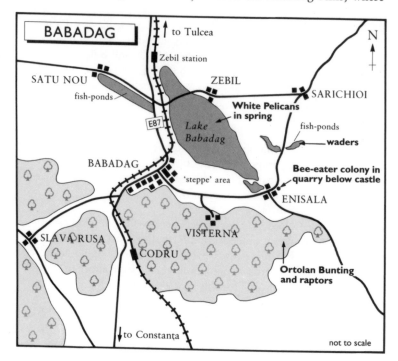

woodlands are good for Black, Middle Spotted and White-backed Woodpeckers, Golden Oriole, some of the raptors mentioned above, Icterine Warbler and Ortolan Bunting. Any summer visit to the Danube delta should include at least a day here.

CALENDAR
April sees flocks of White Pelicans on Lake Babadag before they head on to the delta to breed. Visit from May onwards for the raptors. This is also a good area for geese from October to February.

SPECIES
◆ *Pallid Harrier* The steppe and grassland here is one of the few areas of Europe where this species breeds, although it is rare.
◆ *Buzzard* Hybrids of the nominate race *buteo* and the eastern race *vulpinus* are common here.
◆ *White-backed Woodpecker* An few isolated pairs of the *lilfordi* race are said to inhabit the woodland south of town.
◆ *Bee-eater* An easily watched colony sits by the roadside at the foot of Enisala castle.
◆ *Pied Wheatear* The stony steppes around Lake Babadag are a likely spot.

ACCESS
Babadag lies on the E87 around 35 km (22 miles) south of Tulcea and 90 km (56 miles) north of Constanţa. Most of the area can be freely explored, although permission should be sought before entering the fish-pond systems. An IBA.

LAKE CEAMURLIA

44°42N 28°47E
Lake Ceamurlia is one of several smaller lakes and lagoons linked to Razelm and Sinoie. There are also reedbeds, salt-marsh, grazing meadows and agricultural land, which are easy to work in contrast to the larger areas nearby. Most typical Black Sea coast birds are here with Purple Heron, Great White and Little Egrets, Ferruginous Duck and Savi's Warbler in summer. This area is worth checking for Paddyfield Warbler, too. The farmland has Calandra Lark and Black-headed Bunting. In early spring Ceamurlia is one of the spots where pelicans gather before moving on to the delta to breed, and in winter thousands of geese roost on sandbanks beyond the lake. Fields of winter wheat between Lunca and Ceamurlia de Jos to the north, and the whole region west and south of the lake are regular feeding sites for Red-breasted and White-fronted Geese. There can be huge numbers of ducks in autumn and winter, with Teal, Gadwall, Wigeon, Pintail, Red-crested Pochard, Goldeneye, Smew and the occasional flock of Whooper Swans. Not surprisingly, with all this potential prey White-tailed Eagles also winter. If conditions underfoot permit, as the sandbanks, lagoons and inlets of this area are in a constant state of flux according to wind and wave

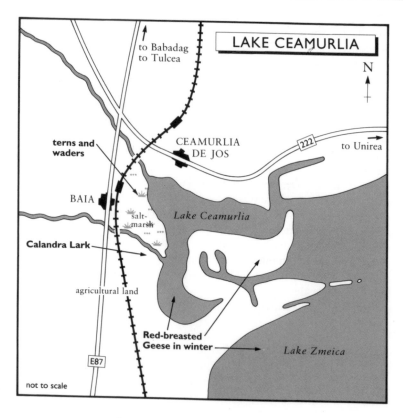

movements, a walk around the south shores of the lake towards Lakes Golovita and Zmeica may reveal offshore wildfowl roosts.

CALENDAR

April is a good month for passage birds on their way to the delta and beyond. May and June are best for locally breeding birds. October sees the arrival of geese, with peak numbers usually in December. By mid-March most of the geese have gone.

SPECIES

♦ *Red-breasted Goose* In good winters, flocks of several hundreds can be found dotted around the lake, and dusk flights can be spectacular.
♦ *Caspian Tern* This is a regular site in spring for wandering birds.
♦ *Calandra Lark* Try the agricultural land between the lake and the railway line near Baia.

ACCESS

The lake is just to the east of Baia, a village on the E87 about 70 km (44 miles) north of Constanţa. Babadag is 20 km (12 miles) further to the north. Approach the lake from either Baia or Ceamurlia de Jos to the north. For geese, the whole lake area will have to be explored, as the situation varies from year to year. The area is open, except around a military installation near Ceamurlia. Part of a larger IBA.

SINOIE LAGOON

44°35N 28°50E

This large, shallow lagoon and surrounding fish-ponds, steppe and agricultural land form a major area for passage birds in spring and autumn. Most of the summer visitors that breed in the Danube delta stop here to feed or roost during migration and are, in many ways, easier to observe then. The environs of Sinoie village are a good place to start for many of Dobrudja's typical breeding birds, and this is also a favoured roosting and drinking spot of Red-breasted Geese in winter. A few miles beyond the village, a long, narrow strip of land, Grindul Lupilor, separates the lagoon from Lake Zmeica. The shoreline, marshes and reedbeds here are excellent for passage waders and passerines and in summer have White Pelican, Great White and Little Egrets, Squacco Heron, Little Bittern, Ferruginous Duck, Spotted and Little Crakes, Black-winged Stilt, Stone Curlew and Savi's and Paddyfield Warblers, to name only a few. Ruddy Shelduck, Marsh Sandpiper, Collared Pratincole, Mediterranean and Slender-billed Gulls and Caspian and Gull-billed Terns are on the cards, too. The surrounding farmland and steppe has Red-footed Falcon, Quail, Calandra and Short-toed Larks, Tawny Pipit, Black-headed Wagtail, Lesser Grey and Woodchat Shrikes and Spanish Sparrow.

CALENDAR

There is something of interest in each season. Except in very harsh winters, hundreds of thousands of geese use the lagoon from October to February. April and early May are good for passage birds. From May to July all of the region's special breeding birds occur. Return wader passage begins as early as mid-July.

SPECIES

◆ *Red-breasted Goose* As with the other wetlands of the Black Sea coast, numbers and exact locations change annually – the Sinoie area is one of the most regular sites for large flocks.

◆ *Smew* Thousands winter, although they may be far from the lagoon shore and out of range.

◆ *Demoiselle Crane* Some occasionally turn up during migration.

ACCESS

The lagoon lies just to the east of the village of Sinoie, about 40 km (25 miles) north of Constanţa. As with Razelm (*see* pages 140–42), the sandbars, islets and lagoon shores here can change, moulded by the wind and waves from the Black Sea. Approach from Histria in the south, or along the Grindul Lupilor from Sinoie in the north. An IBA.

ISTRIA

44°33'N 28°44'E

In the few miles between Istria, a small village that lends its name to the bird reserve here, and Histria, a site of Greek and Roman ruins, lies one of the Black Sea's, and Europe's, greatest bird areas. The road that leads to the ruins and adjacent, rather basic, campsite passes between Lakes Nuntasi and Istria and is one of the most productive roads for birds I have ever been along. In summer, the steppe, salt-marsh, pools and reed-fringed lake edges here can produce Squacco Heron, Glossy Ibis, Little Bittern, Spoonbill, Ferruginous Duck, Ruddy Shelduck, Black-winged Stilt, Kentish Plover, Marsh Sandpiper, Avocet, Stone Curlew, Collared and Black-winged Pratincole and Paddyfield Warbler. There are large colonies of Little and Common Terns with Whiskered, Black and Gull-billed Terns around, too. White and a few Dalmatian Pelicans often feed on Lake Nuntasi. In spring and autumn more pelicans, egrets, herons, storks, raptors and waders pass through, and the ancient ruins are good for falls of passerines. Winter can also be spectacular with hundreds of thousands of geese, mainly White-fronts, but with flocks of several thousand Red-breasted Geese regular in good years. Quite simply, Istria should be on every birdwatcher's list of essential places to visit.

CALENDAR
January is the usual peak period for geese with hundreds of thousands in the area in recent years. April and August to September are best for passage waders, and May to August for breeding birds.

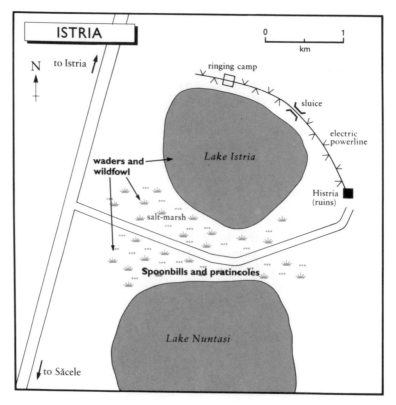

SPECIES

◆ *Ruddy Shelduck* A few pairs of this declining bird hang on here.
◆ *Black-winged Stilt* This is a good site with up to sixty pairs nesting each year.
◆ *Black-winged Pratincole* All pratincoles should be carefully checked for some of the few pairs of this species that occur.
◆ *Paddyfield Warbler* A ringing camp in August 1991 produced over 400 specimens in two weeks, many thought to be local birds.

ACCESS

Istria is around 45 km (28 miles) north of Constanţa and the Mamaia resorts along minor roads. The E87 passes just west of the area. The road through the area to the ruins and campsite is a good vantage point. A dyke can be followed on foot from the ruins to a ringing camp to the north of Lake Istria, which operates as a fish-farm. The salt-marshes should not be entered. A Bird Reserve and an IBA.

LAKE HASARLÂC

*c.*50°45N 27°50E

By Dobrugean standards this is a small lake, but it is thus somewhat easier to work than most other sites. There is some open water, extensive reed cover, dry sloping grassy shores and sandy cliffs. Little Bittern, Purple and Squacco Herons, Little Egret and Whiskered Tern are all numerous, and there are also Pygmy Cormorant, Spoonbill, Glossy Ibis, Ferruginous Duck and occasionally Ruddy Shelduck. The low cliffs on the eastern shore host a varied range of breeding birds, including Roller, Hoopoe, Bee-eater, Little Owl and the *melanoleuca* race of Black-eared Wheatear. There may also be Pied Wheatears here; the terrain certainly looks suitable.

CALENDAR

Visit in spring and summer.

SPECIES

◆ *Black-eared Wheatear* The most northerly known breeding site in the country.

ACCESS

Conveniently situated alongside road 2a just before the junction with the E60 at Hirsova. Tulcea is about 90 km (56 miles) to the north-east. Apparently now privately owned, but access is allowed via convenient farm tracks which run between the lake and the cliffs. Not listed as an IBA.

CHEIA

*c.*44°30N 28°28E

Cheia is Romanian for gorge. Besides rocky walls there is also scrub, stony steppe and dry grassland set amongst the large agricultural fields which typify Dobrudja. Birds include Short-toed and Booted Eagles, Bee-eater, Red-backed Shrike, Hoopoe, Rock Thrush and

Ortolan Bunting. The dry grassy and stony areas surrounding Cheia are worth some attention as larks, wheatears and scrub warblers could prove interesting. In winter, the gorge is silent, but fields in the area are feeding places for large flocks of geese.

CALENDAR
Visit in spring and summer
ACCESS
Cheia is 2 km (1.25 miles) south of the village of the same name, and 5 km (3 miles) north of Tirgusor. Mihail Kogalniceanu is 16 km (10 miles) to the south on the E60 from Constanţa. Exploration of the gorge is straightforward from the road. Not listed as an IBA.

LAKE TAŞAUL
44°21N 28°35E
This is a noted winter feeding site for White-fronted and Red-breasted Geese, although, as always, the situation changes from year to year with much depending on temperatures. Although typical of the lakes of Dobrudja in being slightly brackish, in harsh winters Taşaul can freeze over forcing the geese to move on to nearby unfrozen lagoons or south into Bulgaria. In most years Red-breasted Geese roost in the water and feed in the surrounding agricultural fields. They are always outnumbered by White-fronts. The odd party of Lesser White-fronts is likely here, too. Fields around Constanţa Airport just to the west are used during the day by the geese, with high concentrations possible. Spring and autumn passage sees good numbers of waders and all three marsh terns. The north-western end of the lake has some reed and marsh areas which can be reached by taking the E87 and then a minor road to the village of Piatra. This is the best spot to explore in summer, with both bitterns, Squacco Heron, Red-footed Falcon and the usual wetland warblers.

CALENDAR
This is another site which is better in winter (the geese arrive in October), although it is probably worth a stop in summer if one is based at the coastal resorts or Constanţa.
SPECIES
◆ *Ferruginous Duck* Perhaps the most interesting breeding duck species here, occasionally winters.
◆ *Caspian Tern* Regularly occurs at the end of summer.
ACCESS
Lake Taşaul is 15 km (9 miles) to the north of Constanţa just beyond Navodari. A minor road runs northwards from this town to Corbu, where there is a smaller lake. Another heads westwards just to the south. Set in open land, the lake can be viewed easily from roads and farm tracks. Use common sense when watching the fields around the airport, as this is a also a military base. The lake is an IBA.

CONSTANȚA

44°14N 28°38E

This international port and the major city of the region is a convenient base from which to explore southern Dobrudja. In winter, the only reliable hotels, petrol stations and restaurants are here, and in summer, the nearby beach resorts offer quite cheap packages from Britain which eliminate some of the inconveniences of arranging things locally. Just north of the city, a coastal strip lined with hotels separates Lake Siutghiol from the Black Sea. Despite the sunseekers, birdwatching here in summer can be quite productive, with gulls and terns on the sea, Little Bittern, Ferruginous Duck, Savi's and Great Reed Warblers breeding, and Little Egret, Squacco Heron, Marsh Harrier and often Mediterranean Gulls as well. An excursion inland will pick up typical birds of the Dobrudja plain. A visit at the end of summer has the double bonus of a build-up of non-breeding and early migrant birds and less crowded resorts. In winter the port at Constanța offers good sea-watching, with Black-throated Diver, Great Crested, Red-necked and Black-necked Grebes, Red-breasted Merganser and Mediterranean, Little, Common and Yellow-legged Gulls amongst others. Avoid the busy main port and try the smaller harbour around the Palace Hotel.

CALENDAR

Lake Siutghiol is worth a look in summer, and the port and sea at Constanța, best in winter. April and September see particularly good movements along the coast.

SPECIES

◆ *Black-necked Grebe* Thousands winter close in around the port at Constanța and along the whole coast.
◆ *Caspian Tern* April and August are two regular months.
◆ *Scops Owl* In the gardens and parkland at Mamaia.
◆ *Spanish Sparrow* Breeds in colonies in parks and at roadsides.

ACCESS

Constanța sits on the Black Sea around 210 km (130 miles) east of Bucharest. In the summer season there are various charter flights direct from the UK to Constanța, serving Mamaia and other beach resorts. Some discretion should be exercised when sea-watching at Constanța as this is also a naval base and officials are sensitive to foreigners with optical equipment. Lake Siutghiol is an IBA.

LAKE TECHIRGHIOL

44°01N 28°29E

This brackish lake to the south of Constanța is famous as a health resort to which people flock each summer to cover themselves in therapeutic mud. This does not rule out a worthwhile visit for breeding birds, although the lake itself is perhaps not a particularly productive place in summer when compared to the other wetlands on

Farmland surrounding the shores of Lake Techirghiol is good for Calandra Lark.

the coast. The saline nature of Techirghiol means that it seldom freezes over completely, and is thus a key wintering area for wildfowl. In particular, this is the best, and often only, site in the region for White-headed Duck, although the species is getting scarcer and can take some finding. Throughout the winter, any open water should have good numbers of Black-necked Grebes, Whooper Swan, various ducks such as Shelduck, Teal, Pintail, Shoveler, Tufted Duck, Pochard, Ferruginous Duck and Smew, as well as the odd vagrant gull. Numbers vary from year to year depending on conditions elsewhere. A marshy, reedy area at the southern end of the lake has Great White Egret and Bittern. The windswept, open shore rises high above the water at several points around this large lake, offering the chance to scan the water for wildfowl concentrations. The surrounding area is good in summer for Stone Curlew, Hoopoe, Calandra and Short-toed Larks, Black-eared and Pied Wheatears, with Black-winged Stilt, Avocet and other waders on the shore. Hen Harrier, Merlin and Rough-legged Buzzard winter.

CALENDAR
Wildfowl begin to congregate in October and, as is the case with all the local wetlands, stay as long as the weather permits. Visit from October to March for White-headed Duck.

SPECIES
- *Black-necked Grebe* Winter numbers can be in the thousands.
- *White-fronted Goose* Freshwater springs along the south shore attract birds to drink.
- *White-headed Duck* A visit in January 1991 produced only five birds. December 1993 saw 75.
- *Shelduck* This is an important nesting site for the species which is a rare breeding bird in Romania. More winter.

ACCESS
Techirghiol is 10 km (6 miles) south of Constanţa along the E87. The lake is separated from the sea by a narrow land-strip along which the E87 runs. Heading south from the city, pass over the huge Black Sea–Danube Canal and then turn right on a minor road running near the western shore for the village of Techirghiol. In dry weather the southern shore can be followed. No permission is needed. An IBA.

HAGIENI
43°48N 28°27E
In complete contrast to most of southern Dobrudja, this excellent reserve is a mosaic of rolling oak woodland, conifer plantations, wet-meadows, patches of reed and a stream valley. There is the more typical habitat of scrub and limestone hillsides, too. All this results in a good blend of birds, some of which are difficult elsewhere in the region. Raptors include Honey Buzzard, Short-toed and Booted Eagles, and Marsh Harrier. As it is relatively easy to work from an access road and reasonable track, Hagieni probably offers the best chance hereabouts for crakes. As usual, Corncrakes give themselves away by calling; Spotted and Baillon's Crakes will need more skill and a degree of luck. Even a casual stroll through the reserve should produce singing Grasshopper, Savi's, River and Great Reed Warblers, Red-backed and Lesser Grey Shrikes, Golden Oriole and Ortolan Bunting without too much effort. Roller, Nightjar, Syrian, Great Spotted and Middle Spotted Woodpeckers, Wryneck, Icterine and Barred Warblers and Sombre Tit are all here, too. Although less common, Olivaceous Warblers also occur. Raptor and passerine passage through Hagieni in late summer is very interesting.

CALENDAR
Hagieni is an ideal spring and summer site for anyone staying south of Constanţa. Visit from April to August for songbirds and raptors.
SPECIES
- *Ortolan Bunting* This is probably south Dobrudja's best site, with the species quite common.
- *Rock Bunting* Try the wooded hillside to the right of the road just before the river.
- *Olive-tree Warbler* Could be around here as this species seems to be expanding its range northwards from Bulgaria.

ACCESS

The Hagieni Reserve is approximately 9 km (5 miles) to the west of Mangalia, a beach resort 43 km (27 miles) south of Constanţa. There is a border crossing with Bulgaria 20 km (12 miles) to the south. From the E87 to the west of Constanţa, take the road towards Negru Voda, then the first minor road off it to the right. After a couple of miles a track across open land to the left leads to the reserve. An IBA.

LAKE DUNĂRENI
44°11N 27°46E

This large lake functions as a fish-farm, although it is a natural-looking lake, with much vegetation including extensive reedbeds in the centre, patches of trees along dykes and an arm of the Danube just to the north. Pygmy Cormorant, Little Bittern, Spoonbill, Glossy Ibis, Purple and Squacco Herons, Little Egret and Whiskered and Black Terns all occur in summer. Both pelicans also sometiems feed here. The lake seldom freezes in winter, being fed by a warm spring, and thus some birds hang around. The village itself has White Stork, Syrian Woodpecker and Spanish Sparrow, although the latter should be scrutinized carefully as various hybrid sparrows are widespread.

CALENDAR

Best from April through to September.

SPECIES

♦ *Spoonbill* Romania's largest colony is here.

ACCESS

The lake is just to the west of Dună reni, which can be reached by taking a minor road north from road 3 at Ion Corvin and then turning left just before Aliman. The bridge over the Danube at Cernavoda is 30 km (19 miles) to the north-east. The village of Dunăreni overlooks the lake from its hill-top position. A road winds down through the village to the fish-farm entrance where permission to enter should be sought. An IBA.

LAKE OLTINA
44°10N 27°37E

This large open lake lies to the north of Fetii valley (*see* opposite) and can easily be combined with a visit there. The wooded valley of the Danube lies just to the north and is a good raptor area. The lake itself is not particularly good for breeding birds, rather more interesting are surrounding habitats which have some typical Dobrudjean species. The south-east shore has sharply rising sandstone cliffs with a phenomenal number of breeding Sand Martins, as well as Roller, Bee-eater, Tawny Pipit, Spanish Sparrow and Red-backed and Lesser Grey Shrikes. The eastern shore from the village of Oltina to the cliffs has orchards and vineyards with Syrian Woodpeckers and Golden Orioles. At the southern end of the lake, reeds hold herons and warblers.

CALENDAR
Visit in summer.
SPECIES
◆ *Pied Wheatear* This is another seemingly suitable site. Indeed, such cliff-edged lakes along the Danube have proved to be traditional sites for isolated pairs.
ACCESS
The village of Oltina is approximately 18 km (11.25 miles) north of Baneasa in the vary south of Dobrudja. Constanţa is about 90 km (56 miles) to the east. The lake is to the west and south of Oltina. Just before the village several tracks from the road lead down to the shore through vineyards. Not listed as an IBA.

FETII VALLEY
44°05N 27°39E
Formerly too close to the Bulgarian border to make a visit with binoculars wise, this rocky karst area is tucked away in the south-east of Romanian Dobrudja. Raptors find the combination of rock walls and craggy slopes, quarries, deciduous woods and agricultural land ideal. Levant Sparrowhawk, Short-toed, Booted and Imperial Eagles,

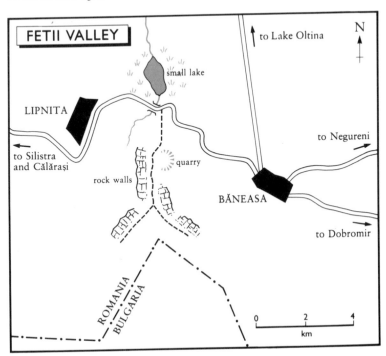

Honey and Long-legged Buzzards, Egyptian Vulture and Lesser Kestrel are all possible. Eagle Owl is resident and Scops Owl is about in summer. Nightjar, Roller, Barred Warbler, Red-backed and Lesser Grey Shrikes, and Cirl and Ortolan Buntings all seem to be quite common in and around the patches of oak and scrub. Woodpeckers include Black, Middle Spotted and Syrian. There are also Alpine Swift, Rock Thrush and Rock Bunting. Much remains to be discovered in this corner of Europe, and Fetii is yet another place where more time and a careful search may produce such Balkan specialities as Semi-collared Flycatcher, Olive-tree Warbler, Black-headed Bunting and Rose-coloured Starling.

CALENDAR
Summer is the season to visit, from May to July, for raptors and songbirds.
SPECIES
♦ *Booted Eagle* This is an excellent place to observe both phases of this normally elusive eagle.
♦ *Egyptian Vulture* One of the few places where this species has a hold in Romania.
♦ *Syrian Woodpecker* Seems to be the most common woodpecker here.
ACCESS
Fetii's rocky slopes and walls lie mainly on one side of the valley. The area is just south of road 3 in the very south-eastern corner of Romania between the villages of Lipnita and Baneasa. Silistra is about 35 km (22 miles) to the east on the way to Bucharest, and Constanţa is about 95 km (59 miles) to the west. As they are less paranoid these days, any border guards or officials encountered can usually be reassured by describing oneself as an 'ornithologist', although I did spend some hours in the local barracks in 1993 explaining myself. A Nature Reserve and an IBA.

LAKA CĂLĂRAŞI
44°15N 27°12E
Although not so impressive as it once was, this remnant of the once-numerous Danube wetlands that lay south-east of Bucharest is still worth a visit. As with most lakes in the region, Călăraşi is now a working fish-farm and similarly a feeding site for bands of pelicans from Bulgaria. There are large open lakes and smaller ponds by road 3 a few kilometres before the city of Călăraşi. Little Bitterns, Little Egrets, Purple and Squacco Herons and Whiskered Terns are all quite common in summer. White Pelicans regular fly in from the south. Useful marshes with Collared Pratincole and other waders lie by the concrete road south of the main road near an ugly mining complex. In spring and at the end of summer, waders such as Ruff and Marsh Sandpiper pass through.

CALENDAR
Best from April to September.
ACCESS
Just 6 km (3.75 miles) west of the industrial town of Călăraşi, itself
120 km (75 miles) south-east of Bucharest along road 3. Access to the
fish-farm depends on the gatekeeper, however, good smaller ponds lie
by the roadside, and a concrete road which leads southwards to the
Silistra ferry cuts through the marshes. Not listed as an IBA.

CIOCĂNEŞTI FISH-PONDS

44°10N 27°05E

This busy fish-farm has ponds of all sizes with some reed and tree
cover. There are relatively few breeding birds but it is a favoured
feeding site for pelicans: mostly White, but Dalmations are also
possible. Other birds include Red-necked Grebe, Ferruginous Duck,
Garganey, Squacco and Night Heron, hordes of Little Egrets and
Whiskered Terns, which are very common. In autumn, waders and
more wildfowl pass through.

CALENDAR
Best from April to August
SPECIES
◆ *Cormorant* Do not be surprised if birds are shot, as the farm is quite
within its legal rights to cull the flocks which nest on islands in the
Danube and take tons of the small fish in which the farm specializes.
◆ *White Pelican* Parties from Lake Srébarna just over the border in
Bulgaria regularly visit the ponds to feed.
ACCESS
The vilage of Ciocañeşti is about 30 km (19 miles) west of Călăraşi.
The fish-ponds lie between the village and the Bulgarian border and
can be reached along a cobbled road from the centre of the village.
Permission to enter the farm must be sought from the usually
obliging gatekeeper. Not listed as an IBA.

POIANA BRAŞOV

45°35N 25°30E

This resort is a good base from which to look for the montane
species of the Southern Carpathians. High peaks such as Mt
Cristianu and its spruce forests hold Golden Eagle, Ural Owl, Alpine
Swift, Three-toed Woodpecker, Alpine Accentor, Wallcreeper,
Nutcracker, Water Pipit, Ring Ouzel, Crested Tit, Crossbill and Rock
Bunting. At lower altitudes mixed beech and conifer forest has Honey
Buzzard, Goshawk, Red-breasted Flycatcher and Siskin, among
others.

CALENDAR
From April to June for breeding birds.

SPECIES
- *Wallcreeper* Sometimes on the cable-car buildings on Mount Cristianu besides being on the peak proper.
- *Nutcracker* Can seemingly disappear when breeding in spring, otherwise it is even found around the resort itself.

ACCESS
The resort is just 10 km (6.25 miles) south of Braşov, which is the main city of the area. Mount Cristianu (1960 m, 6370 feet) can be reached by cable-car, and has chalets which should be booked in advance. The forests are easily accessible from the resort. No IBAs are listed.

ROTBAV FISH-PONDS
45°58N 25°30E

These five ponds with their reed, willows and conveniently high dykes topped by tracks, provide a birding contrast in what is otherwise decidedly mountainous country. Lying alongside the River Olt, a migration route through Transylvania, a good selection of ducks, waders and songbirds take the opportunity to rest here during both spring and autumn passage. Breeding birds include White Stork, Little Bittern, Marsh Harrier, Marsh and Great Reed Warblers, Bee-eater and various Yellow Wagtails. Lesser Spotted Eagles hunt over the ponds and surrounding farmland. Autumn passage sees both storks, parties of Little Egrets, various herons, Green, Wood and Marsh Sandpipers and Ruff.

CALENDAR
Worth a look at almost any time of year.

SPECIES
- *Yellow Wagtail* As if this group was not complicated enough, a curious blend of black-headed and blue-headed hybrids occurs.

ACCESS
Just to the east of the main E60 road near the village of Rotbav, about 30 km (19 miles) north of Braşov. The small station of Vadu Rosu on the main railway line to Braşov overlooks the ponds. Proposed as an IBA.

SÎNPAUL FISH-PONDS
46°11N 25°23E

This is a somewhat isolated wetland site nestling in the foothills of the Carpathians and the best place for miles around for wetland birds. There are large reedbeds, meadows and oak and pine woods around the shallow ponds, all set in a remote rolling landscape of crops, grasslands and plantations. By Romanian standards the fish-ponds cover a small area, but are thus quite easy to work. White Storks nest in the village, there are Corncrakes nearby and Little Bittern, Ferruginous Duck, Garganey, Marsh Harrier, Spotted and Little Crakes and Savi's and Great Reed Warblers are all at the ponds. In spring, the fish-ponds are an important stop-over for migrating waders such as Black-tailed Godwit, Ruff, Wood and Marsh Sandpipers, and all three marsh terns. Autumn passage, in late August and September, is good for the occasional diver, groups of White Storks, Black Stork, Little Egret, Spoonbill, Osprey and Great Snipe. Although Sînpaul cannot compete for species or numbers with the Black Sea wetlands, its very location makes it an important site well worth a visit if one is birdwatching elsewhere in Transylvania.

CALENDAR
April and early May for spring passage birds. From May on for the breeding species. September is the best time for groups of storks.

SPECIES
◆ *Ferruginous Duck* The best site in the region.
◆ *Spotted Crake* Considering its accessibility and size this is an excellent site for this species with around half-a-dozen pairs.
◆ *Lesser Spotted Eagle* This is a regular hunting area for locally breeding birds which should be seen in summer on even a brief visit.
◆ *Yellow Wagtail* Many hybrid forms of the black-headed and blue-headed *flava* races occur here.

Sînpaul fish-ponds in Transylvania are a good site for finding Spotted Crake.

ACCESS
The fish-ponds are situated near the village of Sinpaul about 15 km
(9 miles) south-east of Odorheiu Secuiesc in Eastern Transylvania. As
the crow flies, Tirgu Mures is 75 km (47 miles) to the north-west.
The ponds can be observed via their raised banks and adjacent road.
The SOR has a chalet for visitors here. A Bird Reserve and IBA.

BICAZ GORGE
46°48N 25°51E
Another of the Eastern Carpathian's gems, this is probably the most
spectacular gorge in the country. Besides the sheer roadside walls of
granite where several pairs of Wallcreepers and Eagle Owl, Alpine
Swift, Alpine Accentor and Golden Eagle breed, there are also spruce
forests, a rushing stream and grazing pastures. Lake Rosu to the west
of the gorge proper is not particularly good for birds itself but the
surrounding forests, which are accessible here, have Ural and
Tengmalm's Owls, Hazelhen, Capercaillie, Three-toed Woodpecker,
Firecrest and Nutcracker.

CALENDAR
Visit in spring and summer when the road is passable.
SPECIES
♦ *Wallcreeper* Certainly, a bit of luck is needed as much of the
suitable habitat towers frustratingly high.
ACCESS
The gorge is cut by the winding road from Bicaz to Gheorgheni.
Piatra-Neamt is about 50 km (30 miles) to the east. There are a few
lay-bys in which to park, but finding vantage-points can be a
problem. An IBA.

LAKE BICAZ
47°00N–26°04E
This 30-km-long (19 mile) man-made reservoir sits amid spectacular
Transylvanian highland scenery. Also known as *Izvorul Muntelui*,
and marked on some maps as such, it is a perhaps unusual site for
divers, grebes, geese and ducks in auutmn and winter. Before the
reservoir was created, migratory birds presumable passed high
overhead here as they crossed the Carpathians. The surrounding
beech and conifer forests hold most of Transylvania's special
woodland birds: Ural Owl, Three-toed, White-backed, Grey-headed
and Black Woodpeckers, Red-breasted Flycatcher, Hazelhen, Crested
Tit, Ring Ouzel and Nutcracker included. But this is an area
requiring time and more often than not a good deal of walking.

CALENDAR
Migrating White-fronted Geese roost here in October. The best time
for forest birds is April–June. April is also good for terns and gulls.

SPECIES
- *Nutcracker* Particularly in the spruce forests of the western shore.
- *Slavonian Grebe* Regularly recorded in winter but difficult to observe from the shore.

ACCESS
Going north from Bicaz on the winding road out of town, the elephantine dam which holds the reservoir is soon crossed. Access into the forests is straightforward, to the water less so. One option is to take the passenger-service boat which runs daily from near the dam linking settlements along the reservoir and returning in the afternoon. Alternatively, it might be possible to hire a boat locally. The resort of Piatra-Neamt is 30 km (19 miles) to the east. An IBA.

GURGHIU MOUNTAINS
46°12–46°55N 24°50–25°50E

This is one of the wildest places in Europe, home to Brown Bears, Wolves and many good forest birds. The vast coniferous forests that blanket most of the mountains are the haunt of Eagle, Ural, Tengmalm's and Pygmy Owls, although finding them needs time and a good deal of luck as potentially suitable areas of habitat are huge. Diurnal birds of prey include Golden and Lesser Spotted Eagles and Peregrine. Above all, this is excellent grouse country; Capercaillies

Scattered populations of Sombre Tit in Transylvania are at the very north of the species' range.

are a speciality, and Hazelhens are common. Woodpeckers, too, are represented with Black, Grey-headed, White-backed and Three-toed all possible. Birds such as Red-breasted and Collared Flycatchers, Black Redstart, Ring Ouzel, Sombre Tit, Dipper, Crossbill, Nutcracker and Raven are found throughout the mountains. The key to finding them is to know one's habitats. Part of the eastern Carpathians, this is not a region that should be taken lightly as there are few such facilities as petrol stations, and decent maps are often out of print. Then again, this is spectacular country. Come prepared for an expedition, not a bird walk, and who knows what may be waiting.

CALENDAR
Although conditions can be tough well into April, the best time to visit is probably early spring when the grouse are lekking and the owls are calling.

SPECIES
◆ *Capercaillie* If weather permits, a visit in April may be rewarded with lekking cock birds.
◆ *Hazelhen* Said to be common.
◆ *Ural Owl* Certainly here, although its exact status, like that of most birds, is unknown.
◆ *Red-breasted Flycatcher* Breeds in old beech forest, of which there is plenty.
◆ *Three-toed Woodpecker* Small numbers inhabit the dense spruce forests here.

ACCESS
Tirgu Mures, the largest town in the region, is around 35 km (22 miles) to the south-west of the mountains. Road 15 heads north from here, passing through Reghin at the western foot of the range before arching round to follow the northern border of the mountains along the River Mures. From Reghin a minor road with several smaller branch roads cuts eastwards through the mountains. Not listed as an IBA.

TURDA GORGE
46°31N 23°40E

Transylvania has many beautiful spots and this is one of them. This deep gorge cut through the limestone of the Trascau mountain range is an easy mile-long walk of scenic birdwatching opportunities. There are sheer rock walls and caves and ledges, interspersed with bushes and woodland along the stream that runs through the gorge floor. Farmland and grasslands surround the area. Woodlark, Red-backed Shrike, Barred Warbler, Red-breasted and Collared Flycatchers, Black Redstart, Serin and Tree Sparrow are all quite common. Not surprisingly, this is ideal habitat for Golden Eagle, Eagle Owl, Rock Thrush and Rock Bunting, but the special bird

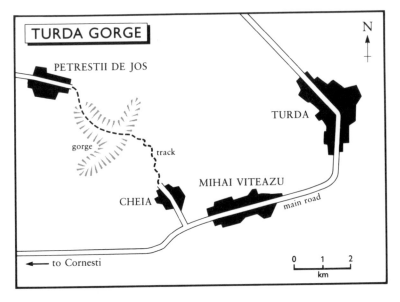

here is Wallcreeper. A couple of pairs are said to breed and no high-altitude trekking is needed, just a good pair of eyes, as these birds are not always easy to locate on the high rock walls. Honey Buzzard, Alpine Swift and Raven also occur. The gorge is also a good place for woodpeckers with Black, Grey-headed, Syrian and Lesser Spotted here all year round. In summer they are joined by Wryneck.

CALENDAR
The best season to visit is summer, from late May onwards, when the scenery and birds are at their best. Although some good birds are resident, heavy snow can cut off the gorge in winter.

SPECIES
◆ *Eagle Owl* A couple of pairs are resident.
◆ *Rock Thrush* A regular and good site from the end of May for what is a difficult bird in this part of the country.
◆ *Wallcreeper* Certainly here, but, as is often the case, a good deal of neck strain can be expected.
◆ *Crag Martin* May also be here. It bred in the 1970s but since then seems to have disappeared.

ACCESS
The gorge lies 8 km (5 miles) to the west of Turda between the settlements of Cheia and Petrestii de Jos. The largest town in the region is Cluj Napoca 32 km (20 miles) to the north along the E60. Although the gorge is huge, it is well-hidden. From Cheia, a path winds through agricultural land and then through the gorge. This is a popular recreation and climbing spot, but do not be tempted to scramble about away from the paths. An IBA.

MT BAISOARA

46°31N 23°15E

The whole of Transylvania has excellent and relatively unexplored tracts of mountains covered in vast forests. Mt Baisoara is one convenient site within easy reach of a good base at Cluj Napoca. Being a ski resort, there are decent approach roads and some tourist facilities, important factors when birdwatching in this wild region. Hazelhen, Black Woodpecker, Nutcracker, Crested Tit, Firecrest and Crossbill are all quite common birds in the spruce forests. Grey-headed and Three-toed Woodpeckers can also be found, and there may be interesting owls – try exploring the slopes up from the ski resort at Baisoara in the off season. Higher up Water Pipit and Ring Ouzel can be seen, and, around the resort itself, Black Redstart and often Nutcracker. Lower down are Sombre Tit and Serin. With the exception of other similar mountain ranges in the Balkans, this is one of those few places left in Europe where significant bird discoveries could be made.

CALENDAR

Spring and summer visits are probably best when the ski resort is not so busy and many birds are active.

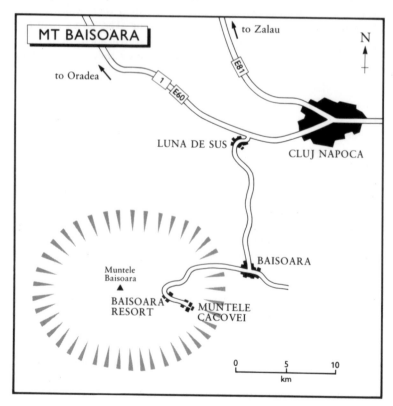

SPECIES

◆ *Nutcracker* Quite common and often semi-tame around the resort.

◆ *Crested Tit* Common in conifers at all altitudes.

◆ *Sombre Tit* The parks and orchards around Cluj Napoca itself are worth a stop for this species.

ACCESS

The mountain lies around 40 km (25 miles) south-west of Cluj Napoca along minor roads. From the city drive west to Luna de Sus on the E60, south to Baisoara and then west climbing to Muntele Baisoara resort and Muntele Mare. Most of the mountain can be explored on forest paths and ski runs. Not listed as an IBA.

ÎNTREGALDE AND RÎMETI GORGES

Întregalde Gorge 46°15N 23°24E Rîmeti Gorge 46°20N 23°30E

These two gorges and the area between them are real gems. The limestone crags and walls, surrounding farmland, hay meadows and oak and beech woodlands all offer good birdwatching. There are other, smaller, gorges in the general area which, as a whole, is a fine raptor site with Short-toed, Booted, Golden and Lesser Spotted Eagles here in summer. Eagle Owls also breed. Quite common birds include Nightjar, Hoopoe, Grey-headed and Middle Spotted Woodpeckers, Woodlark, Red-backed Shrike, Dipper, Black Redstart and Rock Bunting. Two specialities are Rock Thrush and Wallcreeper, with several pairs of each said to breed. Hazelhen, Black Woodpecker and Red-breasted Flycatcher are in the adjacent woodland. Sombre Tits can be found in more open areas with scattered trees. Besides the presence of some fine birds, the proximity of the gorges to villages and roads means that this is, by Transylvanian standards, a relatively easy place to explore. Although rock climbers find the walls ideal, birdwatchers can leave their ropes at home.

CALENDAR

Summer is best, from mid-May on, but several good species are resident and, weather permitting, technically possible in any season.

SPECIES

◆ *Rock Thrush* Both gorges are regular sites from the end of May for this colourful bird.

◆ *Rock Bunting* Not surprisingly, rather common.

ACCESS

The two gorges lie in the Trascau Mountains near the villages after which they are named, approximately 25 km (15 miles) and 15 km (9 miles) respectively west of Aiud. To reach Rîmeti, head north-west from Teius to Stremt and then follow the river valley for about 26 km (16 miles). For Întregalde, turn right a couple of miles south of Teius, towards Galde de Sus, and continue along the Galde Valley for about 30 km (19 miles). Several tracks cross between the two gorges, which are Nature Reserves, so keep to the paths. Jointly listed as an IBA.

RETEZAT NATIONAL PARK

45°22N 22°41E

This scenic mountain range deep in the Southern Carpathians is mostly high alpine habitat with vast beech and spruce forests, dwarf pine in the alpine zone, meadows, glacial lakes, tarns and rocky tops. There are easier places in Europe, indeed in Eastern Europe, to see typical birds of these mountains, but few as scenic or as challenging. This is yet another area that offers the chance of ornithological discoveries. Golden and Lesser Spotted Eagles are both here and owls include Eagle, Pygmy, Ural and possibly Tengmalm's. There are Black, Grey-headed, Middle Spotted, White-backed and Three-toed Woodpeckers, although a good deal of walking would be needed to get them all. The spruce forests of Retezat are home to Hazelhen and Capercaillie, and the beech forests at lower altitudes best for Red-breasted and Collared Flycatchers. Ring Ouzel and Water Pipit breed and there may be Alpine Accentors. More widespread birds include Goldcrest and Firecrest, Willow and Crested Tits, Hawfinch, Siskin, Crossbill, Nutcracker and Raven. Wallcreeper and Alpine Swift occur in the rocky limestone areas of the southern Retezat.

CALENDAR

In winter, conditions are unsuitable for birdwatching. The mountains can only be realistically explored from late May to September.

SPECIES

◆ *Rock Partridge* The status of this species is far from clear. I would be interested to hear of sightings.

◆ *Tengmalm's Owl* This is one of the species which is almost certainly here, but little or only old information exists. So, if anyone is bored with stake-outs . . .

◆ *White-backed Woodpecker* Beech forests are home to this species.

ACCESS

The Retezat National Park is around 390 km (242 miles) north-west of Bucharest by road. The area is best approached from roads 68 and 66 (the latter is part of the E69) which skirt the northern edge of the range. Roads head up from Piu and Clopotiva to mountain resorts. A section of the Retezat is a 'scientific reserve', with restricted access. This is not an area suited to a brief visit, rather a well-planned mountain trekking holiday with every conceivable item of equipment. It may be possible to arrange a stay at mountain chalets run by the Romanian Academy of Sciences. An IBA.

CEFA FISH-PONDS

46°55N 21°41E

This area of large and small ponds, reedbeds, grassland and woodland in an agricultural setting, corresponds to the Biharugra fish-ponds over the border in Hungary. A state-owned man-made and managed wetland, Cefa is an important place for many breeding birds that have declined elsewhere in western Romania. In summer there are Red-necked Grebe, Purple, Squacco and Night Herons, both bitterns, Little Egret, Ferruginous Duck, Garganey, Marsh Harrier and Whiskered and Black Terns. Although they do not always breed, Great White Egret, Spoonbill and sometimes Glossy Ibis occur. A bit of luck and concentrated effort might turn up Spotted and Little Crakes. There are Savi's, River, Marsh, Great Reed and Moustached Warblers and Penduline Tit. The area around the ponds has White Stork, Red-footed Falcon, Lesser Grey Shrike and probably a few Great Bustards, as a population lies just over the border. Some Great Bustards may reside in the grassland between the ponds and the border but, so far as I can tell, the area has not been surveyed. There is good spring passage, especially of waders, and Cefa is a key stop-over for wildfowl in autumn, mostly White-fronted Geese but with some Greylag and Bean Geese, and vagrants always possible. Flocks of Cranes sometimes use the area from late September to November.

CALENDAR
Cefa is at its best in two periods: from May to August for breeding birds and October and November for geese and Cranes. However, if one is passing this way at any time of year it is worth a visit as one of the best wetland sites in this part of the country.
SPECIES
♦ *Night Heron* More than fifty pairs breed alongside Little Egrets in nearby woodland.
♦ *Squacco Heron* Probably the best Romanian site for this species west of the Carpathians.
♦ *White-fronted Goose* By far the most common goose in autumn and winter with several thousands usually recorded in November.
♦ *Whiskered Tern* This is the northernmost nesting site in Romania.
ACCESS
The fish-ponds lie just to the west of the village of Cefa which is 24 km (15 miles) south-west of Oradea along the E671. There is a border crossing with Hungary just before Oradea at Bors. Strictly speaking, the fish-ponds are out of bounds, but permission to explore can be obtained by asking the farm workers. Border guards here can still be a little sensitive to foreigners and the border itself is mostly unmarked, so common sense is required. An IBA.

MURES FLOOD-PLAIN
46°00N 21°05E
These meadows lie along the River Mures for a few miles before it passes through the town of Arad. The adjacent Ciala-Pecica area, prone to spring floods, has oak, elm, willow and natural poplar woodlands and plantations dotted with ponds, marshes and stands of reeds. There are always good raptors here with Black Kite, Honey Buzzard, Lesser Spotted Eagle, Marsh Harrier and Red-footed

The flood-plain of the River Mures near Arad is ideal for Black Kite.

Falcon in summer, Osprey, Hen and Montagu's Harriers passing through in spring and autumn, and wintering White-tailed Eagle and Rough-legged Buzzard. In such an area there is always the possibility of a Saker. The flood-plain habitat is ideal for White Stork, Little Egret, Night Heron and Little Bittern. There is also Ferruginous Duck, possibly Little Crake, Black and Syrian Woodpeckers, River and Marsh Warblers, Nightingale, Penduline Tit, Short-toed Treecreeper and Golden Oriole. Most of these birds can be found without having to thrash through the mosquito-infested and soggy undergrowth, in fact, most are around, or not far from, settlements. Try the area around the hamlet of Bodrogu Vechi. There are also some dry spots within the woodland where Nightjar, Bee-eater, Hoopoe, Tawny Pipit and Red-backed and Lesser Grey Shrikes are likely.

CALENDAR
Visit from mid-May to July for breeding birds. August and September are good for storks, passage raptors and waders, but not in large numbers. November is the best month for Crane and sees the arrival of wintering raptors and Great Grey Shrike.
SPECIES
♦ *Crane* This is one of a series of autumn stop-overs along Europe's eastern flyway.

◆ *River Warbler* One of the most common birds here.
◆ *Olivaceous Warbler* Probably quite common.
ACCESS
The area lies either side of the River Mures, between Pecica and
Arad in south-western Romania. Timisoara is 50 km (31 miles) to
the south along the E671, and a border crossing into Hungary at
Nadlac 30 km (19 miles) to the west along the E68. The area is
framed to the north by the E68 and to the south by a minor road
into Arad. Although it can be freely explored, it is a case of finding
entry points into the area as there are no bridges across the Mures
here. An IBA.

SATCHINEZ
45°58N 21°04E
This well-known wetland is a refuge for birds which were common
throughout the region before drainage schemes and intensive farming
transformed the area. Satchinez is another link in the chain of
autumn migration stop-overs which are dotted through this part of
Eastern Europe. It is now an island of marshes, ponds, wet-meadows,
willow copses and large reedbeds in a sea of agriculture. Birds include
Black-necked Grebe, both bitterns, Grey, Purple, Squacco and Night
Herons, Little Egret, White Stork and Marsh Harrier. The herons
nest in noisy mixed colonies in the reeds and willows. These reedbeds
offer the best chance in this part of the country for Spotted and Little
Crakes. A few Corncrakes breed in the surrounding meadows. There
is an impressive list of 'reedy' warblers with Grasshopper, Savi's,
River, Marsh, Reed, Great Reed and Sedge all here. There are some
Penduline and Bearded Tits, although Bluethroat has disappeared. In
spring, Satchinez sees parties of all three marsh terns passing through.
In winter, the reserve and surrounding area are good for Rough-
legged Buzzard, Hen Harrier, Merlin, Short-eared Owl and Great
Grey Shrike.

CALENDAR
A visit at almost any time of year is worthwhile. May is best with late
passage birds moving through and summer visitors settling in. The
end of summer, August and September, see storks, egrets, waders and
some wildfowl. Mild winters have wintering White-fronted Geese.
SPECIES
◆ *Ferruginous Duck* This is the best site in the region.
◆ *Night Heron* In some years up to a hundred pairs nest.
ACCESS
Satchinez is a Bird Reserve, near the village of the same name, tucked
away in the very south-west corner of Romania. Timisoara is 24 km
(15 miles) to the south-east along minor roads. As is often the case,
most of the same birds can be seen outside, as well as within, the
actual protected area. An IBA.

BULGARIA

GENERAL INFORMATION

Bulgaria is predominantly a mountainous country, yet from the
birdwatcher's point of view probably of most interest for its
coastal and lowland birds. There are birds here which are totally
absent from western Europe, and others that are found in a few
places farther north and west but which are widespread and common
here. It is also one of the least birdwatched countries in Europe,
offering the visitor the chance of discovery. For such a poor country
the range of available accommodation is remarkable and obviously
because of the importance placed on tourism. Bulgaria is generally
inexpensive by any standards, but, as in the other countries dealt
with in this book, this is changing. Hotels can be overpriced. Credit
cards and even traveller's cheques are usually rather useless in most
of the country. The unit of currency is the leva.

January is the coldest month with temperatures of about 0 °C
(32 °F) almost everywhere. The coast is usually a little milder than
the mountains, where the temperature can drop to well below zero.
In July and August, expect something around 23 °C (74 °F) in the
mountains and often above 30 °C (86 °F) on the coast.

Basic medicines to cope with such complaints as diarrhoea and sunburn should be taken. A reciprocal health agreement apparently exists between Bulgaria and Britain, although there may be a charge for medicines. It seems safe to drink the water, although, as *glasnost* has dug up some frightening statistics elsewhere in the region on water quality, it may be wise to stick to bottled water or local wines.

Unless one reads the Cyrillic alphabet, some road signs, are difficult to follow. However, Bulgarians are generally very helpful if a common language can be found. In larger hotels in Sofia, and in the Black Sea resorts, people know English, German and often another language or two. Elsewere, a small amount of Russian helps. With the exception of the border region with Turkey, and obviously closed areas and reserves, which are often fenced off or have signs in several languages, the Bulgarian countryside can be freely explored.

IMPORTANCE FOR BIRDS

Although much is unknown about the bird populations of Bulgaria, particularly the vast montane areas inland, it is clear that the country is of great importance for the avifauna of Europe. The globally threatened Pygmy Cormorant, Dalmatian Pelican, Imperial Eagle and Lesser Kestrel all have significant populations, there are some White-tailed Eagle pairs, and Black Vultures have recently returned after a period of extinction. Credit must go to dedicated local ornithologists for enticing this species back with their 'vulture restaurant' project. Vast tracts of forest and mountain ranges surely support good populations of grouse, owls, woodpeckers and flycatcher species, as well as some interesting subspecies such as the Balkan races of Alpine Accentor and Shore Lark. Wetlands along the Black Sea coast and the Danube are better known and support colonies of various herons and egrets, Glossy Ibis, Spoonbill, Ruddy Shelduck, Collared Pratincole and Gull-billed Tern. These same wetlands are important sites for passage birds, too, with White Pelican and various raptors particularly numerous in the autumn. In winter, the coastal wetlands also provide refuge for three more globally threatened birds; White-headed Duck, some Lesser White-fronted Geese and varying numbers of Red-breasted Geese. A variety of raptors breed in significant numbers, although, again, more data are needed. Egyptian Vulture, Short-toed Eagle, Levant Sparrowhawk, Long-legged Buzzard, Booted Eagle and Saker are just some of the threatened species that can be found in Bulgaria.

GETTING THERE

At the time of writing, the only scheduled flights from London are to Sofia, which is ideal for most of the mountain sites but far from the Black Sea. Packages to the coast are worth considering as they land at Varna or Burgas and are a good springboard for birdwatching along the Black Sea. I have heard of two-centre holidays combining Golden Sands and Sunny Beach and, with a hire car for one or two days, this could in theory be an easy way of doing the whole coast from Turkey to Romania. Bulgarian taxi rates are quite reasonable and local buses very cheap; both are good ways of getting from resorts to sites up and down the coast. Driving across Europe from the west involves crossing Romania or Serbia and, unless one has other reasons, is not advised. One can drive in from Greece, Turkey and the Romanian Black Sea resorts if one is there. Reserves require permission to enter and only marked paths can be followed. However, it is probably fair to say that getting permit information is not straightforward, and that the rules and protection concepts are somewhat out of date. In some places the emphasis seems to be on keeping birdwatchers and naturalists out, whilst ignoring the often damaging habits of local people. In compiling the following list of sites, considerable thought was given to accessibility, as some good bird areas, particularly in the wilder mountain ranges, are difficult to work.

CONSERVATION

There is little tradition of nature conservation and bird protection amongst Bulgarians, although an awareness of environmental health has blossomed since the end of the former regime. Problems do exist with, for example, illegal hunting in some regions. However, a network of National Parks and Nature Reserves does exist. The state authority dealing with nature conservation matters is the Ministry of Environment, located at 67, William Gladstone St, 1000 Sofia, Bulgaria. Write to them for permits for protected areas. The Bulgarian Society For The Protection Of Birds (BSPB) is a non-governmental organization founded in 1988. It has over six hundred members which makes it the largest body of its kind in the country. The tasks it faces are huge, but already its dedicated volunteers have made an impression both at home and internationally. The BSPB concentrates on active field work such as 'vulture restaurants' and habitat management, public awareness in general and educational work with young people. For further information write to the BSPB, 1421 Sofia, 8 Blvd. Dragan Tzankov, Bulgaria.

HABITATS

As well as the well-known wetlands on the Black Sea coast, Bulgaria is blessed with a variety of other bird habitats. Its relatively under-developed agricultural industry means that there is a great diversity of bird species, from eastern steppe species like Pallid Harrier and Pied Wheatear to alpine breeders such as Shore Lark. However, at the same time, valuable wetland habitat has been lost to agriculture, and some upland areas ruined by overgrazing. Most of the countryside is

Bulgaria is arguably Eastern Europe's best country for raptors such as Egyptian Vulture.

either farmed or covered in forests, some of which are old deciduous woodlands of the type long since gone from most of Europe; others are high-altitude conifer forests. There are also alpine meadows and a few peaks with almost permanent snow cover. Some steppe habitat remains in the Danube plain, along the coast and particularly in Dobrudja in the north-eastern corner of the country, where some of the country's most interesting birds are to be found. Many places in the country are, of course, reminiscent of other Balkan countries with scrub and pasture grazed by sheep and goats, where various larks, shrikes, warblers and buntings are common. The Black Sea coast is an important flyway in both spring and autumn, particularly for pelicans, storks and raptors. Finally, there is the sea, which is an important bird habitat in its own right. Bulgaria's bird habitats, both natural and man-made, are indeed remarkable.

SEASONS

SPRING
April sees good passage north along the Black Sea flyway, with gulls, terns, waders and passerines stopping off at the coastal wetlands. Early May has a combination of migrants and arriving breeding birds. The higher mountains are still under snow and difficult to reach.

SUMMER

This is the time to make a grand tour of the country, with the mountains of the west and centre at their best in terms of both weather and birds; and the specialities of the Danube and Struma valleys and coastal plain also all present. There are many possible treks in the uplands. The end of July sees the beginning of migration.

AUTUMN

There is a bottle-neck at Burgas on the Black Sea coast where large numbers of storks, pelicans and raptors pass from the end of August through September to early October. Although the birds can travel over Bulgaria very high up, on most days there is a steady stream. River valleys farther west are also minor flyways.

WINTER

Without doubt, the really productive places to visit in this season are in the north-east and east of the country. From Srébarna through Dobrudja to the Black Sea, thousands of wintering geese are possible. The vast majority are White-fronts but flocks of Red-breasts occur every year. Early 1993 saw tens of thousands of the latter. If conditions are harsh farther north in Romania, numbers here can be spectacular. The Rhodopes Mountains have overwintering vultures.

BIRDWATCHING SITES

DANUBE ISLANDS

40°37–43°40N 20°10–25°28E

From the Black Forest to the Black Sea, the River Danube is lined with good, and often exceptional, birding sites, and the Bulgarian stretch is no exception. One famous spot is Belene Island, which is covered in wet willow thickets, poplar woods, marshes, pools, meadows and farmland, and is a sanctuary for colonies of Cormorants, with some Pygmy and Little Egrets, Squacco, Purple and Night Herons, Glossy Ibis and Spoonbill. Good numbers of Whiskered Terns nest, and there is a chance of Black Kite and White-tailed Eagle. Warblers include River, Great Reed, Icterine and Olivaceous. About 20 km (12.5 miles) downriver, near the village of Vardim, a somewhat similar but smaller island has most of the above birds, too. Indeed, all the semi-temporary islets and sandbars along this stretch are worth checking in summer.

CALENDAR
Visit in the summer when breeding colonies are in full swing and water levels are at their lowest revealing sandbars and making access to the river slightly easier.

SPECIES
◆ *Little Egret* Besides hundreds of breeding pairs good numbers often overwinter.

ACCESS
Belene Island lies between the village of the same name and the town of Svistov about 70 km (45 miles) north-east of Pleven. Almost the whole of Bulgaria's border with Romania is formed by the Danube, which for birdwatchers presents the problem of access as, despite *glasnost*, frontier officials are still suspicious of cameras, binoculars and telescopes. It is definitely unwise, if not forbidden, to try to reach the islands themselves. Indeed, it is unnecessary, too, as most of the birds entioned are easily encountered from the river bank at Belene or from the road between Svistov and Vardim. Belene Island is a Nature Reserve and an IBA.

RUSENSKI LOM

43°50N 25°57E
This network of limestone gorges and valleys with forests, meadows and dotted settlements is an fascinating place in which to birdwatch. With Long-legged Buzzard, Lesser Spotted and Golden Eagles, Lesser Kestrel, Saker and Egyptian Vulture all possible in summer, this is a very important place for raptors. It can, however, be a slightly confusing place to work, as no decent maps are available and the rolling landscape is deceptive, hiding many of the stream valleys and gorges from view until one is right upon or past them. A picturesque and excellent spot is tucked away down a dead-end road from Ivanovo in the west of the area. There are historical sites here known as 'stone churches', which are, in fact, caves with medieval frescoes. The steps leading to the first one can be followed farther up and on to a rocky outcrop, which overlooks an impressive wooded gorge with Long-legged Buzzard, Eagle Owl and Black Woodpecker. Apparently there are Lesser Kestrels around here, too. Ruins above the village of Cerven and the gorge cut by a stream here are worth exploring for more woodpeckers, Black Stork, Rock Bunting and Rock Thrush. Nisovo, at the centre of the whole area, is similarly surrounded by vertical rock walls. Above and between each settlement are areas of scrub and agricultural land with White Stork, Roller, Tawny Pipit and Red-backed Shrike amongst others.

CALENDAR
Eagle Owl and some of the diurnal raptors are resident but the ideal time to visit is from May to August when the full complement of breeding birds occurs.

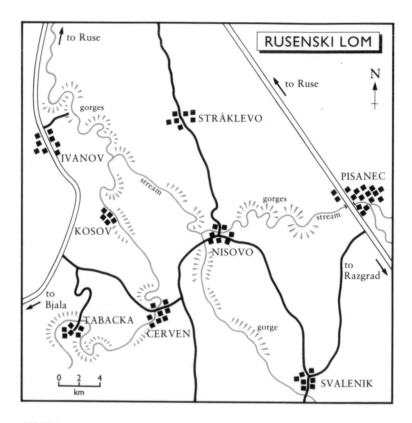

SPECIES

◆ *Long-legged Buzzard* Several pairs breed in the National Park with the gorge to the east of Ivanovo particularly good.

◆ *Eagle Owl* Possible in several of the rocky gorges.

ACCESS

Rusenski Lom begins 16 km (10 miles) south of the Danube port of Ruse via the E85. There is a border crossing with Romania at Ruse, via the 'Friendship Bridge' across the Danube. A trip into Bulgaria from Romania is feasible, although you should perhaps bear in mind that despite its name this bridge and its officials are the unfriendliest that I have ever encountered with long delays the norm. Coming from the Black Sea resorts, take the E70. Rusenski Lom is a National Park but mostly open. Walking through the valleys and gorges and across the karst tops is really the only way to cover the area. An IBA.

LAKE SRÉBARNA

44°05N 27°07E

An internationally renowned wetland, Srébarna is a remnant of the once numerous lakes that lined the Danube's route to the Black Sea. It has extensive reedbeds, adjacent steppe, vineyards and agricultural land and is periodically inundated by the Danube. The only nesting site for Dalmatian Pelican in Bulgaria, it is probably worth a visit for that reason alone, but there are also Red-necked Grebe, Pygmy Cormorant, Great White and Little Egrets, Purple, Squacco and Night Herons, Little Bittern, Spoonbill, Glossy Ibis and White-tailed Eagle. Ducks include Gadwall, Shoveler and Ferruginous Duck (the last in large numbers). Whiskered and Black Terns are quite common. The reeds hold Water Rail, Savi's, Moustached and Great Reed Warblers and Bearded Tit. Marsh Harriers are common and there are some Montagu's in the surrounding area, along with White Stork, Black Kite, Bee-eater, Hoopoe, Calandra Lark, Black-headed Wagtail and Lesser Grey Shrike. Thousands of geese, mainly White-fronts but including some Red-breasts and, occasionally, Lesser White-fronts, occur in winter. If all this is not enough, there are woodlands to search on hills overlooking the lake.

CALENDAR
Lake Srébarna has exciting birds at just about any time of year but from May to July is the best time to visit for the breeding specialities.
SPECIES
◆ *Dalmatian Pelican* The number of breeding pairs fluctuates and estimates vary, but this is still one of the best spots in Europe to see the species.
◆ *Pygmy Cormorant* A small colony regularly breeds.
◆ *Purple Heron* One of the most common herons here, and easily encountered in summer.
ACCESS
Lake Srébarna is 20 km (12 miles) west of Silistra, and lies between road 21 and the Danube. The river forms the border with Romania here, and a ferry service provides an occasional frontier crossing. Srébarna is a Biosphere Reserve and Unesco World Heritage Site and permission is needed for most of the wetland. Alternatively, Balkantourist in Silistra apparently arrange 'official' visits. An IBA.

LAKE DURANKULAK
43°38N 28°30E
This coastal lake in the top right-hand corner of Dobrudja is a feasible day-trip from Golden Sands, or from the Black Sea resorts in Romania just to the north. The slightly saline lake and marsh have many of the birds typical of the coast such as Red-necked and Black-necked Grebes, Bittern, Little Bittern, Marsh Harrier and Savi's, Marsh, Reed and Great Reed Warblers. The main reason for coming this far north is that this is a workable site for Paddyfield Warbler, which, incidentally, may be more common along the Black Sea shoreline than is thought. Other summer birds at Durankulak are Ferruginous Duck, Whiskered Tern and Collared Pratincole, with Calandra Lark, Olivaceous Warbler and Spanish Sparrow nearby. The lake is also a wintering ground for White-fronted, a few Lesser

White-fronted and Red-breasted Geese, various ducks including Smew, as well as Great White Egret. On passage, just about anything seems possible, with White Pelican, Pygmy Cormorant and Ruddy Shelduck regular in autumn. Passage waders could be very interesting, and one gets the feeling that this is the sort of place where regular observers could turn up all kinds of things.

CALENDAR
From mid-May onwards is best for warblers, September for good passage and October for Crane. November to February is the usual time for thousands of geese but much depends on the weather.
SPECIES
♦ *Paddyfield Warbler* Try the marshy vegetation bordering farmland between the lake proper and the campsite.
♦ *Red-breasted Goose* Numbers vary from winter to winter depending upon conditions farther north in Romania, but can reach tens of thousands.
♦ *White-headed Duck* Conditions seem suitable for some wintering birds.
♦ *Spanish Sparrow* Around the pump-house building on the western side of the lake.
ACCESS
Durankulak is 6 km (4 miles) south of the Romanian border at Vama Veche in the very north-eastern corner of Bulgaria. The lake, which is a Landscape Reserve, lies to the east of the E87 between Durankulak and the village of Vaklino. An IBA.

LAKE ŞABLA-EZERETZ
43°30N 28°35E
These two brackish lakes, and attendant smaller wetlands, are separated from the Black Sea by a long sandbar. The varied habitats ensure a good mixture of birds: open water, reedbeds, marsh, agricultural land, Cape Şabla and the Black Sea itself. Perhaps the two most interesting birds here are Ruddy Shelduck and Paddyfield Warbler, both of which breed. There are also Marsh, Savi's and Great Reed Warblers. During passage periods, the campsite is a particularly good spot for falls of passerines, as it is on the coastal flyway; just about anything is possible at the end of summer. There is a smaller, but interesting salt-marsh near the campsite, with Little Egret, Ferruginous Duck, waders on passage and resident and vagrant gulls and terns. Nearby are Red-footed Falcon, Short-toed, Calandra and Crested Larks, Tawny Pipit, Lesser Grey Shrike, Black-headed Wagtail, Spanish Sparrow and Ortolan and Black-headed Buntings. There is also the chance of Rose-coloured Starling flocks. In winter, the lakes host thousands of White-fronted Geese and, as is the case all across Bulgarian Dobrudja, large flocks of Red-breasted Geese when conditions are unsuitable farther north.

CALENDAR
From May onwards is good for breeding birds. September is excellent for waders, Caspian Tern and Red-breasted Flycatcher at the campsite. From November to March divers, grebes, wildfowl and some Pygmy Cormorants occur. In the winter of 1991–92 an estimated 175,000 geese, mostly White-fronts, were counted here. Thus, this an all-year-round site.

SPECIES
◆ *Ruddy Shelduck* About ten pairs are said to breed.
◆ *Red-breasted Goose* Tens of thousands feed in the area during some winters, some 59,000 were there in January 1993.
◆ *Paddyfield Warbler* In the marshy area to the north of the campsite, rather than the reeds proper. I have a feeling that more wetlands on this coast hold this species than is generally thought. It is simply a question of someone doing a thorough census.

ACCESS
The lakes lie between the villages of Ezerec and Şabla in the north-east corner of Bulgaria. Varna is 85 km (53 miles) to the south along the coast. The Romanian border at Vama Veche is only 20 km (12 miles) to the north and so a trip over the border from the Mangalia resorts is feasible. A road runs from Şabla to a campsite at the centre of the area. Parts of the area are fenced off, but this does not really restrict the birdwatching. An IBA.

CAPE KALIAKRA
43°20N 28°30E
The variety of birds that can be seen on this headland is quite remarkable, and is because of the close proximity of several distinct habitats. As one leaves Balgarevo on the road to the cape, scrub and steppe on either side of the road have Red-footed Falcon, Stone Curlew, Short-toed Lark, Tawny Pipit, Lesser Grey Shrike, Hoopoe and Cirl and Black-headed Buntings. In some years, there are flocks of Rose-coloured Starlings. Ravines on the left which lie out of view are said to hold Eagle Owl. Saker and Pallid Harrier are also around here. Farther along, the cape cliffs near the car park are good for Pied Wheatear and Alpine Swift, and, to cap it all, an isolated colony of Shags breeds at the very tip of the cape. A path to the right of the buildings leads to an often much-needed café and bar, and then on to the tip of the cape. Sparrows are worth checking here as Spanish, Tree and House all occur. Birds out over the sea include the Yelkouan Shearwater. Poles and nets in the sea below the cape are favourite roosts for gulls and terns. In the right, or wrong, weather migrants find refuge amongst the cape buildings and bushes with various warblers, Bee-eater and Red-breasted Flycatchers are particularly numerous in autumn. Larger migrants also move through, although they can sometimes be frustratingly high up. Pelicans, storks, harriers, buzzards and eagles all occur in groups

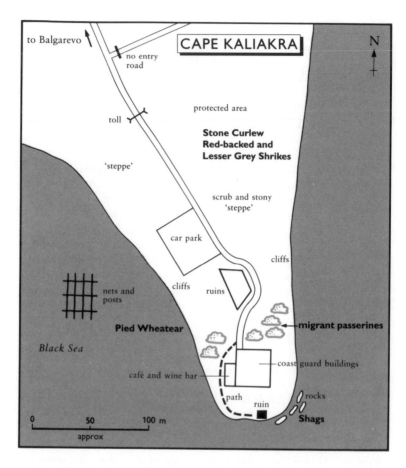

at the end of summer. If the birds are not enough, Monk Seals can also sometimes be seen just off the cape.

CALENDAR

April sees some spring passage. From May to July the weather is milder and the steppe area is at its best. From the end of August through to October birds are moving south. Early September is probably the best time for migration watching.

SPECIES

- *Shag* Bulgaria's only breeding colony, of the Mediterranean and Black Sea race *desmarestii*, is here.
- *Black-eared Wheatear* Also possible on the steppe.
- *Pied Wheatear* Although by no means the only site for this species on the Bulgarian coast Kaliakra is perhaps the most reliable for good views.
- *Alpine Swift* A small colony nests on the cliffs near the café.
- *Pallid Swift* Careful scrutiny of all swifts may produce Pallids as they breed amongst their congeners at several sites around the country.

ACCESS
The cape is about 75 km (47 miles) from Varna and 60 km (37 miles) from Golden Sands north along the E87. At Kavarna, take the road for Balgarevo and then it is straight on along the cape with birds on both sides. In summer, there is a toll. One area of scrub and steppe to the left by a no-entry road is signposted as a reserve. There also seems to be some kind of military installation nearby as officials once stopped me and noted my car registration-number. An IBA.

GOLDEN SANDS COAST

43°20N 28°02E

For many years, the only practical way of visiting Bulgaria was on a package tour to one of the Black Sea resorts with Golden Sands (*Zlatni Pjasaci* in Bulgarian) one of the main destinations. Quite a few birdwatchers have taken advantage of these relatively inexpensive holidays with flight, hotel and meals thrown in, as a base for exploring the coast. In fact, this still remains one of the best ways of birdwatching in the area. The Golden Sands resort itself has some excellent birds. The sea regularly produces Black-throated and Red-throated Divers, Red-necked and Black-necked Grebes and Yelkouan Shearwater. Yellow-legged Gulls hang around the beach, and Slender-billed and Mediterranean Gulls, and Gull-billed and Sandwich Terns are also possible. In parks and gardens around the resort there are Grey-headed and Syrian Woodpeckers, Scops Owl, Crested Lark, Olive-tree Warbler, Hawfinch and Golden Oriole. Just north of the resort, before Kranevo, the road passes cliffs where there is a chance of Red-rumped Swallow and Pied Wheatear. Farther along the coast, the River Batova enters the sea at Albena. The river can be followed along a track on the southern side. Here Purple Heron, Little Bittern, Black Kite, Nightingale and Penduline Tit occur, and this is an exceptional place for warblers with Savi's, Great Reed, Marsh, Olivaceous and Barred all likely in summer. Farmland in the valley holds Quail, Short-toed and Calandra Larks and Black-headed Wagtail. The next village along the coast road is Balchik, where in summer high cliffs are worth scouring for Alpine Swift, Pied Wheatear and Spanish Sparrow. Baltata Forest and the open semi-steppe areas above Albena and Balchik are likely to produce raptors, Bee-eater, Roller, Lesser Grey Shrike and Black-headed Bunting.

CALENDAR
There are good birds around throughout the summer, but the resorts themselves can be rather busy in high season. The two best periods are perhaps May for breeding birds and late spring passage and August–September for autumn passage.

SPECIES

◆ *Alpine Swift* Small numbers nest along with Swifts.

Pied Wheatear is one of the Bulgarian Black-Sea coast specialities.

◆ *Pied Wheatear* This does not seem to be as regular to the south of Golden Sands, although it is quite common in suitable habitat north of here.
◆ *Red-rumped Swallow* Sometimes parties swirl around the tops of hotels at Golden Sands and Albena.
◆ *Eagle Owl* Scan the cliffs just south of Balchik.
◆ *Calandra Lark* Try the open land in from the coast near Obrociste.
ACCESS
Golden Sands is 15 km (9 miles) north of Varna, where charter flights arrive. Albena is around 15 km (9 miles) farther north and Balchik 10 km (6 miles) beyond that. Most of the area can be worked from the coast roads. Access is unrestricted, except for Baltata Forest, which is a Nature Reserve and partly fenced off. No IBAs listed.

YATATA RESERVOIR
43°11N 27°42E
Honey Buzzard, Black Kite, Short-toed, Lesser Spotted and Booted Eagles, Levant Sparrowhawk and Marsh and Montagu's Harriers all pass this way in autumn, sometimes in good numbers. This medium-sized artificial lake is not very far inland and still on the coastal strip before the hills begin to rise. Besides raptors, White Pelican, the occasional Dalmatian Pelican, both storks, Spoonbill and various ducks, including Shelduck and Ruddy Shelduck occur in spring and

autumn. Shallow, vegetation-covered parts of the lake hold marsh terns and some pairs of Black-winged Stilts and Avocet. Crested and Calandra Larks, Tawny Pipit, Black-headed Wagtail, Red-backed Shrike, Barred Warbler and Stonechat may also be found. This is a somewhat neglected site and those who make the effort may be rewarded with a surprise or two.

CALENDAR
April and May are good for spring passage; mid-May to July for breeding birds. August sees some passage but September is probably best.
SPECIES
♦ *Black-winged Stilt* Sometimes up to a dozen breeding pairs.
♦ *White Pelican* If nothing much is happening at the coastal sites try here.
♦ *Ruddy Shelduck* Some pass through and may even breed.
ACCESS
Only 16 km (10 miles) from Varna the lake is an easy day-trip for those based here or at satellite resorts such as Golden Sands. Take the minor road inland from Varna through Ezerovo to Beloslav and the lake is just outside town north of the road to Razdelna. An IBA.

KAMCIJA
43°02N 27°50E
This stretch of swampy woodland, with old oaks, elms and ash trees, at the mouth of the River Kamcija, is a good site for Semi-collared Flycatcher, Olive-tree Warbler, Nightingale, Penduline Tit and determined mosquitoes. There is a colony of Little Egrets, and Black Storks also breed. Parkland of mixed pine and deciduous trees, criss-crossed by tracks and roads around a tourist complex, is worth a little time for Syrian Woodpecker and the more common woodland birds. There is a chance of Scops Owl, and Sombre Tits are probably here, too. A long sandy beach northwards from the river mouth is crowded in summer, but worth a stroll in spring or autumn when hirundines, pipits, wagtails and wheatears move through. Slender-billed, Mediterranean and Yellow-legged Gulls and various terns all occur along the beach. A steady stream of boat-trips head up and down the river in the tourist season, spoiling the atmosphere of what must have been a quiet riverine forest in the not-too-distant past. However, a boat trip may be the only way to get an overall impression of the forest and perhaps to pick up a few raptors.

CALENDAR
Good from May to July for the key woodland birds. The beach and resort are empty of tourists in September, and some passage can be observed at this time, although it must be said that the riverine forest is the main attraction here, and so summer is the time to visit.

SPECIES

◆ *Olive-tree Warbler* Although sometimes difficult to locate visually, its distinctive song can be a giveaway.

◆ *Yellow-legged Gull* The most common gull, often roosting at the mouth of the river.

ACCESS

About 30 km (19 miles) south of Varna. Take the E87 through Bliznaci and then go left on a clearly signposted road to the Kamcija resort. A path runs along the riverbank from the boat-station to the mouth of the river and beach, and a little way inland through woodland. The riverine forest is quite impenetrable, but most birds can be heard or seen from the available paths. Kamcija is a Nature Reserve and an IBA.

CAPE EMINE

42°42N 27°54E

This is another of the headlands that jut into the Black Sea and are good spots for observing spring and autumn passage. Although not so impressive as Cape Kaliakra in terms of habitat and species, Cape Emine is certainly worth a visit if one is doing the Bulgarian coast, and certainly not to be missed for those staying at nearby Sunny Beach. There are cliffs, rocky and scrubby areas, patches of oak and, of course, the sea itself. On a good day in September, thousands of White Pelicans and White Storks pass the cape, along with some Black Storks. Raptors include Honey Buzzard, Black Kite, Short-toed, Booted and Lesser Spotted Eagles. Bee-eater and hirundines can also turn up in large numbers. In summer, birds found locally include Levant Sparrowhawk, Red-backed Shrike, Isabelline Wheatear and Cirl Bunting. Sombre Tits can be seen in the scrub and woodland around Vlas. Divers, grebes and gulls, as well as Yelkouan and sometimes Cory's Shearwaters, are possible offshore.

CALENDAR

May to August for breeding birds; the end of August to September for pelicans and raptors. Cranes pass through mainly in March and October.

SPECIES

◆ *Yelkouan Shearwater* Once thought to be a Black-Sea race of Manx Shearwater, this species is regular offshore here.

◆ *Lesser Spotted Eagle* By far the most numerous eagle on migration.

◆ *Sombre Tit* The woodland on the approach to the cape from Sunny Beach is a good bet.

ACCESS

Cape Emine is 60 km (37 miles) south of Varna and 45 km (28 miles) north of Burgas. Access from the north is difficult: maps are unreliable. Approach from Sunny Beach along the coast road to Vlas, then walk along the cape beyond the tourist developments. An IBA.

SUNNY BEACH

42°40N 27°41E

It was a combination of convenience and cost that put Slanchev Bryag, as it is known in Bulgarian, on the European birdwatching circuit. When, for various reasons, much of Bulgaria was difficult to explore, Sunny Beach offered Balkan birdwatching without hassle, and is still an excellent base for the Black Sea coast and a good site in its own right. The resort is a sprawling complex of hotels and restaurants, but even here there are Syrian and Middle Spotted Woodpeckers, Red-backed Shrike, Spanish Sparrow and Red-rumped Swallow. Early in the morning, the sea is worth a look, particularly at the end of summer, for Red-necked and Black-necked Grebes, Yelkouan Shearwater, Mediterranean, Yellow-legged, Little and Slender-billed Gulls and Sandwich and Gull-billed Terns. At the southern end of the resort, the Hadzijska Reka, a stream lined by reeds, woods, gardens and fields, can be followed inland. Little Egret, Little Bittern, Marsh Harrier, Quail, Bee-eater, Grey-headed and Black Woodpeckers, Wryneck, Great Reed, Icterine and Olivaceous Warblers and Bluethroat are some of the birds here. A quarry where the stream is crossed by the main Burgas–Varna road is a useful spot to check. Isabelline and Black-eared Wheatears are possible on the higher barren ground beyond, and storks and raptors also pass this way during migration. To the north of the resort is a conspicuous windmill which houses a restaurant. The wooded hillside here has Sombre Tit, Cirl Bunting and Golden Oriole. During autumn passage, songbirds occur here in good numbers and raptors include Short-toed Eagle, Levant Sparrowhawk, Long-legged Buzzard, Booted and Lesser Spotted Eagles, Hobby and Red-footed Falcon.

CALENDAR

The summer season stretches from May to September and coincides with the best periods to visit for birds: May for late spring passage and the arrival of the first summer visitors, and June and July for breeding birds and late August and September for autumn pelican, stork and raptor passage.

SPECIES

◆ *Levant Sparrowhawk* Regular in September and may breed.

◆ *Red-breasted Flycatcher* In late September quite numerous in and around the resort.

◆ *Olive-tree Warbler* Also possible around the resort and along the stream valley.

ACCESS

This is Bulgaria's largest resort and on the map in every sense. Burgas and its airport are 35 km (22 miles) to the south and Varna 80 km (50 miles) to the north along the E87. The coast and hinterland are almost totally accessible, although permission should be sought before entering allotments around the resort. No IBAs listed.

Long-legged Buzzards are scattered breeders throughout Bulgaria.

AJTOS HILLS

42°45N 27°30E

This little-known area of grazing and agricultural land, grassy downs, scrub and semi-steppe rising into wooded hills lies just inland from Sunny Beach and Burgas. The area is worth a visit for a contrast from the more famous coastal wetlands. Typical birds of open Bulgarian countryside like Hoopoe, Calandra, Short-toed and Crested Larks, Tawny Pipit, Black-headed Wagtail, Lesser Grey and Red-backed Shrikes, Barred Warbler and Cirl Bunting are all here in their preferred habitats. There are some Nightjars, and flocks of Rose-coloured Starlings periodically invade. In summer, raptors hunting in the area include Levant Sparrowhawk, Buzzard and Long-legged Buzzard and Lesser Spotted Eagle. Sakers are also possible; the area to the south of Brjastovec is worth trying. A visit at the end of the Sunny Beach season may be rewarded with parties of Red-footed Falcons, or even a Pallid Harrier, as they begin to wander from breeding sites. Indeed, being so close to the coast, a good amount of passage occurs over the hills when unfavourable conditions force birds inland from the Black Sea.

CALENDAR

From mid-May through the summer for breeding birds. September for raptors migrating south. Quite quiet in winter.

SPECIES

♦ *Long-legged Buzzard* Try the area to the east of Zitarovo.

♦ *Black-eared Wheatear* The eastern Mediterranean race *melanoleuca* occurs here in open scrubby areas.

ACCESS

The hills are around 15 km (9 miles) north of Burgas and 25 km (16 miles) west of Nesebar. From Burgas take road 6 (E773) towards Ajtos and the hills are to the east before the town. From Sunny Beach or Nesebar take the E87 south until Aheloj then turn right onto a road to Kableskovo which skirts the south of the area. Not listed as an IBA.

LAKE ATANASSOVO

42°30N 27°30E

With the possible exception of Srébarna, this is probably Bulgaria's most famous bird area and, indeed, seldom disappoints. But do not expect a tranquil or picturesque natural wilderness, Atanassovo is a working site for salt extraction complete with scruffy buildings and a busy main road. Yet a rich variety of birds occurs in this semi-artificial habitat. Black-winged Stilt, Avocet, Kentish Plover, Stone Curlew, Collared Pratincole and the occasional Ruddy Shelduck all

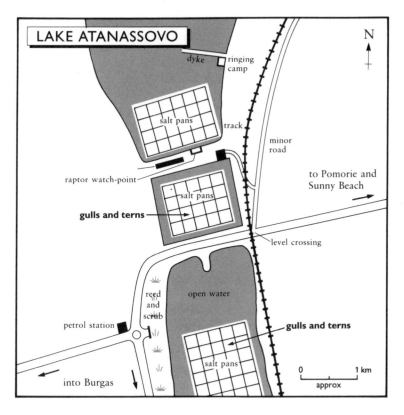

find the saline conditions on and around the lake and salt-pans ideal. Gull-billed, Sandwich, Common and Little Terns all probably breed, and with many hundreds more of these, as well as White-winged Black, Black and Whiskered Terns in autumn, the importance of this site cannot be overstated. The gulls, too, are impressive, with some Mediterranean and Slender-billed always around in summer and large numbers possible in the autumn. Reedbeds, particularly around the northern end of the lake, have Little Bittern, Purple and Squacco Herons, Marsh Harrier, Spotted and Little Crakes and Bearded Tit. The numbers of birds counted passing over the lake from August to October are remarkable, although at times the raptors and pelicans in particular can be very high up and, in practice, could be counted above any of the lakes along the coast. Generally, Spoonbill, Glossy Ibis and Pygmy Cormorant pass through in small parties, along with a few Dalmatian Pelicans. By contrast, the numbers of White Pelicans, Black Storks, Honey Buzzards and Lesser Spotted Eagles add up to thousands by the end of autumn. White Stork numbers can reach six figures. Other birds on passage at Atanassovo include Levant Sparrowhawk, Booted, Short-toed and Steppe Eagles, Osprey, Red-footed Falcon, Marsh Sandpiper, Crane, Bluethroat and various warblers. A minor road skirts the very northern tip of the area and passes through agricultural land and scrub good for Long-legged Buzzard, Hobby, Roller, Red-backed Shrike and Calandra Lark.

CALENDAR

March and April are good months for spring passage, and May to July excellent for a summer visit. Taking into consideration the problems of access, as well as numbers of birds, August and September are probably the best of all as birds can be observed all over the area. If one is in the area, winter also has its attractions with flocks of Shelducks, other wildfowl and gulls.

SPECIES

◆ *Gull-billed Tern* The only regular breeding site for this species in Bulgaria, although it is possible to see birds all along the coast.

◆ *White Pelican* Total autumn passage numbers are usually in five figures.

◆ *Lesser Spotted Eagle* By far the most numerous eagle on migration, but the vast majority pass over very high.

◆ *Slender-billed Gull* Sometimes perches on posts in the salt-pans near the raptor watching point.

ACCESS

The salt-pans begin on the north-eastern limits of Burgas. Take the E87 out of the city towards Sunny Beach and Varna, then cross over a roundabout where the south section of the lake comes into view opposite a petrol station. A little farther on the road bends right and crosses a railway line before passing the airport. Turn left at the level crossing, and the salt-pans and lake proper are on the left. Much of Atanassovo is a Nature Reserve, and entry needs a permit (see 'Conservation' on page 170). Access to the raptor watch point and dykes around the southern salt-pans and those near the roundabout is straightforward, but it must be said that finding good vantage points can be difficult. An IBA.

LAKE BURGAS

42°30N 27°20E

Situated, as it is, alongside the rather bleak town of Burgas, this large lake, or rather its birds, may come as a pleasant surprise. The three shores away from the main road which skirts its eastern bank are lined by reeds, and there are marshy patches and bushes at the southern end in particular. Pygmy Cormorant, Little Bittern, Night, Squacco and Purple Herons, Little Egret, Spoonbill, Glossy Ibis, Ferruginous Duck and Savi's, Reed and Great Reed Warblers all find the mixed saline and freshwater habitat suitable, although it is visibly polluted in places. White Pelicans roost on passage, and, as with most of the wetlands on this coast, it is always worth a second look at a flock for a Dalmatian Pelican. A line of electricity pylons in the water is invariably covered with roosting Cormorants and can be scanned from the main road. The numbers of waders depend on water levels, but Black-winged Stilt and Avocet breed, and Spotted Redshank, Marsh and Green Sandpipers and Ruff are regular in the autumn. Collared Pratincole and marsh terns are also around in summer. Winter sees Greylag and White-fronted Geese, ducks, gulls and sometimes both pelicans.

CALENDAR
May to July is good for breeding species; August to September for heron and pelican passage and the chance of rare waders.
SPECIES
♦ *Pygmy Cormorant* Some usually present all year round.
♦ *Glossy Ibis* A good site with around 100 pairs.
♦ *Black-winged Stilt* A few pairs breed.
ACCESS
The eastern edge of the lake is followed by the main E87 coast road in the southern suburbs of Burgas. A small area is a Landscape Reserve. Access is from the main road at several points, but beware of stopping on this dangerous stretch of road. An IBA.

LAKE MANDRA

42°25N 27°28E

This is the southernmost of the three lakes near Burgas, but still easily reached from Sunny Beach and other resorts. Not surprisingly, Lake Mandra has a similar collection of birds, but is generally regarded as being less interesting than Lakes Atanassovo and Burgas, although I am not quite sure why, as few industrial cities in Europe can have such good birdwatching on their doorsteps. Besides the large open sheet of water visible from the main road, there are wet-meadows, reedbeds, scrub and an interesting strip of marsh with brackish pools between the road and the Black Sea. This lagoon is particularly good in autumn when waders are passing through and Slender-billed, Little and Mediterranean Gulls and Gull-billed, Sandwich, Common and Little Terns are all possible. All three marsh terns occur. In summer, Lake Mandra has Pygmy Cormorant, Night, Squacco and Purple Herons, Little and Great White Egrets, Glossy Ibis, Spoonbill, Little and Common Terns, Penduline Tit and Savi's Warbler. Winter sees an impressive list, including Black-necked Grebe, Bewick's and Whooper Swans, over 100 Pygmy Cormorants, White Pelican, Great White Egret and Greylag and White-fronted Geese. The brackish nature of Lake Mandra and the adjacent lagoon also attracts a few White-headed Ducks every winter.

CALENDAR
Spring passage is in April and May. Breeding birds should all be in place from mid-May onwards, whilst mid-August to October sees the various migratory species passing through. November to February can see White-headed Duck.

SPECIES
◆ *Marsh Sandpiper* The marshy pools between the main road and the sea are worth checking in August and September.
◆ *Dalmatian Pelican* Used to breed, but is now only seen on passage with an occasional couple sometimes wintering.
◆ *White-headed Duck* Lake Mandra is an important wintering site for this rare species.

ACCESS
Just to the south of Burgas to the right of the main road out of town (E87), with the lagoon area on the left. A minor road runs near the southern shore at Dimcevo, where two small rivers drain into the lake. Access is mostly unrestricted, although in the past there have been incidents with 'officials' demanding to see passports. An IBA.

LAKE ALEPU
42°22N 27°43E
This brackish lake and marsh form an important stop-over on the Black Sea flyway for most of the birds associated with the more famed sites farther north around Burgas and Varna. Autumn, in particular, sees groups of Glossy Ibises, Spoonbill, Pygmy Cormorant, White Stork, White Pelican and a few Dalmatian Pelicans resting here on their way south. Spring, too, has its attractions, with many of the same species making the stop in April and May. However, Lake Alepu is also a summer site for several reed-nesting species, and has at present escaped the worst of the tourist developments of the

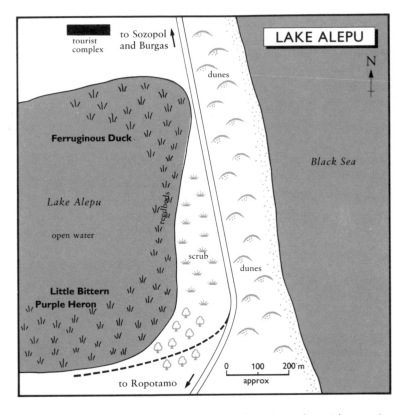

region. It is also somewhat easier to work as it is alongside a main road. Little Bittern, Squacco and Purple Herons, Ferruginous Duck, Marsh Harrier, and Great Reed and Cetti's Warblers are all relatively easy from the roadside. Areas of scrub and woodland to the south have Cirl Bunting and Olivaceous Warbler. Raptors pass over the area in September, with Lesser Spotted Eagle in summer. On the other side of the road from the lake there are dunes, a long beach and the Black Sea itself. In summer, the beach is inhabited by sunseekers, but gulls and terns can still be seen. Black-necked and Red-necked Grebes occur on the lake and on the sea at the end of summer.

CALENDAR

From May onwards, the reedbeds at Alepu are occupied by breeding herons and warblers. The coast can be busy with tourists from the adjacent resort in midsummer, but it is not as crowded as the resorts farther north. September is the best month for passage. Winter should produce several partial migrants from farther north seeking unfrozen wetland habitat.

SPECIES

◆ *White Pelican* Small groups drop in during migration, but do not expect them in summer.

- *Ferruginous Duck* A few pairs breed.
- *Scops Owl* Can be heard in the gardens of the nearby resort.
- *Moustached Warbler* I have a hunch that this is a wintering site. If anyone is here in winter, then this might provide another chance to fill in the blanks.

ACCESS
Lake Alepu lies to the south-east of Burgas along the Black Sea coast road (E87) about 10 km (6 miles) south of Sozopol. The lake and reedbeds can be watched from almost anywhere along the road, although the water can be obscured by the high reeds. There is a good track at the southern end of the lake just before the road bends to the right. An IBA.

ROPOTAMO

42°16N 27°44E
Before it reaches the Black Sea, the River Ropotamo is flanked by broadleaved woodland, lily-clad marshes and rocky hillsides covered in scrub. There are Semi-collared Flycatchers here, along with Kingfisher, Red-backed Shrike, Cetti's, Icterine, Olivaceous and Olive-tree Warblers, Nightingale, Sombre Tit, Short-toed Treecreeper, Hawfinch and Golden Oriole, all of which inhabit the riverine

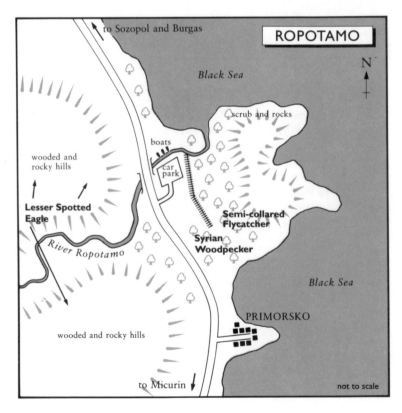

woodland. Cirl and Ortolan Buntings can be found in the more open woodland that covers the surrounding hillsides. This is also a good place for woodpeckers, with Grey-headed, Middle Spotted, Syrian, as well as Wrynecks. Raptors around here include Red-footed Falcon, Levant Sparrowhawk, Goshawk, Honey Buzzard and Lesser Spotted and Booted Eagles. Arkutino is part of the Ropotamo Reserve, just north of the river. Here Pygmy Cormorant, Purple and Squacco Herons, Great White Egret and wildfowl are likely, but with fences all over the place it is a difficult site to explore. Morski Pelin is another part of the reserve, this time on the right bank of the river where it enters the sea. A path from the car park heads in this direction, but again is met by an ugly wire fence, which formerly enclosed a former Communist Party residence. Tourist boats regularly ply along the river to and from the sea here.

CALENDAR
Being mainly a forested wetland area particularly good for songbirds, Ropotamo is worth a visit in spring and summer with May and June probably the best months.

SPECIES
◆ *Semi-collared Flycatcher* Try the deciduous woodland along the river and before Primorsko.
◆ *Cirl Bunting* Quite common in the more open rocky areas.
◆ *Olive-tree Warbler* Rather skulking, but in summer listen out for its characteristic song.
◆ *Syrian Woodpecker* Around the car park and at the quay from which the boat-trips run.
◆ *Rufous Bushchat* Has never been recorded breeding in Bulgaria, but has been seen in the river valley here in summer. Another chance for discovery perhaps?

ACCESS
Around 18 km (11 miles) south of Sozopol on the main E87 coast road. A little way on from Lake Alepu, the road winds through forested hills before crossing the River Ropotamo. Immediately after the bridge, turn left to a car park in the trees. There is a departure point for boat-trips and snack bars here. Parts of Ropotamo require permission to visit. Many of the key birds also reside outside the protected areas. Not an IBA.

STUDEN KLADENEC
41°36N 25°03E
This huge reservoir, filling a valley along the River Arda in the Eastern Rhodopes Mountains, is at the heart of an outstanding raptor area. The vertical cliffs, crags, rocky banks and surrounding wild terrain are ideal for Eagle Owl and satisfy the hunting requirements of Long-legged Buzzard, Short-toed, Booted, Golden, Imperial and Lesser Spotted Eagles, Egyptian, Black and Griffon

Vultures and Lesser Kestrel – an impressive list by any standards. Perhaps not surprisingly, birds such as Rock Nuthatch, Rock and Blue Rock Thrushes and Rock Bunting are also here. Black Storks are quite common and other birds include Chukar, Pallid Swift, Isabelline and Black-eared Wheatears, Spanish Sparrow, Sombre Tit and an interesting collection of warblers which includes Subalpine, Sardinian, Orphean, Barred and Bonelli's. This is one of the best regions in the country for Masked Shrike, too. Besides all these delights there is still plenty of scope for confirmation and discovery here, as elsewhere in Bulgaria.

CALENDAR
Many of the key species are summer visitors only, and so a visit from May onwards is best. Winter has its attractions, with parties of Griffon and Black Vultures feeding in the region: the relatively mild climate makes the Eastern Rhodopes the only really worthwhile montane habitat to visit in Bulgaria in this season.
SPECIES
♦ *Black Vulture* Sadly, numbers have declined drastically in Bulgaria and this is now probably the best area for the species.
♦ *Chukar* Birds here are of the *kleini* race. Care should be taken with identification as one moves westwards, as hybridization with Rock Partridge has apparently occurred.
♦ *Rüppell's Warbler* Is it here? There are some rumours but little exact information. Certainly, this is not that far from populations in Turkey and Greece.
♦ *Orphean Warbler* The Rhodopes Mountains are the Bulgarian stronghold for this species. Birds are of the Levant race *crassirostris*.
ACCESS
The area begins just to the east of Kardzali which is 85 km (53 miles) south-east of Plovdiv. Despite its apparently remote location, Kardzali is served quite well by road and rail links. It may be wise to ask for permits from the police authorities to explore the mountains if one intends to head towards border areas. Under no circumstances approach the nests of raptors as this is illegal. An IBA.

THE BALKAN RANGE
c.42°50–43°40N c.22°30–26°30E
This wild mountain chain cuts right across Bulgaria, beginning just to the east of Sofia and continuing to the spectacular Shipka Pass and beyond. There are several reserves and parks, but the whole range has good birds. The Steneto National Park is a scenic subalpine karst region of meadows, valleys and beech, hornbeam and conifer forests with Long-legged Buzzard, Booted, Golden and Lesser Spotted Eagles, Hazelhen, Capercaillie, Rock Partridge, Black, Grey-headed, Middle Spotted and White-backed Woodpeckers and Red-breasted Flycatcher. The Tzarichina Reserve farther west is mixed forest with most of the

Although common nowhere, Semi-collared Flycatchers breed throughout Bulgaria.

above as well as Ural and Tengmalm's Owls and, higher up in an alpine zone, Shore Lark, Alpine Accentor and Ring Ouzels. Farther west still, and a feasible day trip from the capital, is the Boatin Reserve which is almost completely blanketed in old beech forests and particularly good for Semi-collared Flycatcher. Griffon Vultures are possible throughout the range, although these days they are certainly far from common.

CALENDAR
The Balkan Range's owls and woodpeckers are early breeders and thus an exploration in March and April is best for these, although the weather can be tough at this time. In summer things are better on both the weather and songbird fronts.

SPECIES
- *Ural Owl* There are birds scattered across the range, which indeed is the only region in Bulgaria where the species is known to breed.
- *Rock Partridge* Scattered throughout the mountains with the Tzarichina Reserve being a noted site.
- *White-backed Woodpecker* The old beech forests are ideal. The *lilfordi* race breeds right across the range.
- *Semi-collared Flycatcher* Try the deciduous forests of Boatin. Has bred on the outskirts of Sofia itself.

193

ACCESS
The foothills of the Balkan Range begin around 50 km (31 miles) east of Sofia. For Boatin and Tzarichina head north-east from Sofia on the E79 and then east for Etropole and on via minor roads to Divcevoto or Ribarica. For Steneto, take road 6 from Sofia to Karnare and then a minor road north to Trojan and on to the village of Cherni Osam, although you should ask permission locally from the Water Board first. The range is a popular hiking area with trails and some core reserves which require permits. Tzarichina and Steneto are IBAs.

RILA MOUNTAINS
*c.*42°07N 23°07E
The Rila range has typical layers of montane habitat going from river and stream valleys at lower altitudes, to mixed deciduous woodland, then coniferous forests, areas of dwarf pine interspersed with alpine meadows, tarns and finally rocky ridges and bare rugged peaks. By virtue of its famous monastery, Rila is on the tourist track in Bulgaria and thus not as forbidding a site as some mountain spots in the Balkans. Most of the typical high mountain specialities are here, with Water Pipit, Alpine Accentor, Ring Ouzel and Alpine Chough usually quite easy to find around or above the tree-line. Shore Larks are also possible, but more difficult, requiring a trek up to open areas. Regular spots for Wallcreeper are the rock faces beyond the Maljovica resort, below the peak of the same name at 2729 m (8953 feet). Other somewhat easier birds in the Rila area include Alpine Swift, Crag Martin and Red-rumped Swallow, which are often around the buildings near the campsite, hotels and monastery. Firecrest, Dipper, Rock Thrush, Rock Bunting, Crossbill and Nutcracker are also quite widespread. White-backed and Grey-headed Woodpeckers are in the older forest stands lower down. Hazelhens are also possible, and there are Golden Eagles here, too. Considering its proximity to Sofia, its facilities and its birds, Rila is an ideal introduction to mountain birdwatching in Bulgaria.

CALENDAR
June is probably the best time to visit, when the weather is reasonable, breeding birds are present and the summer walking season not quite underway. However, there can still be ice and snow at higher altitudes even in July.
SPECIES
◆ *Pallid Swift* This is the rarest of the three swifts here.
◆ *Wallcreeper* Inhabits the vast rock walls of the high glacial valleys, but, as is often the case, a bit of luck is needed.
◆ *Alpine Chough* Is rather common in the alpine zone.
◆ *Shore Lark* Any birds encountered will almost certainly be of the Balkan race *balcanica*.

ACCESS
The Rila Mountains lie 60 km (37 miles) south of Sofia. There are two main routes from the capital up into this range: one via Samokov to the Maljovica resort and its ski-lifts, and the other through Stanke Dimitrov along the E79 to Rila village and on to the monastery. Once at the end of these routes, there are numerous trails, but one should come properly equipped for alpine walking. Not listed as an IBA.

KRESNA
c.41°45N 23°13E
The small town of Kresna nestles in the valley of the River Struma amid seemingly barren, rocky, scrub-dotted hillsides. It is, however, a particularly good area for Masked Shrike. Of course, all the typical birds of Bulgaria's dry lowlands and rocky arid terrain are here, too: Rock Partridge, Red-rumped Swallow, Crag Martin, Tawny Pipit, Short-toed Lark, Woodchat and Lesser Grey Shrikes, Barred Warbler, Black-eared Wheatear, Blue Rock Thrush and Rock, Ortolan and Cirl Buntings. For the intrepid, a minor road from Kresna takes one to Vlahi in the foothills of the Pirin Range, arguably Bulgaria's wildest, and which is good country for large raptors.

CALENDAR
From May to August for summer visitors: September sees some songbird passage down the valley.
SPECIES
◆ *Masked Shrike* This is a relatively new species to Bulgaria, and the Kresna area is a stronghold.
◆ *Ortolan Bunting* Seems to be very common here.
ACCESS
About 110 km (70 miles) south of Sofia on the E79, Kresna is a more than useful stop on the way to Sandanski (*see* below). Most of the countryside along the river can be explored freely. No IBAs are listed for the area.

SANDANSKI
41°35N 23°16E
This spa town in the extreme south-west of the country lies at the centre of an excellent region comprising Mediterranean-like habitats with many birds that are difficult elsewhere in Bulgaria. This is basically an agricultural area with orchards, vineyards and woodland along the River Struma. North of the town is an area of rocky hill-sides and scrub where Egyptian Vulture, Lesser Kestrel, Roller, Rock Partridge, Rock Sparrow, Rock Nuthatch, Short-toed Lark, and Lesser Grey, Masked, Woodchat and Red-backed Shrikes occur. The environs of Ploski village have Long-legged Buzzard, Scops Owl (also in Sandanski town itself), Red-rumped Swallow and Subalpine Warbler.

One of the most familiar songbirds of the Balkans, Olivaceous Warbler is common throughout Bulgaria.

South of the town towards Melnik are steep sandstone cliffs set in impressively rugged terrain with, apparently, real Rock Doves, Alpine and perhaps Pallid Swifts, Bee-eater and Rock Bunting. The quarries towards Petric are also worth a look. Birds such as White Stork, Syrian Woodpecker, Calandra Lark, Cetti's, Olivaceous, Olive-tree and Orphean Warblers, Black-eared Wheatear, Sombre Tit, Black-headed, Cirl and Ortolan Buntings and Spanish Sparrow are quite widespread throughout the whole Struma valley. Bonelli's Warblers are also possible, although they seem to be less common. As if all this were not enough, 25 km to the north-east are the Pirin Mountains where Lammergeiers may still occur. There are some reports, but little definite information.

CALENDAR
For most of the above-mentioned birds, mid-May to mid-June is the ideal time. Early May sees some songbird passage up the valley and, of course, many species can be observed right through the summer. Winters are not too harsh here, and so some good birds are resident.
SPECIES
♦ *Sombre Tit* Quite common, particularly in patches of oak woodland.
♦ *Masked Shrike* Only seems to be in the steppe-like area to the north whereas its congeners are widespread.

◆ *Black-eared Wheatear* Can be seen on telegraph poles, rooftops and posts in vineyards.
◆ *Bonelli's Warbler* Not the most typical warbler here, but try the wooded river valleys near Ploski to the north of Sandanski.
◆ *Spanish Sparrow* Often nests in colonies in acacia trees in villages.

ACCESS
Sandanski lies just off the E79 about 22 km (14 miles) north of the Greek border at Kulata. There is a border crossing into Macedonia 30 km (19 miles) to the south-west. Sofia is 160 km (99 miles) to the north. Much of the area may be freely explored, although it is probably not wise to stray too close to frontiers. For the south of the Pirin Range, take the minor road from Sandanski up through Liljanovo to the Begovica chalet. No IBAs are listed for the region.

MELNIK
41°30N 23°25E
The town of Melnik sits inside craggy walls, rocky screes and sandstone cones fashioned by the elements, with high mountains as a backdrop, in an out-of-the-way corner of Bulgaria. The area around is an arid landscape of stony hillsides, vineyards and fields of tobacco broken only by the River Melnishka. If one gets this far then it is worth spending some time watching for Egyptian Vulture, Long-legged Buzzard, Imperial Eagle and Lesser Kestrel among the other birds of prey. There are Scops Owls in the town itself. Nightjar, Alpine Swift, Crag Martin, Red-rumped Swallow, Woodchat Shrike, Black-eared Wheatear, Spanish Sparrow, Rock and Blue Rock Thrushes and Rock, Cirl and Black-headed Buntings are all typical birds in and around the town. Nearby stony hillsides are good for Rock Partridge, Rock Nuthatch and Rock Sparrow. Orchards, vineyards and scrub areas have Bee-eater, Sombre Tit, some Orphean, Subalpine and Sardinian Warblers, with Olivaceous, Great Reed and Cetti's Warblers along the river. Short-toed and Calandra Larks, Ortolan Bunting and Woodlark are widespread.

CALENDAR
From May to August for breeding birds, although some do winter.
SPECIES
◆ *Red-rumped Swallow* Often breeds in small colonies under bridges.
◆ *Pallid Swift* It is worth keeping an eye open here for this species among its congeners.
ACCESS
Melnik is on a dead-end road which leads to the Rozhen Monastery from the E79. The border crossing with Greece at Kulata is about 25 km (15.5 miles) to the south, and the largest town in the region, Petrich, about 28 km (17.5 miles) to the south-west. With the exception of obviously private vineyards, the area can be explored freely. No IBAs listed.

THE BALTIC STATES, EUROPEAN RUSSIA, BELORUSSIA AND THE UKRAINE

I only have space here for the briefest outline of the birdwatching possibilities in a region which is both very large and contains a rich diversity of habitats. There are some spectacular landscapes and exciting birds awaiting those who venture into the various countries which make up the European states of the former Soviet Union. When one considers just a few of the breeding birds of this vast region – Dalmatian Pelican, Pallid Harrier, Black Vulture, Spotted and Steppe Eagles, Demoiselle Crane, Little and Great Bustards, Great Snipe, Terek Sandpiper, Slender-billed and Great Black-headed Gulls, Pied Wheatear, Greenish Warbler, Siberian Tit and Pine Grosbeak – the appeal is almost irresistible. Moreover, although there are some renowned and remarkable ornithologists in each country, much still remains to be discovered. This is, of course, another good reason for visiting. In a very short while these countries will become essential destinations on the agenda of all travelling birdwatchers.

TRAVEL

Independent travel is now legally possible, with most of the zones formerly out of bounds to visitors today technically accessible. At the time of writing, however, travelling in some parts of the region is, it must be said, far from simple. This has nothing to do with travel restrictions, as in the past, but rather with the current poor social and economic conditions as these countries restructure themselves and adapt to a new market-orientated system. It is not unknown for flight tickets to become strangely invalid or for flights to be cancelled suddenly or become horrendously overbooked. Aeroflot (Soviet Airlines), once the largest airline in the world, has been split into independent state airlines and co-operation and scheduling between these is at times less than satisfactory. Train travel is suffering similarly, is always an adventure in Eastern Europe and, in any case, can be very slow because of the vast distances involved. It is, however, now possible to hire cars in Moscow and the other capitals and large cities. Although, after these comments, it may all seem more effort than it is worth, the experienced travelling birder should not and will not be put off: there are too many birding delights lying in wait.

ESTONIA

This is the smallest and most northerly of the Baltic States with an avifauna similar to that of southern Finland which lies just to the north across the Gulf of Finland. Indeed, Estonia is a significantly less expensive alternative to that fine birding country, although the Arctic species are mostly absent. The Estonian capital, Tallinn, can be reached by ferry from Helsinki and other Baltic ports, and is now linked to most European capitals by direct flights.

BIRDS

Quite common breeding birds include Common Eider, Hazelhen, Black Grouse, Corncrake, Ruff, Black Tern, Ural Owl, Grey-headed Woodpecker, Thrush Nightingale, River Warbler, Blyth's Reed

Warbler, Red-breasted Flycatcher, Crested Tit, Scarlet Rosefinch and Ortolan Bunting – tempting by any standards. Exploration and/or local knowledge could produce Red-throated and Black-throated Divers, Slavonian Grebe, Lesser Spotted Eagle, Capercaillie, Crane, Great Snipe, Caspian Tern, Tengmalm's and Pygmy Owls, White-backed Woodpecker, Nutcracker and Parrot Crossbill.

SITES

To the east of Tallinn via the E20 the Lamemaa National Park is an area of lakes, marshes and forests with many of the above birds.

Estonia's stretch of the Baltic coast is littered with rocky islands, inlets and salt-marshes which are particularly good during passage periods when divers, ducks, including some Steller's Eider, and various waders all move through. In spring and autumn, the straits between the mainland and Muhu Island, and particularly Matsalu Bay, see tens of thousands of wildfowl, including Whooper and Bewick's Swans, Bean, White-fronted and Barnacle Geese, Common Scoter and Long-tailed Duck. In summer, Matsalu Bay also has breeding ducks, gulls and terns, including the only Caspian Terns on this side of the Baltic Sea.

Parnu in the south-west, on the main road from Tallinn to Riga in neighbouring Latvia, is a good base for exploring both the southern coastline and inland forests and bogs along the River Parnu. On no account forget the mosquito repellent here.

LATVIA

The Latvian capital, Riga, sits conveniently at the base of the Gulf of Riga. Ferries reach here from numerous Baltic ports, and direct flights are now possible from most European capitals. Despite rising costs, which locals find difficult to keep pace with, prices for most things remain well within the reach of most westerners.

BIRDS

Latvia's birdlife is, not surprisingly, similar to that of Estonia to the north and Lithuania to the south. Elk, Beaver and mosquitoes may also be encountered. Typical breeding birds which in summer should be found without too much difficulty include Black Stork, Crane, Green Sandpiper, Whimbrel, Black Tern, Great Grey Shrike, Woodlark and Scarlet Rosefinch. A little time and effort, and Black-throated Diver, Black Grouse, Hazelhen, White-winged Black Tern,

The bulk of Europe's Crane population breeds in the countries of the CIS.

Spotted and Lesser Spotted Eagles, Ural and Eagle Owls and White-backed and Three-toed Woodpeckers might oblige.

SITES

There is good birding to be had within easy reach of Riga. Lake Babite just to the west of the capital lies close to the Gulf of Riga and is a stop-over for passage wildfowl in both spring and autumn.

Farther along the coast near Kemeri, a mosaic of lakes and marshes has breeding Black-throated Diver, Slavonian Grebe, Little Bittern and Crane.

Farther north still, Lake Kanieris is a site for White-tailed Eagle and has a large gull colony.

Once away from the coast and the capital city, Latvia is very much a land of bogs, marshes, lakes and wild forests of beech, alder and pine. A particularly good area for Black Grouse, Capercaillies and breeding waders are the peat-bogs along the River Daugava to the north of Jekabpils around 120 km inland from Riga.

Large mixed colonies on marshes to the north-east of Lake Lubana have Little Gull and Black and White-winged Black Terns.

Cape Kolka, at the tip of the Kurzeme Peninsula to the north-west of Riga, is a watch-point for migrating birds, particularly in spring. Honey Buzzard, Buzzard and Sparrowhawk make up most of the raptor numbers and songbird passage is at times phenomenal. The forests and wetland habitats of the peninsula are also good in summer for birds of prey, with Spotted Eagle possible, and Black Grouse, Hazelhen, Crane, Corncrake, Nightjar, Black Woodpecker and Red-breasted Flycatcher also here. Lake Engure lies on the coast roughly halfway between Riga and Cape Kolka and in summer has Red-necked and Slavonian Grebes, Spotted and Little Crakes and various gulls and terns. The surrounding forests hold Black Stork, Hazelhen, woodpeckers and flycatchers.

LITHUANIA

The capital city, Vilnius, lies inland in the south-east of the country, close to the border with Belorussia, and has an international airport. The southernmost of the Baltic states, Lithuania also has its fair share of wild birch and alder forests, vast peat-bogs, marshes and traditionally farmed meadows. anyone who has visited north-east Poland will find much to remind them here in terms of habitats and birds.

BIRDS

Widespread birds include Black and White Storks, Crane, Ruff, Black Tern, Grey-headed and Black Woodpeckers, Woodlark, Thrush Nightingale, Icterine, River and Grasshopper Warblers, Crested Tit, Golden Oriole and Scarlet Rosefinch. These should be located easily in summer. Rather more difficult, but possible, are Spotted Eagle, Corncrake, Great Snipe, Roller and Greenish Warbler. Spruce forests hold Hazelhen, Capercaillie and Nutcracker but one has to time it right for these often elusive species, generally the earlier in the year the better.

SITES

Kursiu Bay on Lithuania's coast is sheltered from the Baltic Sea by a long spit and is a haven in autumn for thousands of migrating wildfowl and waders. White-tailed Eagle, Spotted Crake and reed-dwelling warblers also breed here. The River Nemunas enters the bay near Rusné and forms a delta of islets, channels, pools and reedbeds. Bittern and Little Bittern, crakes, gulls, terns and various warblers all breed.

To the north-east of Vilnius a 'lake district' with rivers, marshes, wet-meadows and mixed forests has in summer Lesser Spotted Eagle, Marsh Harrier, Corncrake, Ruff, Roller and perhaps breeding Slavonian Grebe and Great Snipe.

To the south-west of the capital, towards the Polish border, the flood-plain of the Nemunas and its tributaries is good in summer for both storks, Crane, various wildfowl, Black and Red Kites, Montagu's and Hen Harriers, Lesser Spotted and Spotted Eagles, Great Grey Shrike and, again, probably Great Snipe leks.

EUROPEAN RUSSIA

Where can one begin with a country so large as Russia? The sheer size of the area covered and the great range of habitats contained render the birding possibilities endless, even if we limit ourselves to European Russia, which stretches from the Arctic Circle in the north to the Black Sea in the south.

BIRDS AND SITES

Moscow is served by major airlines and offers the chance of Greenish Warbler and Thrush Nightingale in its parks. North of Moscow is the Rybinsk Reservoir which is good from spring to autumn for wildfowl. Between here and Moscow is a vast flood-plain area of wet forests,

EUROPEAN RUSSIA

N

KOLA
PENINSULA

FINLAND

LAKE
LADOGA

RYBINSK
RESERVOIR

ESTONIA

LATVIA

LITHUANIA

MOSCOW

RIVER OKA

POLAND

BELORUSSIA

UKRAINE

0
km

● VORONEZH

bogs, lakes, farmland and reservoirs with many of Russia's boreal birds including Crane, Slavonian Grebe, Spotted Eagle and Azure Tit.

East and south-east of the capital various habitats along the Oka and its tributaries host White-tailed Eagle, Osprey, White-winged Black Tern, Great Snipe, Terek and Marsh Sandpipers and Pygmy Owl. This is also a good area for passage wildfowl and waders.

Farther to the south towards Voronezh and beyond, vast agricultural lands and remaining steppe areas offer the chance of lowland species such as Imperial and Steppe Eagles, Saker, Red-footed Falcon, Pallid Harrier, Great Bustard, Black-winged Pratincole, Demoiselle Crane and Rose-coloured Starling. Farther to the south and east the chances of Isabelline Wheatear and invasion species such as White-winged and Black Larks and Rose-coloured Starling are greater.

Excursions from the relative comfort of Saint Petersburg in the north-west of Russia are a way of seeing some typical northern European birds. The city has an international airport and is served by ferries from most Baltic ports. The huge Lake Ladoga to the north of the city sees large numbers of divers, grebes, ducks, swans and geese on passage as does the Gulf of Finland to the west. Forests here hold Pygmy, Tengmalm's, Eagle, Great Grey, Ural and Hawk Owls, although some time, skill and probably also local knowledge are needed to track down this impressive selection. As one moves northwards and eastwards other possibilities include Siberian Jay, Arctic and Greenish Warblers, Siberian Tit, Pine Grosbeak, Parrot and Two-barred Crossbills and Yellow-breasted Bunting.

If one can get as far north as the tundra of the Kola Peninsula and the Barents Sea and its islands and cliffs then breeding birds such as Velvet Scoter, Red-necked Phalarope, Brünnich's and Black Guillemots, Willow Grouse, Ptarmigan, Gyrfalcon and Long-tailed Skua come into play. Flocks of Common, King and Steller's Eiders winter here.

Clearly, the birds are outstanding but the question remains in many regions of Russia of just how to get to them. Several British birding tour companies offer holidays in Russia, often with local experts as guides and, all things considered, this may for the moment be the best way of seeing this country's birds.

BELORUSSIA

Belorussia's capital, Minsk, lies at the heart of the country on the main E30 Warsaw–Moscow road and can also be reached from some European capitals by direct flights. This little-known country is criss-crossed by rivers and dotted with wetlands and has an extremely impressive selection of birds. Who knows what secrets lie in store for those prepared to undertake a prolonged exploration?

BIRDS AND SITES

Slavonian Grebe, Spotted and Booted Eagles, Eagle and Ural Owls, Great Snipe and White-backed Woodpecker are certainly tempting. The legendary Pripet Marshes, which cover a vast area in the south and spread into the Ukraine, have in places been drained and converted to agricultural land, but nevertheless remain a wetland wildlife paradise of marshes, bogs, fens, lakes, reedbeds, conifer forests, birch woods, dunes and farmland. Nearly 200 breeding bird species occur, including five species of grebe, both storks, Ferruginous Duck, Spotted, Lesser Spotted, Booted, Short-toed and White-tailed Eagles, Hazelhen, Black Grouse, Capercaillie, Crane, Barred Warbler, Black-tailed Godwit, Thrush Nightingale, Great Grey Shrike and Scarlet Rosefinch. Are there Aquatic Warblers here? There is a border crossing in the west of the region at Brest on the main E30 route from Warsaw to Minsk.

The Belorussian side of the primeval forest known in Poland as Białowieża (*see* page 33) is equally good for birds, although somewhat

less visited. Besides the forest proper there are several small rivers, bogs and marshes. Quite common birds include White Stork, Green Sandpiper, Black Woodpecker, Collared and Red-breasted Flycatchers, Thrush Nightingale and Scarlet Rosefinch. Spotted Eagle, Hazelhen, Capercaillie, Ural Owl, Three-toed and White-backed Woodpeckers and Great Snipe are also said to be here. Greenish Warblers must be a possibility and there are Bison, Elk and Beaver here, too.

UKRAINE

The Ukrainian capital, Kiev, is linked directly to several other European cities by air and rail. Odessa, on the Black Sea, and Simferopol, on the Crimea, also have airports, and Odessa and several Crimean ports can also be reached by ship from other Black Sea countries. By road, the Ukraine can be entered from Romania in the south and Hungary, Slovakia and Poland in the west. The Ukraine has a rich range of exciting birds, some of which are often not even considered to be typical European species. As soon as travel to this rather out-of-the-way country becomes easier, western birders will no doubt flock in.

BIRDS

As far as birding goes, the Ukraine's attraction undoubtedly lies in its steppe species. Indeed, the Ukraine arguably offers the best steppe birding in Europe, although there are also the forests and peaks of the Carpathians, the varied habitats of the Crimean Peninsula, the Danube Delta and the northern coast of the Black Sea. The Ukraine's impressive list of breeding birds includes such exciting species as Demoiselle Crane, Pallid Harrier, Steppe Eagle, Saker, Griffon and Black Vultures, Great and Little Bustards, Black-winged Pratincole, Great Black-headed and Slender-billed Gulls, Gull-billed and Caspian Terns, Ural Owl, Chukar, Pied Wheatear and Paddyfield Warbler.

SITES

Large areas of typical Ukrainian virgin steppe lie in the south-east of the country and stretch southwards to the Sea of Azov. These are good raptor areas with Long-legged Buzzard, Red-footed Falcon and Pallid Harrier and other typical steppe birds such as Demoiselle Crane, Tawny Pipit, Pied and Isabelline Wheatears and sometimes Rose-coloured Starling. Askania Nova is a famous steppe reserve with agricultural lowland which has spectacular birding potential. Pallid Harrier, Steppe Eagle, Demoiselle Crane, Little and Great Bustards, Calandra and Short-toed Larks, Roller, Lesser Grey Shrike, and wheatears are the draws here. Askania Nova is in the south of the country near Cherson, which has an airport.

The Crimea has a wide range of bird habitats ranging from the coastlines of the Black and Azov Seas, salt-lakes, extensive steppes and high rocky mountains. The coastal mountain range and the Yalta area hold Egyptian, Griffon and Black Vultures, Saker, Lesser Kestrel, Eagle Owl, Chukar, Rock Thrush, Pied Wheatear and Alpine Swift. The Sea of Azov is almost an inland sea having only a relatively small outlet to the Black Sea. Its heavily indented coast, islets and numerous adjacent wetlands host breeding herons, egrets, Black-winged Stilt, Collared and Black-winged Pratincoles and large colonies of terns and gulls. Migratory birds, including Red-breasted Geese, pass through in huge numbers. Sivash Bay nestles into the north-east of the Crimean Peninsula and along with its associated lagoons and marshes is an exceptional wetland with breeding Night Heron, Little Egret, Glossy Ibis, Great Black-headed, Mediterranean and Slender-billed Gulls and Gull-billed and Caspian Terns. Divers, grebes, ducks, geese and waders pass through in phenomenal numbers, too. The western shore of the Crimea is also dotted with steppe and wetlands with Paddyfield Warbler a speciality of fish-ponds and rice-fields and Karkinitsky Bay good for wildfowl and waders.

The Ukrainian section of the Danube Delta (see also pages 137–9) is not so well known as the larger Romanian part, but has similarly spectacular birds such as both pelicans.

The Black Sea itself lies on major migration routes and, besides the gulls and terns already mentioned, has Yelkouan Shearwater and the Mediterranean/Black Sea race of Shag.

The Carpathian Mountains stretch into the Ukraine in the west near the Romanian and Hungarian borders and offer a contrast to steppe and wetland birding. Species include Lesser Spotted Eagle, Hazelhen, Capercaillie, Eagle and Ural Owls, White-backed Woodpecker and Red-breasted Flycatcher.

INDEX

Figures in *italics* refer to illustrations and those in **bold** to species highlighted in the text for particular sites.

HAMLYN

NATURAL HISTORY BOOKS

A complete range of Hamlyn Natural History titles is available from all good bookshops or by mail order direct from the publisher. Payment can be made by credit card or cheque/postal order in the following ways:

BY PHONE
Phone through your order on our special *Credit Card Hotline* on **0933 410 511**. Speak to our customer service team during office hours (9 a.m. to 5 p.m.) or leave a message on the answer machine, quoting your full credit card number plus expiry date and your full name and address. Please also quote the reference number NATHIS 1.

BY POST
Simply fill out the order form below (photocopies are acceptable) and send it with your payment to:
Cash Sales Department,
Reed Book Services Ltd.,
P.O. Box 5,
Rushden,
Northants, NN10 6YX

SPECIAL OFFER: FREE POSTAGE AND PACKAGING FOR ALL ORDERS OVER £10.00, add £2.00 for p+p if your order is £10.00 or less.

Whilst every effort is made to keep our prices low, the publisher reserves the right to increase the prices at short notice.
Your order will be dispatched within 5 days, but please allow up to 28 days for delivery, subject to availability.
Registered office: Michelin House, 81 Fulham Road, London SW3 6RB.
Registered in England no 1974080.

If you do not wish your name to be used by other carefully selected organizations for promotional purposes, please tick this box ☐